UNE

EST

NIES

KFOR®

2009

People may not remember exactly what you did or what you said, but they will always remember how you

made them feel.

— Tony paraphrasing various authors

99

00

01

02

03

04

05

06

07

08

10 + 10 = 2009

10 YEARS
10 CORE VALUES

2009 CULTURE BOOK

AS DEFINED BY
OUR EMPLOYEES,
PARTNERS
AND CUSTOMERS

CONT

ENTS.

10 + 10 = 2009
CORE VALUES

I   Deliver WOW through service

II   Embrace and drive change

III   Create fun and a little weirdness

IV   Be adventurous, creative and open-minded

V   Pursue growth and learning

VI   Build open and honest relationships with communication

VII   Build a positive team and family spirit

VIII   Do more with less

IX   Be passionate and determined

X   Be humble

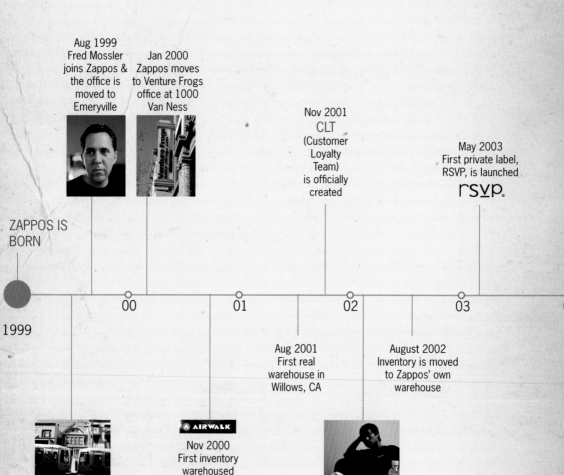

Aug 1999
Fred Mossler
joins Zappos &
the office is
moved to
Emeryville

Jan 2000
Zappos moves
to Venture Frogs
office at 1000
Van Ness

Nov 2001
CLT
(Customer
Loyalty
Team)
is officially
created

May 2003
First private label,
RSVP, is launched

rsvp.

ZAPPOS IS
BORN

00   01   02   03

1999

Aug 2001
First real
warehouse in
Willows, CA

August 2002
Inventory is moved
to Zappos' own
warehouse

June 1999
Zappos'
first office in San
Francisco

AIRWALK

Nov 2000
First inventory
warehoused
First brand is
Airwalk

2002
Tony's hair might
be different but
the t-shirt attire
is just about the
same

HISTORY

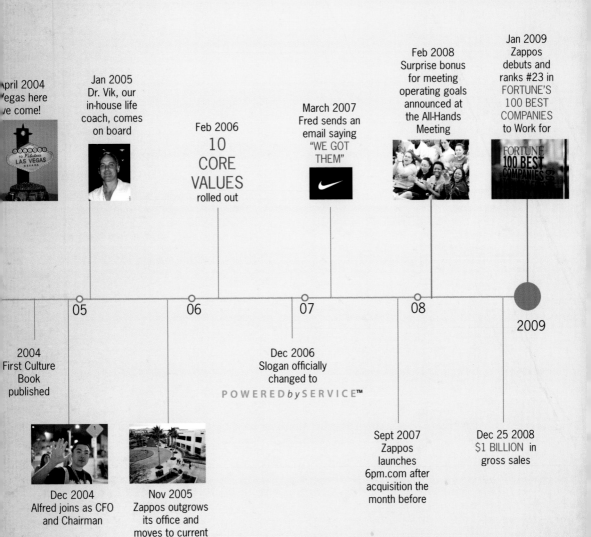

April 2004
Vegas here
we come!

Jan 2005
Dr. Vik, our
in-house life
coach, comes
on board

Feb 2006
10
CORE
VALUES
rolled out

March 2007
Fred sends an
email saying
"WE GOT
THEM"

Feb 2008
Surprise bonus
for meeting
operating goals
announced at
the All-Hands
Meeting

Jan 2009
Zappos
debuts and
ranks #23 in
FORTUNE'S
100 BEST
COMPANIES
to Work for

05   06   07   08

2009

2004
First Culture
Book
published

Dec 2006
Slogan officially
changed to
POWERED by SERVICE™

Dec 2004
Alfred joins as CFO
and Chairman

Nov 2005
Zappos outgrows
its office and
moves to current
location in
Henderson, NV

Sept 2007
Zappos
launches
6pm.com after
acquisition the
month before

Dec 25 2008
$1 BILLION in
gross sales

FOREWORD.

Welcome to the 2009 edition of the Zappos culture book!

Over the past 10 years, Zappos.com has grown at an extraordinary rate. In 1999, the year the company was founded, we had almost no sales. Since then, our historical gross merchandise sales numbers have been:

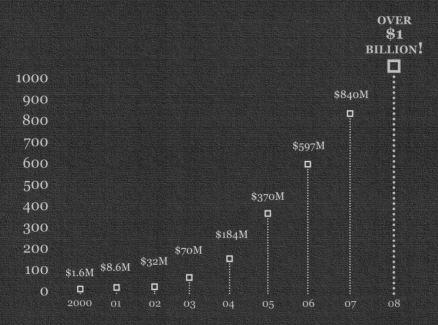

OVER
$1
BILLION!

$840M

$597M

$370M

$184M

$70M

$32M

$8.6M

$1.6M

1000
900
800
700
600
500
400
300
200
100
0

2000   01   02   03   04   05   06   07   08

Back in 2003, we set the goal of hitting $1 billion in gross merchandise sales by 2010, so we are really excited that we were able to hit that goal early.

But what we're even more excited about is another goal that we set early on, which was to make FORTUNE magazine's "100 Best Companies to Work For" list. In January 2009, we finally made the list. We came in at #23, making us the highest ranking newcomer for 2009!

We've been asked by a lot of people how we've grown so quickly, and the

Fig F-1. Tony preparing for his keynote speech at SxSW (South by SouthWest), as the 2008 Culture Book keeps him company. *March 2009.*

Fig F-2. Checking email, Twitter, SMS. What you'll find Tony doing 99% of the time.

Fig F-3. Giving his keynote at SxSW. (They're from Donald Pliner and he has a total of three pairs of shoes used on a semi-regular basis.)

Fig F-4. Tony traveling in a single engine airplane with a shoe on his head.

answer is actually really simple. We've aligned the entire organization around one mission: to provide the best customer service possible.

Online shopping can be a scary experience, especially if you're shopping for clothing or shoes. At Zappos, we believe that if we constantly strive to provide the best online shopping experience possible, then our customers will be loyal and buy from us again and again.

Rather than focus on maximizing short-term profits, we instead focus on how we can maximize the service we provide to our customers. Internally, we call this our WOW philosophy. We want every interaction with every customer to result in the customer saying "WOW" — so that they will become customers for life. Incidentally, we've found that this also results in a lot of word of mouth advertising for us, which means rather than spend a lot of money on marketing, we can instead put that money towards improving the customer experience, and the cycle continues. In the long term, we want people to associate the Zappos name with great service, not with shoes.

While this all sounds good in theory, the challenge in doing all this is focusing the entire company around service. At Zappos, customer service isn't just a department. It's the entire company.

Internally, we have a saying:

"We are a service company that happens to sell shoes.

And clothing.
And handbags.
And accessories.

And eventually anything and everything."

In order for us to succeed as a service company, we need to create, maintain, and grow a culture where employees want to play a part in providing great service. I've been asked a number of times what the company's biggest asset is, and my answer is always the same: the culture.

As we grow as a company and hire new people, we need to make sure that they understand and become a part of our culture. That is the purpose of this book -- to provide a glimpse of what the Zappos culture is all about to new hires, prospective new hires, our vendors and partners, and anyone else who might be interested.

So what is the Zappos culture? To me, the Zappos culture embodies many different elements. It's about always looking for new ways to WOW everyone we come in contact with. It's about building relationships where we treat each other like family. It's about teamwork and having fun and not taking ourselves too seriously. It's about growth, both personal and professional. It's about achieving the impossible with fewer people. It's about openness, taking risks, and not being afraid to make mistakes. But most of all, it's about having faith that if we do the right thing, then in the long run we will succeed and build something great.

Our culture is based on our **10 core values**:

1) Deliver WOW Through Service
2) Embrace and Drive Change
3) Create Fun and A Little Weirdness
4) Be Adventurous, Creative, and Open-Minded
5) Pursue Growth and Learning
6) Build Open and Honest Relationships With Communication
7) Build a Positive Team and Family Spirit
8) Do More With Less
9) Be Passionate and Determined
10) Be Humble

Unlike most companies, where core values are just a plaque on the wall, our core values play a big part in how we hire, train, and develop our employees.

At Zappos, in addition to trying to WOW our customers, we also try to WOW our employees and the vendors and business partners that we work with (and in the long run, our investors). We believe that it creates a virtuous cycle, and in our own way, we're making the world a better place and improving people's lives. It's all part of our long

term vision to deliver HAPPINESS to the world.
Of course, the Zappos culture means different things to different people, so I thought the best way for people to learn what the Zappos culture was all about was to hear from our employees directly. Below is the email that I sent to our employees in January 2009:

FROM: TONY HSIEH
TO: ALL ZAPPOS EMPLOYEES
SUBJECT: ZAPPOS CULTURE BOOK

IT'S TIME TO PUT TOGETHER A NEW EDITION OF THE ZAPPOS CULTURE BOOK, TO BE DISTRIBUTED TO EMPLOYEES, PROSPECTIVE EMPLOYEES, BUSINESS PARTNERS, AND EVEN SOME CUSTOMERS.

OUR CULTURE IS THE COMBINATION OF ALL OF OUR EMPLOYEES' IDEAS ABOUT THE CULTURE, SO WE WOULD LIKE TO INCLUDE EVERYONE'S THOUGHTS IN THIS BOOK.

PLEASE EMAIL ME A FEW SENTENCES ABOUT WHAT THE ZAPPOS CULTURE MEANS TO YOU. (WHAT IS THE ZAPPOS CULTURE? WHAT'S DIFFERENT ABOUT IT COMPARED TO OTHER COMPANY CULTURES? WHAT DO YOU LIKE ABOUT OUR CULTURE?) WE WILL COMPILE EVERYONE'S CONTRIBUTION INTO THE BOOK.

WHEN WRITING YOUR RESPONSE, PLEASE DO NOT REFER TO ANY PREVIOUS CULTURE BOOKS, ANY TRAINING/ORIENTATION MATERIAL, THE COMPANY HANDBOOK, OR ANY OTHER COMPANY-PUBLISHED MATERIAL. WE WANT TO HEAR YOUR THOUGHTS ABOUT THE COMPANY CULTURE.

ALSO, PLEASE DO NOT TALK TO ANYONE ABOUT WHAT YOU WILL BE WRITING OR WHAT ANYONE ELSE WROTE. AND FINALLY, IF YOU CONTRIBUTED TO LAST YEAR'S CULTURE BOOK, PLEASE DO NOT LOOK AT WHAT YOU WROTE LAST YEAR UNTIL AFTER YOU'VE WRITTEN AND SUBMITTED THIS YEAR'S ENTRY.

PS: If you'd like to learn more about our culture at Zappos, check out our blogs at:

http://blogs.zappos.com

You can also learn more about Zappos at:

http://about.zappos.com

If you're interested in working at our corporate headquarters in Las Vegas, our job openings are online at:

http://jobs.zappos.com

Also, we offer free tours of our headquarters in Las Vegas. Just send an email to tours@zappos.com if you're ever planning on being in the Las Vegas area!

There's so many ways to describe Zappos culture, sometimes it's better just to see it for yourself.

Take, for example, the Zappos Peep Contest.

(Note: no Peeps were harmed during the competition.)

A-1. Recreation of the battle between King Leonidas and the Persians, as told in the movie *300*. Except at Zappos, the actors come in marshmallow Peep form.

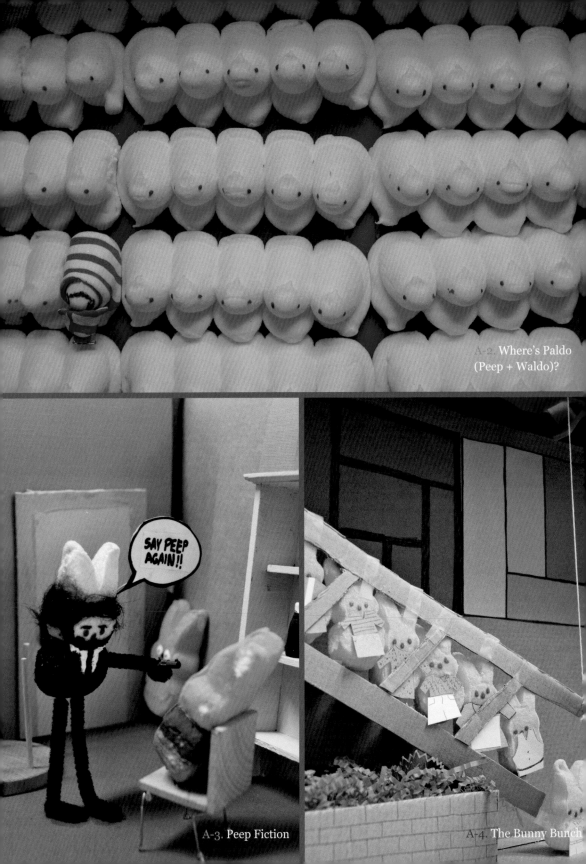

A-2. Where's Paldo (Peep + Waldo)?

A-3. Peep Fiction

A-4. The Bunny Bunch

A-5. The infamous shower scene in 'PeePsycho'.

A-6. Just another night at the 'Peep-a-Boo Club'. (No chicks allowed.)

Or how about the Polar Bear Plunge in Kentucky, an annual fundraiser for the Special Olympics.

Jumping into freezing water in winter for a good cause would be one way, dressing up as nerds beforehand would be the Zappos way.

(Note: no nerds were harmed during the fundraiser.)

THE BEST WAY TO CHEER
YOURSELF UP IS TO TRY TO CHEER
SOMEBODY ELSE UP.

MARK TWAIN

I.

CUSTOMER SERVICE
CUSTOMER LOYALTY TEAM AND PIPELINE TRAINING TEAM

Fig I-1. Instead of hiring interior decorators, every conference room has been designed by different teams of Zappos employees. An example of 'Doing More with Less' (Core Value #8) while 'Building a Positive Team and Family Spirit' (#6) with Creativity (#4).

Abbie 'Abster' M.

EMPLOYEE SINCE SEPTEMBER 26 2005

The Zappos Culture to me is unlike anything I've ever experienced before. It's always fun and weird, we're all creative and open-minded, passionate and determined, but most of all, we're humble. I think it's because most of us have worked horrible dead-end jobs before and can cherish our Zappos Culture for what it is. It's what makes me want to come in every day, even my weekends :) I'm surrounded by happy faces and feel supported in every personal and professional endeavor I embark on. Here, there are people who genuinely care about my success inside and outside of Zappos. There are friends who cheer me on and keep my spirits high. There are co-workers who care about the bigger picture and are passionate about seeing the end result.

I hear so many horror stories from friends about the places that they work and it only makes me feel that much more fortunate to be a part of the Zappos Family. I can't imagine my life without Zappos, and the amazing people that I work with. After 3 1/2 years, you'd think I'd be tired of writing these entries, but I look forward to this time of year for yet another chance to proclaim my love for Zappos! I've seen a lot of change in that time, but one thing remains the same ... our Zappos Culture! That, in itself, says it all! You stay classy, Zappos!

Abby N.

EMPLOYEE SINCE MARCH 12 2007

Zappos is the greatest thing that has ever happened to me. The minute I came to the job fair, I knew this company was something extraordinary. I have worked in customer service my whole life and always enjoyed helping people, but not in the various environments where I was helping them. Since being given the privilege to work at Zappos, I am able to give great service to people – because I am receiving great service from my job. I am so proud and lucky to work for this company. Whenever I hear Zappos mentioned when I am out and about, I make a point of listening to the conversations people are having. I know it is a little freaky to be following awkwardly close behind a couple in the bath section at Bed, Bath and Beyond, listening to their conversation, but it is worth it to me. I am OK with it because it gives me a chance to hear and introduce myself if I hear anything that I would like to bring up to the company. In short, this company is amazing. It gives us the tools to grow professionally and individually while creating many great friendships in the process. If I ever have to leave Zappos, I will know that the experience of working here has made me a better person and I will be forever grateful.

Abraar H.

EMPLOYEE SINCE JULY 29 2008

Let me start off by saying that I love Zappos, and that I am honored to be part of such a great company. I have never been part of a company that has set realistic core values for its employees to follow, not the "yes we can" cliché that most other companies I have worked for try to set as their motto, but which seem so transparent in most cases. You can truly apply Zappos' simple but important Ten Core Values to your everyday life outside of work and use them to better yourself. I want to thank Tony and everyone responsible for making this such a great company to be a part of. I am still fairly new here, but I hope to continue to grow with Zappos, and hopefully one day I can retire a happy Zapponian.

Adrienne C.

EMPLOYEE SINCE MARCH 28 2005

Over the last three years, the culture at Zappos for me has changed in some ways and yet has stayed the same. We still have that "family" type feeling. From the first day I started at Zappos, I've felt this and I continue to feel it every day. People are friendly, genuinely happy to see you and want to help you in any way they can. None of that has ever changed.

So how has our culture changed?? Zappos as a company has changed; therefore our culture had to change accordingly. We all know that we play hard and work hard together. And with the challenges we faced last year, we now know we can get through the hard times together as well. All of us bonded in a way we haven't before. That, in itself, changed us.

I've formed relationships here that have become much stronger than I thought they could ever be. It makes me want to protect our Zappos Culture (my family) even more. Every person at Zappos has a special place in my heart. I can't say that about any other place I've worked.

Fig I-2. Elvis. We're not saying he's dead or alive. All we're saying is that he stands in one of our Pipeline (training) rooms to wake us up if we drift asleep.

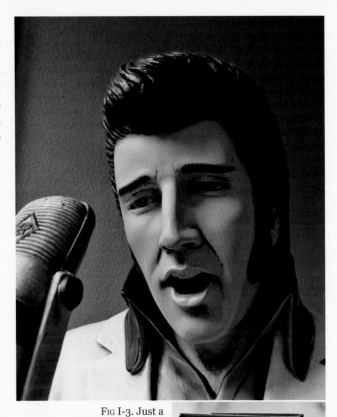

Fig I-3. Just a reminder, in case you ever forget.

Fig I-4. Each team in CLT came up with a theme to design their piggy banks. Moons over my Hammie.

Alan O.

EMPLOYEE SINCE OCTOBER 1 2007

The Zappos Culture, to me, is having such a diverse group of people doing such a great job. We have been able to pull together in the bad times, and have all enjoyed being together in the good times. I am grateful for the ability to be myself here, and I marvel at all the different types of people that work here and still have the ability to not just to get along ... but to actually care about each other.

Alexa F.

EMPLOYEE SINCE AUGUST 29 2008

I have been blessed with the opportunity to work for Zappos for the last seven months or so. Never, in my wildest dreams, could I have ever imagined that I would ever have the opportunity to work for such an incredible company! Having never worked in a call center, I was a little uneasy about what to expect when coming here to Zappos. Little did I know that this company was the company that I had been dreaming about working for someday. I had only heard about the greatness that is Zappos and the only thing I can regret is not listening to my friend and applying sooner! I have worked for many big companies, and speaking from experience, you can't find there what you find at Zappos. Zappos Culture is unmatched by that of any competitor. The culture we have ever so carefully cultivated here is one of the main reasons why I love this company the way that I do. We all share the quality of wanting to provide service through excellence in anything that we do. It's that spirit that continues to allow us to grow to what we are today. In this family, we all strive to develop and improve, not just one person but the entire company as a whole. I feel as if Zappos has broken the mold, creating an elite, integrated group of people that come together with each individual bringing something unique to the family. Ultimately, our culture here is compiled by all of us sharing beliefs, values, goals, attitudes and practices that characterize us as a family, one that each and everyone has helped cultivate and grown to love. I love my job and my new family and friends. I look forward to growing and further developing our culture here at Zappos!

Alicia L.

EMPLOYEE SINCE JANUARY 28 2007

Zappos Culture = I love coming to work every day. I love working in a building full of smiling faces. I love being able to be myself. I love parades, picnics, potlucks, parties and random cake. I love being able to use my amazing coloring skills on random occasions. I love using social media to show the world what we're like. I like being an ambassador of

WOW, everywhere I go, I'm the face of Zappos. I love my Zappos family and I am proud to call this home.

Amanda C.

EMPLOYEE SINCE NOVEMBER 12 2007

Oops! I didn't have time to come up with something funny and clever this year, so how about a Pecan Pie recipe?! Karo® Syrup is the secret to creating the perfect pecan pie. It adds a smooth texture and rich flavor, ensuring that this holiday favorite will have your friends and family begging for more.

CLASSIC PECAN PIE
Prep Time: 5 minutes
Cook Time: 55 to 60 minutes
Chill Time: 2 hours
Yield: 8 servings
INGREDIENTS:

> 1 cup Karo® Light OR Dark Corn Syrup
>
> 3 eggs
>
> 1 cup sugar
>
> 2 tablespoons butter, melted
>
> 1 teaspoon Spice Islands® Pure Vanilla Extract
>
> 1 1/2 cups (6 ounces) pecans
>
> 1 9-inch unbaked or frozen deep-dish pie crust

1. Preheat oven to 350°F.
2. Mix corn syrup, eggs, sugar, butter and vanilla using a spoon. Stir in pecans. Pour filling into pie crust (If using frozen crust, see step 4).
3. Bake on center rack of oven for 55 to 60 minutes. Cool for 2 hours on wire rack before serving.
4. If using frozen pie crust, place a cookie sheet in oven and preheat oven as directed. Pour filling into frozen crust. Bake on preheated cookie sheet.

RECIPE TIPS:
Pie is done when center reaches 200°F. Tap center surface of pie lightly – it should spring
   back when done.
For easier cleanup, spray pie pan with cooking spray before placing pie crust in pan.
If pie crust is overbrowning, cover edges with foil to prevent burning.
To reduce calories, substitute new Karo® Lite Syrup for the Karo® Light or Dark Corn Syrup.
High Altitude Adjustments: Reduce sugar to 2/3 cup and increase butter to 3 tablespoons. Reduce
   oven temperature to 325°F.

Amanda K.

EMPLOYEE SINCE JUNE 19 2006

Zappos is just like every family I associate myself with. Every family member is unique and we all have unique relationships based on our various quirks. And like every family, there are good times and bad. Luckily, the good outweighs the bad in most circumstances, and that makes it that much easier to drag myself out of bed every morning. It makes a huge impact to watch the entire company come together to support each other when we are faced with harsh si¬¬tuations. It's that support and care that creates the loyalty we have to Zappos, our customers, and each other!

Amanda R.

EMPLOYEE SINCE FEBRUARY 20 2007

The Zappos Culture is very unique and I am glad to say that I look forward to coming into the office everyday because of it. My only hope is that more companies will adopt a similar culture to improve the lives of their employees as well their customers.

Amy R.

EMPLOYEE SINCE APRIL 2 2007

I know everyone else says this too, but Zappos Culture means family to me. I imagine that other people say it due to the simple fact that it's so true. Arriving at 2280 every morning is like seeing members of my extended family on a daily basis. I have had a couple of other jobs, and after a while I would always dread coming into work. I have been with Zappos for two years now and I can honestly say that I look forward to coming in every day. Now that's saying something about how different and amazing our culture is here.

Ana L.

EMPLOYEE SINCE APRIL 2 2007

Zappos Culture means working with your friends, and partying with your friends. It means prioritizing your duties without taking yourself too seriously, and remembering that everyone has to work, so you might as well have fun while you're at it. I feel fortunate to have found a place like Zappos.

Andre N.

EMPLOYEE SINCE MAY 5 2008

The Zappos Culture is simply amazing. I love how Zappos not only embraces everyone's individuality, but also encourages it. With all the different people that work here, it is awesome to see everyone striving to ultimately accomplish the same goal. It truly is one team, one dream here at Zappos! I feel privileged to work for a company that not only takes care of its employees, but takes care of its customers as well. Thanks, Zappos!

Andrea B.

EMPLOYEE SINCE JULY 29 2008

Zappos Culture is definitely "different", in a really good way. Seriously, what other company wants you to be fun and a little weird sometimes? That was probably the hardest thing that I had to adjust to, but with all of my colleagues, (friends/family is more like it) here at Zappos being so open, friendly and just warm-hearted, it has really helped me open up. Not just with them, but with our wonderful customers as well. Zappos Culture is just plain awesome and it's because of the Ten Core Values that we embrace. It has also helped me grow into such a better person. I smile more, I laugh more, I live more than I used to, not just here at work, but everywhere. I've learned that once you've let the culture here run through your veins, it changes you in so many great ways, some ways that I thought were impossible to change, but it does.

Andrea R.

EMPLOYEE SINCE FEBRUARY 20 2007

I have been here almost two years now and Zappos Culture is still the same! It's a friendly place to work. More than that, on a daily basis your surrounded with people who feel more like family than co-workers. I never dread coming in to work in the morning because I know something exciting will happen. There is never a dull moment at work because we're all encouraged to be ourselves. The culture here at work is hard to describe because it's like no other place I have ever worked for. When I try explaining it to people, they don't believe me half the time because it sounds too good to be true!

Andrew T.

EMPLOYEE SINCE MARCH 1 2008

Being part of the Zappos Culture has been the most unique experience in my professional career. It is like reaching a new frontier in terms of customer service as well as corporate culture. For someone with an extensive corporate experience, this is breaking a lot of traditions and is opening up so many opportunities. For a person with limited work experience, it is setting the bar really high, because after the Zappos Experience, moving forward to some other endeavor will be a difficult transition (somewhat like a withdrawal). I need to emphasize that like everything in the world, especially among companies, nothing is perfect. This is a work-in-progress and achievements are accomplished on a daily basis. (So it is great that we are empowered to contribute with our 1%.) I believe we are a positive influence in terms of corporate success. Hopefully, we have pioneered a trend in terms of customer service and loyalty. Someday, our special way of customer service will be the norm (rather than the exception) for both brick-and-mortar as well as online businesses. Our success is measured not only in terms of being a profitable and viable business but as well as being the number 1 company whenever people think about service. I foresee Zappos expanding its business, not only in terms of products, but into other business services in the years ahead. I would also like to take this opportunity to proudly say that this company is powered by PEOPLE.

Anna C.

EMPLOYEE SINCE DECEMBER 3 2007

I have worked for several different companies in my lifetime and Zappos.com is probably the best. Zappos tries very hard to make the employee/work experience enjoyable. I work with the nicest people and they all make coming to work very enjoyable.

Anonymous.

The Zappos Culture is what sets Zappos apart from other businesses. For me, it means looking forward to coming to work each day. There is always something fun happening, and my job itself is rewarding. I love my job because it is my passion. I have the ability to problem-solve and organize, and what I do daily makes a difference. At the end of the day, I leave feeling rewarded and happy to work at Zappos. Thank you for the opportunity!

Anonymous.

I think that our company's culture is all about working hard, but having fun while you're doing it. We try to create fun and weirdness in everything we do. Whether it's contests, games, dunk tanks, or parades, we take time out of our day to have fun and foster a very unique family spirit. Because ultimately, that fun and energetic vibe carries over through our daily interactions with our customers, vendors, and business partners alike.

Anonymous.

I have submitted culture essays in the past and I feel the same today as I did back then. Zappos Culture encourages you to learn, grow and achieve. Zappos Culture is everywhere around us. It is what makes us who we are. I appreciate this company and what it does for its team members. I am proud to tell people I work for Zappos.

Anonymous.

This may sound silly, but I looked up the word "culture" in the dictionary to get a feel for how it was defined. I was shocked that I didn't see the word Zappos in there. Our culture is the life and soul of the Zappos body and without it, we would just be another plain company. I have never felt so proud to work for a company that not only works extremely hard, but also plays hard. It's our passion for both that gives us our culture. It's not just going from good to great (a company I used to work from used that slogan, so cliché), but being able to recognize that we are innovators in our industry ... yet we remain very humble as we change the world.

Anthony S.
EMPLOYEE SINCE JAN 28 2008

To me, the Zappos Culture is about making the best out of the toughest times. It is about thinking positively when moving forward and adding a little fun and weirdness along the way.

Aria L.

EMPLOYEE SINCE MAY 23 2005

At every job that I have previously had, I have hit a wall after about two years. Not so here at Zappos. Four years in and every day there is something new and exciting happening. Even better, I have the ability to make it fun and exciting for myself and others. I sit in the front row and I always get asked if I am bothered by people passing by and saying, "Hi" while I am working. Absolutely not! That is one of my favorite parts of my day. I can be having a not so stellar day and the smiling faces that everyone has work to cheer me up, and that is only going to make my day more productive. Here's to four more years!

Ashotta W.

EMPLOYEE SINCE AUGUST 20 2007

I feel like being at Zappos teaches you a lot about life and what it means to be a family. Our family was tested in 2008 but in the end we achieved a lot of goals that, at the time, we didn't know we were gonna hit. At the end of it all, it brought us all closer together and we stuck by each other through the good times and the not-so-good times. This is a phenomenal company to work for and I wish that a lot of people could sit and learn the loyalty and values that we exude on a day-to-day basis. The best part of Zappos is the people in it.

Atrell L.

EMPLOYEE SINCE MAY 7 2005

The Zappos Culture is truly indescribable. I've been working here for four years now, and like our customers, I am still WOWed! Never have I worked for a company that embraces individualism and empowers its employees to make decisions when taking care of customers, as opposed to having them rely on supervisors and managers. Zappos represents the epitome of building relationships, not just with its customers, but also with employees, vendors, and investors. It's amazing! The company clearly reflects the humbleness and determination of our CEO. It has truly been a fulfilling experience to grow with this company. I feel blessed and honored to be a part of such an amazing experience. It just keeps getting better.

Augusta S.

EMPLOYEE SINCE MAY 7 2007

This is my second time writing for the Culture Book. The Zappos Culture is still the "life blood" of Zappos. And it must always be that. It is what flows through all of us, every day, and it even carries over into our everyday life. It is the feeling of being who we are and being the best at it every day. It is a feeling of freedom, happiness, empowerment and gratitude. Other companies' culture? Well, if memory serves me right, it was a feeling of not knowing, not being informed. It is a feeling of not being a part of the big picture, and not being sure what the big picture was. Other companies are mostly driven by numbers, not service or people. What I love about our Zappos Culture is that our culture is us. We make the culture what it is. We are empowered to embrace the culture, which is the way we do things. We put our signatures on everything we do. Assisting customers, embracing change, being open and honest with communication, building our family and team spirits, being passionate and determined about what we do and how we do it. Of course, the fun of being fun and a little weird is great! That's why we must never let it change ... unless the change is only to make it better. Because it is Zappos' future, and my future as well, that would be at stake. It is up to us. As for me, I will continue to champion our Zappos Culture.

Beverly S.

EMPLOYEE SINCE JANUARY 22 2005

When I talk about Zappos to my friends and family, they see how passionate I am about it. My friends back home can't believe employees can feel that way about the company they work for. Before Zappos, neither could I. Since I started at Zappos, I have grown a lot, both personally and professionally. I love the family spirit at Zappos – we laugh and celebrate during the good times, stick together through the bad. It's like the TV show, "Cheers – where everybody knows your name." I am so lucky to be at Zappos and I can't imagine working anywhere else. If Zappos moves to the North Pole, I'm going with them!

Bobby C.

EMPLOYEE SINCE DECEMBER 3 2007

Zappos Culture is the validation for doing what most won't do. Going beyond customer's expectations is like drinking water and getting plenty of sleep. It's a necessary habit. The cool thing is we don't think about it, but customers usually remind us it does make a difference. Truth is that we believe in a bigger picture, a greater goal and this translates into a nurturing, fun place ... not "the daily grind."

Brandon B.

EMPLOYEE SINCE SEPTEMBER 18 2006

Zappos, like "zapatos" with a kick – no pun intended. Fun, like bun, with an "f." Crazy, like daisy, with a c-r-z, and no "i" or "s." You get the picture. Zappos, where dreams are born, nurtured and then let into daycare while you work full time and then pick them up to spend a few hours with them before it's bed time. Zappos, much like your best friend that you've known from the time you were infants, grew up together to one day fall in love and get married after years of not noticing that you actually love your best friend, not the girl you just met by the name of 'Sapphire'. Zappos, much like the hot chocolate that your mom used to make, the perfect temperature, but not so hot that it burns your throat when you drink it and you end up spilling it on your lap or shirt, making you spill more as you get up suddenly due to the severe burns. The culture, much like the cultures across the world, all condensed into two buildings, one warehouse and spread between two states. The culture, just like the model U.N. group you had when you were in junior high, just without the drama or ethnocentricism. The culture, much like the couture brands of Fendi, Prada and Bally but without excluding the everyday brands such as Roxy, Dickies or Nurse Mates. (Sorry, Crocs, but you rest forever in our hearts.) Not much more could be said about Zappos, other than we are a service company that happens to sell shoes, handbags, clothing, video games, global positioning systems, socks, lingerie, hiking tools, lunch boxes, shoe care, barbecues, watches, laptops and also motivational books.

Briana K.

EMPLOYEE SINCE MAY 5 2008

The culture of Zappos is ever-evolving and always alive. The opportunities to learn something new, to exceed expectations, and to better oneself are only made possible because this culture is constantly changing. Whether or not we, as people, know it in the moment, this forces us to grow, only for the better.

Briseida D.

EMPLOYEE SINCE MAY 5 2008

It is what it is … a CULT! I'm sucked into this company with some of the most amazing people that I've ever met. Sometimes it's a little kooky but nonetheless, it's a fun, stress-free and enriching work environment. I also like to brag that I work for the #23 company on Forbes' "Top companies to work for" list.

Britnee B.

EMPLOYEE SINCE MAY 5 2008

I LOVE ZAPPOS! Zappos is the best company to work for by far, even though we have been standing side by side with Core Value #2 since I've been here ... I still think it's the best. I am truly blessed that God has opened the doors to such an awesome opportunity for me to grow in. Everyone here has been great. The customers are fantastic and lunch is yummy. I am in love with the fact that we are encouraged to bring our personality to the table and we are able to do our jobs without limitations. Zappos is not just a place of business but a great learning environment. There are so many possibilities to explore and so many paths to wander down, it's amazing! I know that all the experiences that I encounter at Zappos will help me deliver better "WOW through service," not only on the CLT phones but throughout life in general. The Zappos Culture has taught me how to be a great listener, how to build open and honest relationships with communication, how to build a positive team and family spirit, and how to pursue growth and learning (<---my favorite).

Every day when I come to work, I am overwhelmed with the genuine smiles and happy spirits of my Zappos family. The infectious joy of people I work with inspires me to become more open-minded, creative, and adventurous with each passing day. Each individual is fueled with passion and determination to give the best customer service for our customers, visitors, partners and co-workers ... how can you not be thankful for the culture that surrounds us all day?

Stay Humble!

Candace C.

EMPLOYEE SINCE MARCH 10 2008

The Zappos Culture is an experience of acceptance by all. I sometimes look around and feel we are in a melting pot, and as I look around to my supportive co-workers, I realize all the cream has come to the top and our culture is boiling over! It is boiling over with ideas, inventiveness, understanding, openness, graciousness and creativity. The culture takes you by surprise and embraces you. It is great to be in an atmosphere where you know that whoever you come in contact with that day before work will touch you in some way and you will never be the same person as when you woke that morning. The Zappos Culture makes me a better person.

Candace S.

EMPLOYEE SINCE DECEMBER 4 2006

Zappos Culture is so hard to explain. To me, our culture is about family, belonging, values, fun, service, passion and so much more. I have worked at many companies over the years and have never felt a sense of being a valuable asset to the company, worth investing time and money into, until I came to Zappos. I feel that Zappos invests a tremendous amount of time, training and money into each and every employee, to make us better at what we do not only at work but also in everyday life. Zappos cares about our health and well-being as well as the work that we do. They provide us with paid insurance, (almost unheard of in this time and day), tools for everyday living, fun, our opinions are valued and we are listened to. I still can't believe after over two years that I am excited to come to work every single day! I was actually driving to work the other day, thinking to myself, after this much time at this job, I don't dread going to work. WOW!

Carol T.

EMPLOYEE SINCE APRIL 7 2008

Zappos Culture to me is a celebration of the unique contribution that each person makes to the workload and spirit of the company. It is an environment that encourages a discovery of each person's strengths and an acceptance of their weaknesses. Zappos Culture is like a warm and encouraging embrace.

Chelsea P.

EMPLOYEE SINCE OCTOBER 6 2008

Culture shows your true colors and there's nothing more beautiful than that. Zappos has a carefree culture that accepts everyone the way they are and encourages people to be passionate about things.

Chelsea S.

EMPLOYEE SINCE JULY 31 2007

Zappos Culture, to me, is a way for everyone to be treated equally and to be appreciated for being themselves. Other companies I have worked for don't really have a so-called "culture". What I like about our culture is that diversity and differences are celebrated, not looked down on. Everyone here has the same chance to learn new skill sets and to progress, no matter how little experience they have had in the past. This, in turn, makes Zappos a fun and comfortable environment, which makes you want to come to work to spend time with extended family.

Cheree D.

EMPLOYEE SINCE DECEMBER 28 2004

The Zappos Culture has a culture of its own. It's a culture that no other company can compare to. Zappos Culture is the belief in every employee, and seeks to turn each employee's success story into a company-wide success. It's nice to work for a company that allows you to find your niche and gives you the ability to make the decisions that should make each and every one of our customers happy. My experience with Zappos has been nothing less than wonderful, as I'm headed toward my fifth year here!

Christina C^a.

EMPLOYEE SINCE APRIL 2 2007

What Zappos means to me ... after two years I can sum it up in these three words: Family, Fun, Culture! I have worked in many call centers and none have felt more like a family then Zappos. Everyone embraces the culture and lives the culture in their everyday lives. People see me with my badge all the time and always say how cool it would be to work at Zappos! I love my Zappos family and want to celebrate many more years here!

Christina C^o.

EMPLOYEE SINCE JANUARY 8 2007

What a year it's been. There were painful changes and choices that had to be made. And they hurt. We've had to band together like never before to weather a storm unprecedented in our lives. We've had to refocus and reawaken our passions. We've had to dig deep and dig in and do it together. And we have. And we will continue to. We're determined.

Some say her sweat glands are shaped like Australia and she's never been outside her house, all we know is that she's a STIG Wannabe!!

Christina L.

EMPLOYEE SINCE MAY 5 2008

The Zappos Culture is definitely unique in so many different ways! I love that I can work in an environment that urges me to have a lot of fun! One of my favorite things about being a Customer Loyalty Representative is that I am able to give quality, individualized customer service! Every person that calls in for assistance has a different story and situation. Within my job responsibilities, I am given the tools, power and freedom to assist customers in the way I feel will best suit their customer experience. I am always amazed how far a Zappos employee will go to make someone's day! At Zappos, we are encouraged to grow, learn, communicate and build a spirit of friendship that will last for years to come!

Christine B.

EMPLOYEE SINCE JULY 29 2008

Zappos keeps my rent paid, my tummy full of PBJ's, and my heart full of love for all the wonderful people that I get to work with.

Cierra D.

EMPLOYEE SINCE JANUARY 29 2007

The Zappos Culture to me is a way of life. These people I work with everyday are like my family. We all have something special in common – this amazing company we work for. It's a partnership and a bond in which we all share. We rely on and trust each other in many aspects of life, not just work. The culture brings us together and keeps us there. We are better, smarter, more successful and happier people because of our culture. I love the Zappos Culture because it doesn't define me, it inspires me!

Clarence R.

EMPLOYEE SINCE OCTOBER 6 2008

To me, Zappos Culture is what keeps you from screaming in your car before you walk into the office. It's the antidote to the status quo. The culture gives you the freedom to express yourself, which lets you feel like a real member of a team. To me it's not just some corporate mantra fed to the drones. It's the ability to communicate with anybody, at any time, from middle management all the way to the CEO. It's a rare thing to feel important within a company and Zappos Culture is all about that.

Clarissa R.

EMPLOYEE SINCE MARCH 10 2008

I am enjoying my employment here. This is the only company that not only talks the talk, but also walks the walk. Everyone is friendly, helpful and does their best to help you succeed. I don't have to worry about politics. Everything is what it is and never sugar coated. I am free to be myself, the uniqueness of each person's personality may add some weirdness, but each flavor is a necessary ingredient. Resources are at my disposal to assist each customer, "how to" techniques and yet there is no one watching over my shoulder. Opportunities are given to learn, grow, have fun and just be comfortable in my own skin so-to-speak. Nowhere else that I know of can you be creative in every aspect of your job, enjoy coming to work, and feel like you're part of a big family. I'm humbled, blessed, privileged and honored to be here.

Cody B.

EMPLOYEE SINCE OCTOBER 22 2007

Zappos Culture, to me, means a sense of belonging. There is an underlying feel from everyone that we not only belong to the Zappos Family, but that we belong to something greater than we are. I think working here makes us take for granted the real service we provide, but when we leave here and don't get what we've been trained to think is what should be, we remember just how awesome this company really is. It's an amazing feeling from such an amazing culture. Zappos is us, and we can do anything together!

Corey S.

EMPLOYEE SINCE JANUARY 28 2008

The Zappos Culture to me is the very backbone of this company. I can go out and get a job anywhere doing the very same thing I am now ... or can I? Now that I think about it, I can't. The reason why I would not be able to find a job like this one is because of our culture. Here at Zappos we do have rules, regulations, and guidelines that we work by, but also that we live by. There is a certain feeling of freedom when I come into the office that can be found at no other company. The culture here provides people the opportunity to interact with co-workers in other departments. This gives you a greater understanding on how the entire company comes together as a whole to execute one common goal. That goal is to provide the very best shopping experience and customer service that can be found only at Zappos.

Corina C.
EMPLOYEE SINCE JANUARY 7 2008

The longer I'm a part of the company the more I find out about myself. I've made friendships that will last a lifetime, and bonds that will never be broken. I find myself coming to work not only because it's a job, but also because I love to be here. It's amazing to be at a job where everybody is happy about being there. I hate being scared of the 'big guys' [CEO, CFO, etc] and here, you don't have that sense of fear. We really are just a big family. This has been an excellent experience, and I hope that in the future, somebody will be in my position and have the opportunity to build lasting friendships, amazing bonds, and have a great time while being at work.

Crystal D.
EMPLOYEE SINCE JUNE 2 2008

Zappos is like nothing I've ever seen! For the first few months, I was waiting for the ball to drop ... well I've stopped waiting and it still hasn't! It is amazing when you love your job and one of your main duties is listening to how great you are. That never gets old! Cheers to Zappos! May you have many more years of success!

Crystal M.
EMPLOYEE SINCE AUGUST 30 2005

When I think of what makes Zappos' culture so different, I come up with the following: It is fun, caring, exciting, parades, expos, tours, Twitter, Spoken Word, Zappos Idol, celebrations, awards, carnivals, picnics, milestones, togetherness, family spirit and WOW.

There is always something positive happening at Zappos. It is a very different company to work for in comparison to others. At most companies you will never see the CEO sitting in a cubicle in the same area as the employees. Other CEOs are not approachable but here at Zappos, Tony is very approachable. Most companies do not have crazy parades going through the office during business hours. Here at Zappos you may see and hear a parade at any time during the week. There will be candy or trinkets flying through the air. I was on the phone with a customer one day when a parade came through and the customer was excited that we get to have so much fun at work. Other companies do not have employees singing or reading poetry in front of other co-workers during lunchtime, but here at Zappos we have fun doing these things. We call it Zappos Idol or the Spoken Word. At most companies, you do not hear of them having Expos where you can learn more about the products during working hours. Here at Zappos, we are allowed time to go to these special Expos and learn about the different merchandise we have on our website.

During my three years at Zappos, I have seen our culture grow and change along with our company. We have more exciting co-workers, more celebrations and more milestones accomplished (i.e., a billion dollars in sales in a year). Zappos is an awesome company to work and play at. It is a wonderful feeling to work at a company that has been rated number 23 of Fortune Magazine's "100 Top Companies to Work For." What an accomplishment to be one of the best! It is based on our culture being so different than other companies and Powered by the WOW Factor.

Dail T.

EMPLOYEE SINCE MARCH 12 2007

It is a pleasure to work for a company that has the positive, upbeat attitude we have here at Zappos. I am provided with all the tools and encouragement needed to advance as far as I want. The culture is really refreshing and I love the way Zappos WOWs their external and internal customers every day.

Dan H.

EMPLOYEE SINCE AUG 20 2007

Zappos is more then a company; it is a second home. I have met some special people that will be a part of my life and career for a very long time. Working here has opened up doors that I never even thought existed, and I am grateful and humbled by that.

Dana C.

EMPLOYEE SINCE AUGUST 20 2007

Zappos has changed my life. I love being able to work with people that are so awesome. Everyone here is my friend and second family. Our customers are the best! I get to come to work and talk to the coolest people! I enjoy my job so much! It really makes a difference in your life when you work in such a wonderful environment. Thanks, Zappos!

Daniel H.

EMPLOYEE SINCE FEBRUARY 20 2007

Our culture to me means freedom. Freedom to be yourself, freedom to use talents you might never be able to exercise elsewhere. Just looking at my "Semi-Annual Self Review", I'm the editor of "Zappos in the News" on the Wiki, I'm in 6pm.com now, in the past year I've facilitated Yoga classes in Training and in Leadership & Development, got to help our participants in the JanSport 8000 Meter, helped stage the CLT Zappos Prom as part of the WOW Team, transitioned the training manual for the Resource Desk into electronic form and led a team to make over the Howard Hughes conference room. This type of freedom helps our employees enjoy what their actual jobs are, because they're fulfilled.

Danika J.

EMPLOYEE SINCE JANUARY 7 2008

I can't believe it's been a whole year that I've worked here!!! All right, I know that's the most classic retrospective cliché you can say, but I still can't believe how lucky I am that I work at a company with so much heart, humor and positivity, and I can't imagine where else I would rather be. In the year that I've worked here, the people that work here ARE the Zappos Culture. All the different personalities and backgrounds of everyone who works here are the inspiration for our culture that makes coming to work here every day exciting and fulfilling. We are not just Zapponians, we are Zappos Idols, ping pong champions, Masters of WOW. We can be who we are, whether we're rocking the phones or kicking back at a Zappos happy hour. Long live individuality!!!!

Darlene K.

EMPLOYEE SINCE JULY 29 2008

I would like to contribute my thoughts on Core Value #2, Embrace and Drive Change, and why it's important to me and to the Zappos Culture. My husband and I had moved from Michigan to Las Vegas in January, 2008. We had planned this for at least two years before "jumping in the frying pan" to do it. I was nervous but excited because I had never lived anywhere but Michigan. When I first arrived here, I literally broke down and cried. I'll be honest, I was scared to death!!! Was this the right thing to do?? Did I just waste seven days of driving to get here and have this happen to me??? After that, I took a deep breath and decided it was the right thing to do, and I have to tell you I haven't regretted it. So when I started to look for employment, I had only heard of Zappos from my daughters because I did order from Zappos in the past. I only knew that they sold shoes, so when I heard they were hiring, I did everything possible to make sure that I would be a prospective employee and that I would fit into the culture here. It has been an amazing "wild ride" and I don't want to get off. I love living here in Las Vegas and am proud to be a Zappos employee.

Darren R.

EMPLOYEE SINCE OCTOBER 22 2007

The culture here at Zappos is what really sets us apart from all the other companies I've worked with. There's a million ways I could try to explain it, but in the end it all boils down to bringing everyone all together. No matter what a person's background is, no matter their walk of life, they are not only accepted, but all the different outlooks are pulled together to better everyone.

Dave J.

EMPLOYEE SINCE OCTOBER 23 2006

There is so much to say about Zappos but here is a little bit of it. The past two years working here have been a blast. I have learned there is a work place that can change everyday and still be the same place I started at in October of 2006. The company as a whole is one of a kind – I am honored to work here.

Dawn J.

EMPLOYEE SINCE MARCH 6 2006

To me, the Zappos Culture is about family. The bonds I have formed with people at Zappos will last a lifetime, I only have one friend outside of Zappos and I have been trying to make her work here since I started. Zappos is more than a job to me, it's part of my life and part of who I am, and it's helping me to be the person I want to be. I have learned a lot about myself through Zappos and our culture. The company culture is amazing, and it is what makes us special .We truly do care about our customers and they always come first. The fact that we are empowered to do the right thing still amazes me after years of working here. I am honestly proud to be a part of Zappos.

Deborah H.

EMPLOYEE SINCE AUGUST 28 2006

After two and a half years, I'm still here. I cannot remember the last time I was with the same company for that long. I have worked for some wonderful companies. I have been very lucky. I have never been more proud to work some place. The very ideas that were shared with me on the first day I came to Zappos are still being shared today. These are challenging times, and I believe we have met and will continue to meet the challenge, because we believe that together we can.

Dee M.

EMPLOYEE SINCE DECEMBER 4 2006

Congratulations are in order for me, as I have completed my second year here at Zappos and I am still excited. It is still a fun place to work while pursuing growth, if that is your goal. I think I work with a very wonderful group and everyone seem to be so friendly. This really works. Thanks Zappos, I am looking forward to more years of being part of this great family.

Dennis L.

EMPLOYEE SINCE JULY 29 2008

The Zappos Culture is the greatest asset to the company. It is the main reason I took a pay cut to join. What the culture means to me is acceptance and tolerance. There aren't many big businesses that allow their employees to wear anything (non offensive, of course) to work, i.e., sweats, slippers, basketball shorts, wigs, hats, loose or tight clothes, painted faces, etc. Most companies I worked for, you have to wear a tie or tight uniform for something that doesn't relate to the job. Also, not many companies encourage growth and learning, humility, values the human race should live by anyway! Everyone is friendly. Good vibes! I call it a hater-free work place! If it's your birthday, you had a baby, or it's a special occasion, almost everyone will acknowledge the occasion. How wonderful! How great is a company that can enjoy different ideas and personalities, and doesn't create or expect robots. All companies should embrace culture like Zappos does! Finally, I would just like to say thank you to Tony and everyone! I now know that people (especially in the work place) still have values that we as a society should practice and live with, every day of our life.

Derek C.

EMPLOYEE SINCE JANUARY 8 2007

The Zappos Culture, to me, means camaraderie. It is the understanding that everyone is in this for the team and that it is about helping the company grow as a whole. In other companies, everyone seems to be out for number one, but with Zappos, there is so much selflessness and caring that it really does feel like a family. I would gladly go to great lengths to help anyone here and I know they would do the same for me. Zappos truly is a second family.

Derek F.

EMPLOYEE SINCE APRIL 7 2008

I love being a part of Zappos because it is unlike any other place I have worked. I have never been part of a company that embodies such a fun and wonderful culture. I not only have fun while at work, but the events that are put on outside are unheard of!! We work hard and we play even harder!! I am so glad I am a part of the team here at Zappos and can't wait to see what the future has in store for us.

Derek S.

EMPLOYEE SINCE APRIL 2 2007

Zappos Culture to me is the epitome of balance. As an employee with this company, I've seen it grow and flourish with so many "firsts" that it's hard to recall them all. I'm often excited simply by the fact that I'm with a company that I can be proud of. My grandfather talked about having that same feeling when he was in the aerospace industry and how the lack of true grit and loyalty was the shortcoming of my generation. Unfortunately, he passed on before I started working with this company, but I think he would see that it's not that dedication can't be attained by my generation. It's just that the parameters on how to attain that loyalty have changed. The balance is found in the freedom an employee is given at this company. This is tempered with the understanding that there are also times when you have to knuckle down and get a job done. If there were ever a blueprint of what a company should look like to its customers, employees and competitors, I think Zappos is it. The pangs of lean years to come are trumpeted from all sides. I'm reassured by relatives that no matter what happens in the near future, they'll be there. Yet I can't help thinking, when they attempt to reassure me, that it's all misplaced, I'm with Zappos – and no matter how dark times get, I'm with the team that can weather the storm.

Devlyn T.

EMPLOYEE SINCE JUNE 20 2005

At other companies, going into work would kill any good mood I already had. At Zappos, it's the opposite. If I happen to wake up on the wrong side of the bed one morning, going into work will actually put me in a good mood! Whether it's laughing with a co-worker, teaching a 9:00 a.m. class, or checking out the latest videos on the blogs, coming to work at Zappos never fails to lift my spirits. The positive atmosphere I walk into each morning is, in my opinion, a direct result of our Ten Core Values and everyone's commitment to keeping the Zappos Culture strong. It's an amazing feeling to work for a company with such a great attitude and great people. And it's nice to know that if I ever wake up feeling blah, it won't last long. Because all I have to do is put a little Zappos in my day!

Diana A.

EMPLOYEE SINCE DECEMBER 3 2007

Now it's been a little over a year since I started working at Zappos. I love it here every day, just like on day one. I mean, I love coming to work, the employees are great, the work atmosphere is excellent. You can be yourself; whether you're a little weird or not, you can express yourself freely.

The Zappos Culture means a lot to me. I mean, you can all unite as one and work together as a team and not individually. Zappos is like my second home. You have your co-workers who, over time, become your friends and so forth. Let's aim for two years!

Diana G.

EMPLOYEE SINCE SEPTEMBER 26 2005

The Zappos Culture means everything to me. Our Culture is what makes us different from any other company. I love how Zappos embraces our individuality. On previous jobs, I wanted to forget about my day as soon as I was off the clock. With Zappos it's different. I've never worked in a place where I had so much fun! Every day after work, the first thing I do is share all the crazy stories about my day with my family. Like the Chubby Bunny contest – I didn't think it was possible to put 16 marshmallows in your mouth all at once. Or the Oktoberfest parade. It's our second year having it and all the guys still look great in their lederhosen outfits. The best prank was when Jimmy, Jimmy and Dev, came up with the great idea of challenging Frank to the Chubby Bunny contest and stuffed one of the marshmallows with olives. FYI – Frank HATES olives. I will never forget when he bit into it. His face was priceless! I have so many great memories and they keep getting better through out the years! Create fun and a little weirdness! I Love Zappos!

Diana O.

EMPLOYEE SINCE DECEMBER 5 2005

The Zappos Culture here is truly one of a kind that I have never experienced and I am happy to be a part of the culture we have here. Zappos Culture allows us to be who we really are without being afraid to show our little goofy sides. I am grateful for the freedom that allows us to contribute ideas about the company and the ability to grow with the company. Without Zappos Culture, we would not have the diversity that we have here. We really would not have the different personalities that make us smile and laugh so hard till we cry on a day-to-day basis. Our culture is what allows the company to be fun and a little weird without feeling guilty for having too much fun while we take care of business. :-) Once you experience Zappos Culture, your views and ideas change. Not only do things change but you take it everywhere with you, not just at work but everywhere. That includes the Ten Core Values; they become a part of you. Please, Zappos Culture, don't ever change, without you we would be lost! :-)

Diane M.

EMPLOYEE SINCE AUGUST 16 2004

Zappos Culture is fun and family! Our culture is different than that of other companies, due to standard corporate policies being completely thrown out the window. Zappos actually cares for its employees and we come first!

Dionne L.

EMPLOYEE SINCE APRIL 2 2007

Zappos is home away from home, a place that I can call family, a place that I can be myself. :-)

Donna G.

EMPLOYEE SINCE NOVEMBER 6 2004

Our culture encourages diversity, and thinking outside the box. We are encouraged to be ourselves and contribute ideas to constantly improve service to our customers and our working relationships with each other. It's a pleasure to come to work every day.

Donna H.

EMPLOYEE SINCE JUNE 13 2005

I can't believe I will celebrate my 4th anniversary with Zappos this year! It really doesn't seem possible that that much time has passed. In retrospect, from the first day I walked into the lobby at the Warm Springs office, I have felt extraordinarily fortunate to be part of the Zappos family. Although we have grown enormously in the last four years and many things have changed, one thing that has remained constant is the passion for and focus on making sure we stay true to our culture. I am so happy to see the Zappos philosophy spread and am also proud (humbly so) to have the privilege of being an ambassador of our culture to others.

Donna M.

EMPLOYEE SINCE DECEMBER 3 2007

Zappos has a caring, nurturing environment. I have no doubt that I am a valued team member and my team (everyone at Zappos) wants me to succeed. We are empowered to make decisions on what we think will best serve our customers. We are all about giving our customers the best service they have ever received. That is made easy because that is how each individual at Zappos is treated! It is a happy place to be and that makes one want to work all the harder to give the best they have!

Drew G.

EMPLOYEE SINCE JANUARY 28 2008

My name is Drew and I've worked at Zappos for a little over a year. In my year here, I've had the opportunity to watch our company culture continue to grow and develop. The thing that makes our culture different than other companies that I've worked for in the past is how genuine and organic our culture is. Although we have a list of core values that we always try to live by, every one of us is allowed to interpret and implement these core values in our own way.

Since the economy has taken a turn for the worse, we have had to make changes accordingly. However, we've made no sacrifices in putting our culture on display, both in the office and over the phones to our customers. It's become more and more important that we recognize that our culture is important to us for a variety of reasons. It is not only what keeps us happy at work and what keeps us close as friends and coworkers, but it is also our product. With other companies slashing prices in an attempt to weather this economic storm, we have remained steadfast. We stand by our merchandise, our service and our culture. Because we are so confident in our company, we believe that without cutting our prices, we can keep our customers loyal by letting our culture shine through. I think that as long as we can keep coming up with creative ways to promote and further our company culture, we will not have to worry about what might be going on around us. We can be subtly confident and always figure out a way to put a smile on our face, and on the face of our customers.

DShawn D.

EMPLOYEE SINCE JANUARY 28 2008

Working at Zappos has been an eye-opening experience for me. I honestly never thought that I would find a place that would embrace the weirdness that I have to offer the world. They've shown me how to use my fun and weirdness for good instead of evil. So now, instead of conquering the world, I have decided to conquer the WOW– from customers EVERYWHERE!

Duke C.

EMPLOYEE SINCE JUNE 18 2005

I LOVE THIS COMPANY!!! I've been here for 4 years and this statement still holds true each and every day. Each year brings with it new challenges, and boy, did we have a big challenge this past year with the economy. During the toughest of times, we Zapponians come together as one team, one family, powered by our Ten Core Values. There will always be a light at the end of any dark tunnel. Keep the light burning, Zappos!

Duron P.

EMPLOYEE SINCE MAY 7 2007

Not much has changed in the past year. I'm still blessed to be at a KICK-ASS company like Zappos. I've moved to a different position within CLT and I LOVE IT. I'm looking forward to a lot more wonderful and exciting experiences here. Talk to ya in 2010 :)

Dylan M.

EMPLOYEE SINCE DECEMBER 3 2007

Zappos Culture is different because it doesn't squeeze people into a mold or a preconceived idea of what the perfect employee is. Zappos allows you the freedom to be yourself and work to better your own potential. On a bad day, I think back to other jobs I have had and can't imagine ever going back. Thank you, Zappos!

Ebonique H.

EMPLOYEE SINCE JANUARY 8 2007

I love, love, love Zappos. There isn't a better company in the world to work for at such a young age. If Zappos hired nurses, they would get my first application when I graduate from school. I can't think of a place where I could meet so many genuine friends that all have the same upbeat, silly personality as I do. Yeah, we had a hard year, but we got through it and as a company I feel we are all a little stronger. We had some amazing accomplishments and I personally feel as if I helped to achieve them. I am so glad that two years ago, my friend said "Hey, check out the Zappos job fair." Unfortunately, she didn't get this wonderful job and is forever envious of me, but I bring her to all the fun parties. I couldn't be happier here. Thanks, Zappos.

Eleni D.

EMPLOYEE SINCE JANUARY 8 2007

"BE HUMBLE" & "BE BLESSED"-There's no other way to be!!

Elissa S.

EMPLOYEE SINCE OCTOBER 1 2007

Priceless ... That's what Zappos Culture is to me.

Elsie I.

EMPLOYEE SINCE JUNE 18 2005

Zappos Culture means having the freedom to be yourself and have fun while at work! We are all given the opportunity to grow and to try new and different ways of doing things with one goal in mind: to provide the absolute best customer service ever! Zappos creates a friendly environment that has no boundaries on what we can do to provide a total positive experience for everyone who comes in contact with us. The company truly understands that there is no difference between its external and internal customers. Our feedback and ideas are always encouraged and appreciated. It is a pleasure to work at Zappos; we are all a great big family, the Zappos family!

Eric P.

EMPLOYEE SINCE NOVEMBER 12 2007

Hmmmmmmmm ... what can be said about life at Zappos that hasn't been said before: Often imitated, never duplicated? Where a kid can be a kid? When you're here, you're family? The happiest place on earth? Be all that you can be? I'm lovin' it? Sometimes you feel like a nut, sometimes you don't? These slogans are well known and each one happens to apply to our culture (minus Space Mountain and limitless toys, although we do have an all-you-can eat-salad bar). Still, the one slogan that rises to the top is Powered by Service. No matter how nutty or kid-like or hungry one may be, we are all about the best customer service experience ever ... and we really are family.

Eric S.

EMPLOYEE SINCE MARCH 12 2007

Zappos Culture! Seems complex but yet so simple. It's a way of life that reaches beyond the walls of our company. Nothing new age or religious in nature, it's more like the Golden Rule. It's an attitude that allows a company like ours to prevail in a struggling economy. It's the little things as well as going above and beyond. A mixture of smiles, struggles, accomplishments and failures. Unbelievable customer service! One big happy family.

Erik L.

EMPLOYEE SINCE OCTOBER 1 2007

Just like Zappos is a service company that just happens to sell stuff, Zappos Culture is a bunch of people who hang out with each other and just happen to work together.

Erik P.

EMPLOYEE SINCE JUNE 18 2007

If there were a company out there that would choose a happy-go-lucky individual in worn shoes and jeans over a stern-looking, rigid character dressed in a flawless suit, it would certainly be Zappos. Our company does not always hire the perfect individuals with the 4.0 G.P.A, 780 credit score or model-like stature, but those exact imperfections and the infamous Zappos Ten Core Values make a lethal combination that has propelled this company to the top. I come to work in a white shirt, faded jeans and chucks, and have never been more productive. One time, I was drenched in BBQ sauce from head to toe because I took a BBQ sauce pie in the face like a champ. I was asked to carry the American flag around the call center to the tune of patriotic songs when I was granted my U.S. citizenship. Our culture translates these not-so-perfect instances to priceless moments that can never be drawn from a perfect resume. Fortunately for me, the intangibles come with the job. :)

Ernie L.

EMPLOYEE SINCE MAY 7 2007

When I came in to the Zappos job fair, I was blown away by the company ... but I was waiting for the other shoe to drop. When I came in to start my training, I was blown away by the culture ... but I was waiting for the other shoe to drop. When I went to the floor and started taking phone calls, I was blown away by our customers ... but I was waiting for the other shoe to drop. The other shoe never dropped!

Faby G.

EMPLOYEE SINCE MAY 9 2005

During the time that I have been working for this wonderful company, I have learned so many things, met new friends and filled my life with amazing experiences and memories. I am truly grateful and feel very lucky to work in a place that makes me feel comfortable and has taught me great values to apply to my everyday life. I am proud about all of our accomplishments and vision for the future. I love Zappos, I love what we do and I am very happy about my time here and super-excited about our future.

Floyd S.

EMPLOYEE SINCE JULY 31 2007

At a lot of workplaces, you start out happy in your new job, and then you grow to resent the daily grind. Zappos provides me with structure and boundaries, but our core values allow me to be myself in this environment. In good times or bad, I rely on Zappos to put a smile on my face. How many times do you say you want to help make the world better? I wake up every day happy to go to work and leave with the knowledge I participated in changing someone's day. Greatest feeling in the world!

George T.

EMPLOYEE SINCE MAY 7 2005

I have found that I always learn more from my mistakes than from my successes. If you aren't making some mistakes, you aren't taking enough chances.
   --John Sculley

Wow! Another great year at Zappos! What helps me enjoy the culture is that we are allowed to move forward and take chances to make a great life at Zappos even better. If we make mistakes while we are taking those chances, we can learn from those mistakes and move forward. I never thought I'd be saying this about any place, but my top memories of Zappos Culture are those of people who took chances and made mistakes. It's made Zappos even better over the years. I never want to work anyplace else, ever.

Georgina P.

EMPLOYEE SINCE OCTOBER 28 2006

Wow, where to even begin! I love being a part of this company and its visions. I have taken the Zappos Culture and have applied it to every aspect of my life. To be part of a company that treats their employees the way we are treated is awesome and rare (yes, we are very spoiled). To anybody in any department, it is great to come to work and be looked at as a person and not just a number.

Gerald M.

EMPLOYEE SINCE JULY 29 2008

It's refreshing to work for a company that takes Customer Service seriously and actually gives you the resources and power to make simple, practical, common- sense decisions. We have all received questionable or less than adequate service ourselves, as individuals on a daily basis, from numerous other companies and sometimes I wonder about the future of American or international business. Zappos is bringing back the foundation of true business in any market. The customer makes the business possible, so other companies need to begin to realize that part of the recent downturn is a product of years of abuse and neglect. Take a clue from Zappos, and give a little to get a little.

Gina C.

EMPLOYEE SINCE JUNE 2 2008

The Zappos Culture reminds me of my last job. My husband and I ran a pizzeria in Massachusetts. We were very customer-oriented and the employees were like family. I really didn't think that I would ever find that kind of atmosphere in the workplace again. Everyone at Zappos is friendly, helpful, and really cares for one another. I am so blessed to have found my home away from home. :-)

Gina W.

EMPLOYEE SINCE NOVEMBER 1 2 2007

I believe the Zappos Culture is all of us. It's our individuality, enthusiasm, positive energy and amazing customer service skills. I believe that we all have a zest for life that allows us to create positive relationships within Zappos and thus provide better service to our customers. I also believe that our individuality contributes to our unique culture. All of our unique perspectives and personalities, I think, help to shape our culture into what it is today. After a whole year of working here at Zappos, I am constantly reminded of how lucky we truly are to work at a company that is so culture-oriented.

If Zappos had an 11th Core Value ...

Some people come to work in pajamas, some people come dressed for a fashion show and some people just come to work. If I had to make up an 11th core value, it would probably be, "Embrace diversity," because that is virtually non-existent in the corporate world. That is my favorite thing about working here at Zappos. I love that we are encouraged to be ourselves here.

Most work places encourage people to fit the standard "corporate mold" and that's one of the many things that separates Zappos from other employers. Most employers require a certain attire in their daily dress code although they may never come into contact with their customers. For instance, in most call centers employees never even come face-to-face with their customers. This is quite contrary to working at Zappos.

Here at Zappos, you can literally dye your hair neon green or multi-colored and not worry about getting strange looks for it. In fact, it's quite the opposite here in this unique environment. People don't have to hide their tattoos or piercings in this workplace either. Even when customers or partners come in to visit our office, they are welcomed by diversity across the board. We have no dress code, which encourages people to come to work as they are.

Working at Zappos has shown me a different and fresh approach to running a business. It shows that not everyone needs to fit into the "corporate mold" to work for a thriving and successful company. Walking into the office and seeing people's tattoos, piercings and creatively colored hair is extremely refreshing and unique. It reminds me of what a diverse company that we work for, daily. It's actually easy to see that diversity is one of the main driving forces to maintaining our culture.

Although I think that our Ten Core Values exemplify our culture here at Zappos, I think that "embrace diversity" would be a complimentary addition to our core values. I think the best way to sum it up is: some people say you should dress for success. At Zappos, we dress to be ourselves ... and success follows.

Giovanna W.

EMPLOYEE SINCE FEBRUARY 20 2007

We're Zappos. We expect the best of ourselves and remind ourselves daily of the principles and values that help nurture our positive nature. We expect the best of others. We then receive the best. We give by nurturing the highest part of human nature, by going above and beyond the norm, by treating each individual with the ultimate in courtesy and respect. We then reap the benefits and, in turn, become a benefit ... all the while never taking ourselves too seriously, and always remembering to have fun. We become the positive inspiration, and people take us with them, with a smile and fond memories wherever they go. The good we continue to put out, we will receive back – many, many times over.

Grace H.

EMPLOYEE SINCE JANUARY 28 2008

My name is Grace. I just had my one-year anniversary on January 28!!! Yay, me!!!! Zappos has brought a lot of good into my life!!! I have awesome people to work with! Every day I come to work happy, and get to see everybody around me happy too!! For someone who's only 19, I think the CULTURE is what makes Zappos. Working here, you can be any age, as long as you have a positive attitude and be the best you can be!! When you work at Zappos, you get way more then a job! You get a great learning experience, awesome benefits, and most of all, you gain a whole new FAMILY!!! I plan to be here for many more years, learning my way to the top!! I owe a shout out to my Mom (Debbie H.) for bringing Zappos to me!! Thanks, Mom!! Love you!!!! Big Thanks to Tony and Zappos!!!! Love you all!!!

Hawanda A.

EMPLOYEE SINCE MARCH 10 2008

Zappos Culture is the best thing that could have happened to this company. Employees are encouraged to be themselves and can dress comfortably. We can have fun while we work, and still be productive. Every day is a great day at Zappos. I LOVE IT!

Heather C.

EMPLOYEE SINCE JANUARY 8 2007

I have been at Zappos for a little over two years, and though this past year has been difficult, I have never felt more a part of a family at any other job. I have met so many awesome people and made so many amazing friends here that I pretty much owe my happiness in Vegas to Zappos. From making breakfast in the lunchroom with my co-workers to spending New Years with friends that I have made through this job, I have so many memories that involve our tight-knit culture and can't wait to see what the future brings for both our company and ourselves.

Hector G.

EMPLOYEE SINCE NOVEMBER 13 2006

Zappos Culture can be described as unique, weird, fun, family-oriented, crazy, particular, friendly, etc ... I can go on and on, but all I can say is: "There is not other company like Zappos and nobody is, was, or will be like this unique company." Thanks.

Helena D.

EMPLOYEE SINCE APRIL 7 2008

Z is for zany
*A*nd a lot of brainy
*P*eople
*P*ursuing their dreams
*P*roductive in teams
*O*ver $1 billion in
*S*ales

Helene T.

EMPLOYEE SINCE JANUARY 28 2008

I have one word to describe our Zappos Culture, "AWESOME"!

Holly F.

EMPLOYEE SINCE SEPTEMBER 18 2006

I can honestly say that I love my job! I get to work at a great place where everyone is like family, we are all encouraged to learn and grow, and we have a lot of fun everyday. I come in every morning with a smile on my face, and it's still there at the end of the day when I leave. Good times!

Holly K.

EMPLOYEE SINCE JANUARY 8 2007

When we decide what company to work for, its like we have to make the decision between the Red Pill and the Blue Pill. All of the standard, everyday same stuff is the Blue Pill. If you want to have the same, predictable, monotonous workplace, then you want the Blue Pill. But if that just doesn't cut it for you anymore and you need something better, something real, choose the Red Pill, a.k.a. Zappos Culture. While our culture may seem a bit stunning or eccentric to others, Zappos Culture is really the way all companies should be. We've opened up our minds and have moved beyond imaginary boundaries that dictate what a company should and shouldn't be like. Our Zappos Culture is simply amazing. We can be ourselves, dress the way we want and speak our minds without having to worry about how it'll affect our position. We work hard and play hard, making for a wonderful mix. So if any of your friends are torn between choices, suggest the Red Pill.

Hope L.

EMPLOYEE SINCE JULY 16 2007

Culture at Zappos ... WOW, what a topic. I think for me it really hit home when my mom asked me, "How are you doing at work?" And I said, "Well let me put it this way, if someone came along and offered me a very significant amount of money to work somewhere else, I wouldn't take it." I think that says it all. But it's not just the job as a trainer that I love but the way that the culture of Zappos permeates everything that Zappos is, was and will be.

Ijeoma I.

EMPLOYEE SINCE JUNE 5 2006

Zappos is different from other companies because our individuality is both celebrated and appreciated. When you walk through the halls, there is such an array of individuals from different walks of life and I love it! With the uniqueness of our company, we are able to learn so much about where other people have come from and how those experiences have shaped them into being such a good part of Zappos.

Irene V.

EMPLOYEE SINCE MARCH 12 2007

Zappos is unlike any other company I have ever worked for. The feeling you get when walking into the building, the smiles on everyone's faces ... it genuinely feels like people like to be here. I know that I never dread coming to work – I actually look forward to it. The culture here is definitely the main reason for my love for the company. You are treated like family, not just employees. I love that we are encouraged to have fun, also, the fact that people choose to spend time together outside of work. That definitely sends a very positive message about Zappos and its employees.

Jacki M.

EMPLOYEE SINCE JULY 31 2007

I have been here a year and a half and I couldn't ask to be part of a better family. I have made some amazing friends and I love coming to work every day! I am extremely thankful each and every day that I work for a company that genuinely cares for its employees as well as its customers.

Jackie M.

EMPLOYEE SINCE JANUARY 29 2007

To me, Zappos Culture means coming to work with a smile every day. Helping one another when a fellow co-worker needs it. Creating a fun atmosphere to work in. I love the Zappos Culture because I feel that I can express myself artistically here. I have gotten a lot of chances to create what I want. The most important thing here is the friendships I have established. I have met lots of awesome people along the way and I can say that they will be my friends for a very long time. Being away from my family is hard, but Zappos creates a family atmosphere that makes me feel right at home. I love working here and being a part of something so great! I can't imagine the world without Zappos ...

Jackie Y.

EMPLOYEE SINCE JANUARY 7 2008

The Zappos Culture, for me, means, "Be yourself." I've never been a part of a retail company that allows you to be weird and do fun parades and yet still love to do your job. Every morning I wake up to come to work, it's never a drag; I always look forward to my Mondays. For me, self-expression at your work is a big key and here is the perfect fit for me. Especially me being in customer service and still having an impact on the site, it is great. I love how my suggestions don't get waved off like in any other company. I actually have a voice that supervisors and managers will listen to and make an effort to get changes made or find out what they can do. The culture here for me means opportunities ... the opportunity to set your own goals and achieve them... the opportunity to open doors and venture out into other departments. The Zappos Culture is great and we should continue on with the great progression of it.

Jaime S.

EMPLOYEE SINCE OCTOBER 22 2007

Zappos Culture is our way of life. Zappos is a place like no other; it's a lot like when Alice got introduced into Wonderland. I can honestly say people are constantly amazed by the smiles on everyone's faces, and their attitude and demeanor around the workplace.

Through our culture, I believe we can change the world by simply spreading our culture. Just by making an impression on one person, by smiling at some random person walking by on the street or providing outstanding customer service, we can improve the world in which we live.

James 'Jim' G.
EMPLOYEE SINCE SEPTEMBER 10 2005

Zappos Culture has been a consistently evolving thing. Over the years, we have changed, but we have definitely changed for the better, with each other kept in mind. To me, the best part about the culture is the fact that it has remained positive through its years of evolving.

James L.
EMPLOYEE SINCE AUGUST 28 2007

Zappos Culture
        A conscious state of self-awareness
in oneself and others
        to make the world a better place
through one's actions.

Jane J.
EMPLOYEE SINCE JUNE 13 2005

I feel our culture at Zappos is inspiring and honest. It spills over into my day-to- day life outside of work. I believe this positive attitude spreads to everyone I have contact with, making this a more beautiful world, thanks to the sharing of Zappos values. I am proud and fortunate to be a small part of this special company ...

Jasmine K.
EMPLOYEE SINCE DECEMBER 4 2006

Zappos stands alone. It is different, unique, rare, odd, uncommon, extraordinary, incomparable, genuinely unmatched, unrivaled, unprecedented, and even weird. All these words and more are largely part of our culture. It's hard to describe what Zappos Culture means without experiencing it for yourself.

From my first visit here for a job fair, until now, Zappos still has me in awe. Our culture is definitely one-of-a-kind. We keep things fun and innovative, all the while sticking to our core value ... our service. We treat our customers like we treat fellow workers ... like family. We all work hand-in-hand to keep our culture breathing and growing. Even with the changing times, our culture is strong because of our uniqueness. Working here is so much more than a job and I am so privileged and proud to be part of our amazing culture.

Jason B.

EMPLOYEE SINCE JANUARY 28 2008

There is one main thing I have to say about the Culture here at Zappos and that is "Amazing!" The reason for this is that I spent six years in the Air Force, where you must be a mindless robot and just do what you're told. (Let's not mention that everyone looks exactly the same.) If you spoke your mind about something that was wrong or could use improvement, you got yelled at. That makes for a very unfriendly work environment. Here at Zappos, on the other hand, I am simply impressed by how a work environment can work so well when all the individuals are allowed to be themselves. There is no dress code besides the obvious "don't-offend-anyone-with-what-you-wear". You can be yourself. The work place is such a nice place to be, because it is fun when people are allowed to be themselves. I just find it amazing how well we can function as a team without being a bunch of mindless robots. I must say, this has been the best place where I have ever worked!

Jason H.

EMPLOYEE SINCE DECEMBER 16 2007

I'll keep it short since this year's Culture Book will have roughly 1577 entries. Zappos Culture is just plain awesome. If the Zappos Culture were a mad scientist it would be Nikola Tesla. If the Zappos Culture were an intergalactic big-game hunter, it would be The Predator. If the Zappos Culture were a G.I. Joe character it would be Snake-Eyes. If the Zappos Culture were a WWF Superstar wrestler from the late 80s, it would be the Ultimate Warrior. Zappos Culture is that awesome.

Jean D.

EMPLOYEE SINCE JUNE 5 2006

Working at Zappos is not like any job I have ever had. I have worked at many other call centers and this is by far the best! The opportunities here are endless and it is up to each individual to determine how far he or she wants to go. Thank you for hiring me and making it a pleasure to come to work every day.

Jeanine L.

EMPLOYEE SINCE NOVEMBER 12 2007

Zappos is so amazing and the culture here is the best. I don't know anywhere else where you can go to work every day and be totally amazed by the people you work for and with. Although this was a tough year for us, with having to say good-bye to part of our family, the family/team spirit here at Zappos was evident at that time also. The day of the layoff, there were several "get-togethers" just for fellowship and time to be with our team members that were affected. Most companies or people affected by layoffs wouldn't want anything more to do with the other, but here it is truly a "family atmosphere" and there wasn't a second thought about doing it. In fact, there are still many outings that we all attend together. I'm so happy to be here, and I hope I never have to go anywhere else.

Jeffrey L.

EMPLOYEE SINCE JULY 10 2006

This will be my third culture book entry here at Zappos, and wow, has it been one crazy year! To me, the Zappos Culture means sticking by one another during tough times. It means working hard so that you can continue to play hard. It means always striving to better yourself and inspiring those around you to do the same. That, to me, is Zappos Culture.

Jenna D.

EMPLOYEE SINCE FEBRUARY 19 2008

For me, the Zappos Culture is life-changing. Take the Ten Core Values; if you use those values in your everyday life, they can improve the quality of your life dramatically. Every single value is aimed at making us better people. For example, "Doing More with Less" can force you to use your imagination. You don't always have everything you want/need, so you have to be creative in using what you do have. Also, change is inevitable. Without it, no progress would be made, so you might as well embrace it and even drive it. Finally, studies show that people who laugh and smile more tend to live longer, healthier lives. Being fun and a little weird is a great way to laugh more. The culture here at Zappos is incredibly contagious. Ever since I started working here, I've noticed such a dramatic change in the quality of my life and I'm never going to give that up. Thank you so much, Tony and the rest of Zappos!!

Jenna Z.

EMPLOYEE SINCE JUNE 2 2008

Ahhh, Zappos. When someone asks me to describe how I feel about my job, I get kinda stuck with words. This place is just that awesome. I remember when I first started here at Zappos. Everyone was so warm and welcoming, so full of smiles and encouragement, people sharing their stories and laughs. That's just the kind of people we are. People are encouraged to be themselves, and everyone is welcomed with open arms. No judgments, no stress, just people working together towards a common goal – great customer service. The value that is put on each and every one of us here, just for being a part of the family is like no other company I have experienced. There's so much potential for personal growth and development, and I'm happy to be a part of it all. It's definitely a work hard/play hard atmosphere. The culture here is absolutely unreal and Zappos is undoubtedly a blessing in my life.

Jennifer B.

EMPLOYEE SINCE OCTOBER 1 2007

Embracing Zappos Culture this past year has definitely had its share of ups and downs. Luckily for me, there have been more ups. During the second half of the year, there was almost a cloud hanging over the CLT department, due to the recent layoffs – definitely a test in doing more with less [employees] during the busy holiday season. But we all (other departments included) pulled together to get through those long days. For me, our customers' frequent thanks for the service kept reminding me why we should love working here. It's very easy to remember why I was excited to get the job when I get that customer that is truly WOWed by us. Also, I've been very fortunate in having a few fabulous teams this year – they have really meshed and created that true family spirit. It verifies that our company wants to be a huge family. Living with this family for 40 hours a week, I have noticed it spills into my life outside of work, too. People are amazed if you are patient, let them move ahead of you in line, pick up dropped items, etc. ... the longer you are here and the more willing you are, the easier it is to let yourself embrace the Zappos family culture in your entire life.

Jennifer M^c.

EMPLOYEE SINCE DECEMBER 3 2007

It doesn't feel that long ago that I was writing how wonderful Zappos is for last year's edition of our Culture Book. It wasn't that long ago, but I feel like everyone here, myself included, has grown so much over this past year. Zappos is so much more amazing than words can describe and I'm so proud that I can be apart of this fantastic culture, supported by my friends and family!

Jennifer M^y.

EMPLOYEE SINCE JUNE 2 2008

I have had a blast working at Zappos. The culture here is the best thing ever. Going from the WOW team and showing how great our culture is with activities – that is the best thing ever. I love working for Zappos.

Jennifer S.

EMPLOYEE SINCE OCTOBER 6 2008

Zappos is the most amazing company I've ever worked for. You can tell that Zappos is not only passionate about its wonderful customers, but about the employees that help keep it running smoothly! I love that we're allowed to be ourselves & that we don't have to live a scripted work-life!

Jennifer W.

EMPLOYEE SINCE JULY 9 2007

The Zappos Culture? You know how sometimes you meet someone and they're so spectacular and special that you know your life will never be the same, because that person has touched your life? That one person, who will turn every day into a great adventure? Wow … strange to find so many of them in one place. Zappos is more than just a livelihood -- it's a lifestyle.

Jenny B.

EMPLOYEE SINCE MAY 9 2007

One of the places where I see the Zappos Culture manifest itself most visually is in our desire to wear and display Zappos stuff. I can hardly imagine working at another company and getting excited about a new T-shirt, or this year's holiday gift, or anything at all with the company logo on it. We love to show our Zappos spirit wherever we go and that, I think, is a true testament to the power of our culture.

Jerika H.

EMPLOYEE SINCE JULY 9 2007

Zappos Culture is like evolution. It changes over time, but gets better nonetheless.

Jesse C.

EMPLOYEE SINCE SEPTEMBER 12 2005

My Zappos Haiku
Zappos is the best
It has changed my life for good
My friends celebrate
United we stand
We'll change the world call by call
Tomorrow is ours

Jessica B.

EMPLOYEE SINCE OCTOBER 7 2006

Working for Zappos has taught me more than just office skills. My experience has taught me to look at life in a different light, and know that there is always room for improvement. I have learned that my daily betterment of one thing, anything, does contribute to a company-wide progression. We work hard and we play harder! The more you know, the less you don't know. Being honest with yourself and others will create lasting relationships. Approach life with a positive attitude and you will get positive results. It's important to contribute to your team. Our family isn't just our relatives, but our friends too. Make do with what you've got. Follow your passion and the money will follow you. Be determined and never give up. Be modest about your achievements because there's always some one better. Thank you.

Jessica F.

EMPLOYEE SINCE NOVEMBER 12 2007

I think the Zappos Culture is the beating heart of the company, and it's what makes Zappos so successful. People enjoy coming into work and therefore enjoy helping the customers. This creates a great experience for everyone involved and it's why our customers keep coming back.

Jessica O.

EMPLOYEE SINCE JULY 2 2005

The Zappos Culture is totally different from the culture of any other company I've ever worked for. Our culture means freedom to me. I'm free to be myself and reveal my suggestions. Plus, I don't have to feel awkward about how my thoughts will be received. I love that we are welcomed to give all of ourselves, not just told to work. This helps everyone receive people from other walks of life, and want to welcome their ideas, too. I wouldn't trade my three years of Zappos experiences for anything in the world!

Jim C.

EMPLOYEE SINCE SEPTEMBER 18 2006

In the three years I have worked here at Zappos, I can say – without a question of a doubt – that Zappos has not only lived up to my expectations, but has far surpassed them. When I started for Zappos, I quickly got caught up in the excitement of the Zappos experience and it wasn't long after that that I decided that this is the company I want to retire at. Zappos and my Zappos Family is more than a job to me. I feel a strong sense of responsibility to do my part here by cultivating and protecting our culture. I am proud to say that I work for one of the greatest companies in the greatest country in the world! To my Zappos Family – I love you all!

Jo L.

EMPLOYEE SINCE JANUARY 29 2007

What an adventure! All of us are participating in one of those moments in history that will be studied for generations after, like the industrial revolution, the first man on the moon, the introduction of MTV ... we are living and taking part in the story! What creative ideas and new ways of doing business will be born out of this time and out of these walls? What will change about the philosophy of employment? When I am reminded of how much every single one of us is responsible for improving our process, promoting culture, leaving the indelible mark, I can't help but suspect that Zappos will figure prominently in the world story.

Joann C.

EMPLOYEE SINCE DECEMBER 4 2006

Each time I do this, I get this brain flow of ideas about what the Zappos Culture means to me. I think most will talk about the different cultural items, such as Being Humble or Doing More with Less. I want to say something about the impact this company has made on me as to how it treats its employees. I have never worked for a company that holds the success of its employees as close to its culture as this company does. I have worked for companies with structured ideals, such as hotels under union contracts. They are supposed to protect the employees' interests but there is nothing there that gives the individual a sense of purpose and pride. For this reason, I feel that our management team "amplifies" the core value to Build Open and Honest Relationships with Communication. When you can voice your option without fear of reprimand, employees are more inclined to voice the problems that truly retard their growth. This is what I have gained from this company.

Joe A.

EMPLOYEE SINCE OCTOBER 6 2008

The culture that is Zappos is one of many, many faces and beliefs. Being a bartender turned stay-at-home dad for the past three years, I forgot how much fun it would be getting back out in the work field, but if you would have asked me three years ago if I would end up working for a call center of a huge company like Zappos, I would have laughed at you and said, "Give me back my liquor bottles." At first, during training, I was a little scared. Even though I'm a very outgoing person who loves to talk, certain things shook me, but the culture here at Zappos was so similar to that of restaurants that I fit right in. Meeting new people (ones who smile and say hi every time you make eye contact), practicing more PC ways to recycle and do more with less, and just overall quality of life here at Zappos adds to our culture. I've never worked in a call center before, but I can tell you this. This could very well be the last job I'll ever have.

Joe K.

EMPLOYEE SINCE JUNE 2 2008

For me, Zappos is awesome. I have some health issues that have been plaguing me for about four years now, and after my doctor faxed over some info about it, which was requested by the great management team here, they actually accommodated things for me. I was given a longer phone cord so I can move around my workspace easily, and I was given an extra break because I can't sit in one spot for a long period of time. I never asked for this and was given it because Zappos cares!!! I am so happy about that, and have never been treated so well at any job. I'm not looking for special treatment, but because Zappos cares enough about the wellbeing of it's employees, I was given the courtesy of being made comfortable at work and it also helps me keep my health!! That is so important. I think that Zappos is the greatest place I have worked and one that I will ever have the opportunity to be a part of. Thank you for letting me be a part of this company, Tony, and I hope to be here for many years to come. Thank you.

John D.

EMPLOYEE SINCE AUGUST 22 2005

So here we all stand huddled together on this cold day. We are standing in the shape of a great big Z behind the Zappos offices in Las Vegas, NV. We are standing here to have our picture taken for a magazine. We are standing together for a big family portrait. The photographer on the roof is trying to get us to wave our hands and scream and shout and just be seen, the photographer already knows that Zappos employees live for this kind of fun. We are all standing together, screaming, shouting, raising our arms and waving them about, and it's beginning to snow. Everyone standing in the shape of the Z gasps with delight. WOW! It was a moment that had a bit of magic in it. Anyplace else, maybe not, but that day behind the Zappos offices, standing arm and arm with my fellow Zapponians, I believe I felt Ten Core Values.

Jonathan B.

EMPLOYEE SINCE JUNE 2 2008

Zappos is a work environment unlike any other! Just walking the halls and seeing everyone in a good mood is such a great difference, compared to all the other places I've ever worked. I am so glad I applied here and wish I had found Zappos a long time ago!

Jonathan L.

EMPLOYEE SINCE OCTOBER 22 2007

I would say that Zappos Culture has been all about Core Value #2 this last year. As a whole, we all need to Embrace and Drive Change to make sure that we do the best that we can throughout these tough economic times. I'm hopeful that we will also maintain the rest of our values while we press on. I'm very proud to be part of this company as it continues to grow. We're even in Fortune's Top 100! Go, Zappos!

Jonathan W.

EMPLOYEE SINCE JANUARY 7 2008

Zappos Culture is finding that true "family" environment in a workplace. I don't feel like I'm coming to an office with a bunch of people I don't know. I feel like I'm coming to my office, with my friends! I've had jobs that I enjoyed before, heck, I've had jobs that I really, really enjoyed, but I can't say I've ever had a job like this one! I don't ever feel like "why bother" in the mornings. I actually like coming here! I like the company and culture so much that I asked my wife, no, practically begged my wife to come work here too! I knew that she was in a bad place and that Zappos would be a breath of fresh air for her! I can't think of another job where I would pursue getting my wife to come to work at the same company. I know we could get along in a work environment, but with job stresses the way there are in other places, I don't think we'd last very long as co-workers! I can only hope she enjoys it as much as I do! I know it's just what she needed! THANKS ZAPPOS!!!!!!!!!!!!!!

Jordan R.

EMPLOYEE SINCE SEPTEMBER 10 2007

Working the past year and half at Zappos has been a very positive and eye-opening experience. I have been encouraged to constantly expand my horizons while never being asked to change who I am. I have also learned various business techniques that I feel will be applicable throughout my life. Zappos is the best company I have worked for and I greatly recommend working here to anyone who needs an original experience.

Jordan S.

EMPLOYEE SINCE JANUARY 28 2008

Zappos Culture is like nothing I've experienced at any other job. You can feel it in the atmosphere the first time you walk through the doors here. It's being able to do a stupid dance, or break out in random song in front of everyone and no one looks at you like you're crazy, because that's normal here. It means being free to be yourself, and being passionate about your job, because Zappos is passionate about its employees. It's contemplating changing your major in school so you can stay with the company forever! It's being happy to come to work, every day!

Jorge P.

EMPLOYEE SINCE APRIL 3 2006

I think that the best thing I like about our culture is the positivity it contains. I've worked at other places where they didn't care if you made off with a fellow associate's sales or customers, as long as one of you made money for the company. Here, at Zappos, that kind of thinking is so outdated. It doesn't fit in with a positive worldview of what is good for the human race. If all people were proactive in spreading a positive outlook in their actions and words, the world would be a much better place. By improving our culture, we improve our world.

Joseph M.

EMPLOYEE SINCE JUNE 19 2006

For me, the greatest thing about Zappos is the "shared vision" from top to bottom. Everybody pulls on the same end of the rope, and everybody knows where we are because of the openness of communication within the company. In November and December, the "hot button" topic was whether or not we were finally going to put the billion bucks year in the trophy case. Yeas and nays held a mighty tug of war for almost a month, and when Tony sent out the e-mail on Christmas day that the goose was cooked, it was goofy grins and high five time. At Zappos, when we win, everybody wins because EVERYbody plays ...

Josephine R.

EMPLOYEE SINCE FEBRUARY 12 2005

My first day (November 4, 2004) at Zappos was a breath of fresh air. I brought to Zappos a combination of sales, marketing and customer service (commissions and quotas) and experience (24 years). I had only been in the corporate world since 1980 (had just been laid off again in October, 2004). Zappos is my solace, my refuge, my answer to positivity (less stress - no quotas) and the opportunity to provide Superior Customer Service. We are empowered to do our best at every opportunity. We have a sense of one, like family. We are all here to make everything better for everyone we touch. I am thankful and grateful each and every day for the opportunities available to me at Zappos to make a difference.

Josh P.

EMPLOYEE SINCE FEBRUARY 19 2008

Hello, everyone. My name is Josh. I am originally from Northern California, where I was born and raised. I first heard about Zappos from one of my best friends. He has worked here for about three years now and I remember him telling me about this job that he just got and how amazing it really was. I could never understand what the big hype was about ... I mean, he sold shoes over the Internet! It was not until over a year ago when I was in Las Vegas visiting him that I took a tour of the company ... that's when I fell in love! I had never seen anything like it before. Dance Dance Revolution in the lobby, snacks and lunch for the employees, people smiling to be at work! I just couldn't understand why I did not listen to my friend a few years ago! I have been working here for a year now, and I must say that it has been a great experience. In the short time that I have been here, I have met a lot of people ... people that are lifetime friends. Having a culture like ours makes coming to work feel like an honor. I am happy that I made the move from California to Las Vegas. It was the best decision I have ever made. I LOVE ZAPPOS!

Joshua L.

EMPLOYEE SINCE JUNE 18 2007

Zappos Culture, to me, is a fun and friendly environment to work in. I do not know of any other corporate office where you will see such a variety of random stuff everywhere. It makes for a very relaxing and eye-popping place to work. I have worked at Zappos for almost two years now and have seen people come and go, but it seems like the Zappos Culture stays the same. I feel privileged to work for such a great company that truly cares about its employees and its customers.

Josiah B.

EMPLOYEE SINCE JULY 29 2008

The Job ... The Job is WOW. The Job is to WOW. The Job is too WOW, more WOW than

I ever expected, more WOW than the norm can handle. The Job is not a "job," it is an experience. The experience is fun, friendship and family ... the "Three 'F's." The "Three 'F's." is culture – our culture. The culture is monkeys. The culture is aliens. The culture is a parade. The culture is monkeys parading as aliens, wait – what am I saying ... OH NO ... RAISINS, RAISINS, RAISINS!!! Gotta love the "Z." and "Z" is for Zappos, and ZAPPOS IS GREAT!!

Joyce E.
EMPLOYEE SINCE OCTOBER 2 2006

What does the Zappos Culture mean to me? WOW!!! Where do I begin? Okay – from my beginning. I have been with Zappos for two years. The best part of working with this company and adapting to its culture is not only applying the Ten Core Values to my job, but also applying them to my life. When there is a need to call another call center for assistance, I feel that it's MY job to deliver WOW through service. When being adventurous, creative and open-minded, it's easy to make someone laugh and become comfortable. Now, it's easier to do more with less and get that interest rate on that credit card down to at least 4.99%. Yeah – it's the Zappos charm – what a gift. The Zappos Culture has been very, very good to me!!

Julianne "Jewel" R.
EMPLOYEE SINCE JANUARY 29 2007

W-O-W! That's all I have to say about Zappos and its culture. I am always very grateful to have such a wonderful and exciting job. I love that we're encouraged to be our weird selves. Everyone opens the doors for each other, we make friends, we laugh and have a good time, but ...we get the job done! It's amazing to see teamwork happening around the buildings, smiles all around the office, and growth before your eyes. THANK YOU, ZAPPOS! =)

Kara H.
EMPLOYEE SINCE JULY 29 2008

I have worked in the customer service field most of my life but I have never been able to give the customer service I have always wanted to give until I came to Zappos. The Zappos Culture that thrives here is amazing. Not only is Zappos focused on providing the best customer service for our customers, Zappos is even more focused on everyone who works here. For most companies, it's all about the bottom line. Everyone knows everyone like they are part of their family and we hang out with each other even after the work day is over. Most companies don't like to do that but here, we are all family. Working here has definitely changed the way I look at things in all aspects of my life. I do feel privileged to be a part of this wonderful company and I look forward to the future!!

Karen B.

EMPLOYEE SINCE OCTOBER 10 2005

Culture is a group of individuals creating a society. Okay, that was the official dictionary version. The Zappos version is different. Zappos is all about Culture. We are a blending of everything different, and in the beauty of that difference, we create something beautiful. We are a modern-day melting pot of ideas, styles and passions ... every shade and nationality ... short, fat, tall, thin, pierced and un- pierced. No class levels. We accept everyone and everything about each other. Tony is always joking we will start a Zappos Airlines in the future. Maybe we should start with the United Nations ... maybe have the UN take a tour. I have been with Zappos for over three and half years. We have grown so much that at times we have started to strain our Zappos Culture. But then, every Zapponian pulls together. We fix the cracks and go forward. We are people who love people (sorry, did not mean to break into song). But that is our Zappos Culture. We love people!! With no reservations and conditions. Make that UN tour a must-do.

Karen S.

EMPLOYEE SINCE JANUARY 7 2008

Zappos is the most pleasant job I've ever had. It is wonderful to be associated with a company that truly makes the customer and what is best for them its bottom line. All employers talk about the importance of customer service – Zappos actually walks the walk. How does Zappos Culture compare with other company cultures? Well, let's just say I consider Zappos my reward for paying my dues elsewhere!

Kari C.

EMPLOYEE SINCE JULY 31 2007

Hello, I've been with Zappos for over a year and a half and I haven't gotten burned out! Woohoo! Zappos is still and fun and interesting! The culture is a huge part of what makes Zappos the place that it is. Everybody makes you feel welcome and at home. The encouragement to create relationships with your co-workers makes the work environment very comfortable. The company pushes progression and will coach you in any areas that you are having trouble. With most companies, you'd be scared to even mention that you were having trouble with some factor of the job. Here, they encourage us to ask questions and look for the answers. Each day it seems like you are learning something new, so it keeps you thinking and growing. I have plans of becoming live-chat certified and becoming a trainer.

Katheryn G.

EMPLOYEE SINCE OCTOBER 1 2007

I am thankful to have such a wonderful job with such a fantastic company. I have made lasting friendships here. I appreciate the fact that we are allowed to think for ourselves and make mistakes. The benefits are priceless. My kids even brag about the wonderful place Mommy works. I am always talking about it to friends and family. Simply can't get enough of the culture here.

Kathleen H.

EMPLOYEE SINCE NOVEMBER 22 2005

Zappos Culture is like none other! It's great to work for a place where you are encouraged to be yourself! You are also encouraged to continually grow! Zappos is a rapidly growing company that seeks employees' opinions and openly listens to employee suggestions in an effort to continue to be the best customer service company ever! I'm honored to be a part of this team!

Katrina "Hurricane" J.

EMPLOYEE SINCE JUNE 5 2006

"Zappos sells, Zappos sells
Merchandise galore,
Oh, what fun it is to work
for an on-line retail store !! Hey..."

One of the fantastic things about our Zappos Culture – and believe me there are many – is that we are always encouraged to be creative. Whether that means doing a parade, designing piggy banks so we can collect money for one of our charities, writing poetry, dressing as twins for a day, or as you can see, taking a song like "Jingle Bells" and writing new lyrics to describe one of our core values. We are always allowed to think outside the "shoe box". Thanks to Zappos, I am even more than I dreamed I could be and still evolving.

Keir F.

EMPLOYEE SINCE JUNE 2 2008

What does Zappos Culture mean to me?
I have to say that being a native Californian (Northern to be exact), everyone is extremely considerate, friendly and mellow. People are very accepting of one another, and quite often you may see a punk rock kid walking down the street with a hip-hop kid and they are best friends. You might find in one of our most upscale restaurants that your waiter has a tongue piercing. You get that vibe here at Zappos. Acceptance and consideration of one another is key. That is why my friend core value is "Be Humble."

What's different about it compared to other company cultures?
Frankly, I have to agree with Tony that certain companies give their core values within the first 10 minutes of their hiring orientation. If you are lucky, after you are hired, there is a plaque on the wall displaying said core values. Most people within said company do not follow them, and the only person that remembers the company's core values by heart is the training manager.

What do I like about our Zappos Culture?
That it is real and it does exist on a daily basis. That our Ten Core Values are practiced each and every day by all of us and not only do we exercise them here at work, but we often utilize them in our every day lives.

It is an absolute pleasure to work here and I have made some lasting friendships.

Kelly W.

EMPLOYEE SINCE JULY 29 2008

In my experience, Zappos Culture represents respect. We respect our customers, each other, and even the people we encounter outside of our walls. I love that wearing a Zappos shirt makes total strangers approach me and ask if I work here; I love even more that these strangers "get" our culture and us. What I love most, though, is that I can honestly tell them that Zappos is the real deal. Respect is something in such short supply these days. It is refreshing to find such a culture of respect here at Zappos.

Kevin T.

EMPLOYEE SINCE JANUARY 28 2008

I love having another family. That's what Zappos is to me. I think I see the people here more then I see my real family. Not complaining.

Kiana L.

EMPLOYEE SINCE JULY 31 2007

In my opinion, the Zappos Culture is contagious! As you enter the workplace, you are always greeted with a smile, which forces you to start your day off right. It doesn't stop there, though. As I walk to my desk, EVERYONE I come into contact with greets me. This is completely different from other companies, because people may greet you at other companies, but in most cases, they don't really care how your day is going. I also can't ever recall waking up in the morning looking forward to go to work at any other company. We put our customers first and go above and beyond to resolve their issues. Other companies talk about doing it, but we actually do it. Another great thing about the Zappos Culture is the fact that I can be exactly who am, without having to fit some sort of mold. There is nothing like going to work, having the opportunity to be yourself and being appreciated for it.

Kim K.

EMPLOYEE SINCE OCTOBER 6 2008

I am happy to work at Zappos. It is a wonderful place to work. The people are so very friendly and I have made some wonderful friends. I like that we can be ourselves and have fun while working. This is the best job I have ever had.

Kim M.

EMPLOYEE SINCE MAY 5 2008

The Zappos Culture allows us to be ourselves and accept everyone else as themselves. It blends all of our different backgrounds and makes us feel as though we are one big family. With that feeling of family, you know that there is always someone there when you need them. I came to this job from a corporate type situation (big boss, boss, supervisor, me) where I had to conform to their rules – dress code, hair a certain color, nails a certain length, professional appearance. I was happy at the beginning, but then I began to feel that I could not be myself and I was uncomfortable. When I came for my interview and saw Jacob sitting there in shorts, a T-shirt and flip-flops ... my first thought was, "OH, MY GOD! I SO HOPE I GET THIS JOB!" It was exciting to see how everyone was so happy to be here and I wanted that feeling too. I had been so unhappy at my other job that I felt this would be such a great change. Now, months have gone by and I am still so happy to be here ... with hopefully many more to come.

Kim N.

EMPLOYEE SINCE MAY 5 2008

Before I came to Zappos, I had only been working at retail stores. My idea of customer service before was to help someone find a size in a shirt and that was my day. I always despised having to go to work every day. But now, I love coming in to work every day. To walk in those doors and have every single person you walk by say, "Hello," or "Good morning," as you pass by is the best. It is also so great to have such a caring CEO. Tony is so awesome! I did not even know the name of my CEO at my last job. I think I will be working here forever!

Kim W.

EMPLOYEE SINCE MARCH 12 2007

I just want to say, "Thank You" to Zappos! I have been with the company for two years in March and I have never worked for a company as awesome as this one. With the economy being as bad as it is this year. I am very thankful that I still have a job, and with the awesome culture that Zappos has implemented we have been able to sustain ourselves throughout the storm. Thank God for ZAPPOS!!!

Kris Z.

EMPLOYEE SINCE JANUARY 7 2008

The Zappos Culture means so much to me. It means that I get to come to work with a smile on my face and a jump in my step. Zappos is an amazing place to work and the culture only helps to make it that way. Having worked in some other call centers and customer service positions, I have never come across a place like Zappos. Zappos is a place where we can be who we are and not have to worry about fitting a certain mold. Zappos is a place where we can make our customers feel special and do whatever it takes to do that. Zappos is a place where weirdness and fun is celebrated. Zappos is a place where you can be creative and let your imagination run wild. Zappos is a place where you know that you can grow and the possibilities are endless. Zappos is a place where the line of communication is wide open, and relationships are formed. Zappos is a place where family and friends just happen to be your co-workers. Zappos is a place where, we can always find a way to make something out of nothing. Zappos is a place where being passionate and determined go hand and hand with being humble. But most importantly, Zappos is the place I wanna be! Thank you, Zappos for changing my life and making me a better person.

Kristin H.

EMPLOYEE SINCE SEPTEMBER 18 2006

Zappos Culture to me can be described as never getting that sick feeling when I'm driving into work for the day. On my lengthy drives to work at my last job, I would wish that I lived someone else's life because I was incredibly unhappy with the morals the company practiced and tried to make me believe in. I hate to admit it, but after six years, I became selfish and greedy just like them. But by chance, I was forced to leave and start new again. That's when I found Zappos and my life changed for the better – almost immediately! The kindness that Zappos employees pass onto each other is contagious and we all work towards the same common goal of being successful while maintaining our morals. Also, instead of being stuck in the same boring position for my entire career here, I have been encouraged to try out many different departments within CLT and Training until I found the right spot for me. It took almost two years, but Zappos never gave up on me and gave me the time I needed to find what I really enjoyed to do. We are guided to continue our success by advancing in the company with the help of my leadership team. What other company has a management team that will actually train you on how to take over their job? I've never seen one, even when I worked for my family's business back in Wisconsin many a moon ago. Thank you for reading my beliefs on what Zappos Culture means to me. Have a great year!

Krystle G.

EMPLOYEE SINCE JUNE 5 2006

Our Ten Core Values are the basis of our Zappos Culture. If we didn't have them, we wouldn't be Zappos. From #1 to #10, we take pride in each and every one of them ... and it's contagious! I find myself smiling or saying "Hello," to strangers in the grocery store and can't help but think, "Oh yeah, this isn't Zappos!" and that just goes to show you how big of an impact Zappos has made in our lives. We do so much to keep communication open between departments - anything from the awesome Face Game every morning, quickly answered emails to the kind hellos exchanged in passing. The difference between Zappos and every other company I, or anyone else I know, has heard of is that we actually live by our Core Values – which, in turn keeps our Zappos Culture going!

Lacey J.

EMPLOYEE SINCE OCTOBER 23 2006

When I tell people about my place at Zappos, I often take on this real Julie Andrews glow of joy as I rant about all my favorite things. I doubt there is anywhere else on earth that you can find a disguised monk running a shoe store; retail merchandisers, web developers and financial planners having Nerf wars amidst the world's largest standing army of rubber duckies or a gaggle of bearded men in German beer maid dresses singing Oktoberfest songs while parading through the corporate headquarters of a major retailer. Although folks touring our offices often express shock and awe at these things, after a while you get used to them and they become part of your "normal" every day routine. But before I came to Zappos, my idea of a "normal" day at work meant something akin to what I consider a miserable failure of a day now. My own expectations for my own happiness have been raised ... considerably. Zappos doesn't strive to maintain the miserable status quo. We're aiming for pure, unadulterated, exuberant, enthusiastic, unlimited joy ... for our partners, our customers, and ourselves.

LaiLonnie H.

EMPLOYEE SINCE MARCH 10 2008

Working for Zappos is such a pleasure. It is such a peaceful, non-stressful and beautiful place to work. I get to come to work in sweats or jeans and just be myself. I've met some really great people and some are "keepers". On the team that I'm in, we are all so close it's like we are family. The "positive energy" around you is so calming. It's like having sunshine around you all day every day. I feel very privileged to have a "job," but I'm truly blessed to work for Zappos. Gratitude is the best attitude!

Laura C.

EMPLOYEE SINCE JANUARY 8 2007

The culture here at Zappos is amazing. Zappos strives to create a family-friendly and positive workplace. This is done not only by building a very happy and eccentric work force, but also by instilling wonderful values that are often lost in a customer service environment. When you start here, you are given your list of the Ten Core Values. As you continue to work here, you work by these values, which is never hard. You do it without recognition. These values are created to influence each of us to strive for success, be positive while doing it, to enjoy the ride, and to perform above the rest by going above and beyond what would be expected of you. I see their goal as being, "Happy employees create happy customers." After working here for two years, I still come in every day and love it. I have a very special bond with my co-workers. We celebrate each other's successes, birthdays, and family events together. We hang out inside and outside of work, devoting time and energy in one another. We do it because there is a genuine care for the wellbeing of our 'work' family. These friendships can only be created while at work and I was able to meet my best friend here at Zappos. The wonderful energy and experience has given me the ability to do so. I have never felt as if I was just a number, or laborer here. I feel like I am a piece of a very large puzzle. Zappos not only brightens the days of our customers, but also the lives of those who work here. Where else can you have such a good time while making the world a better place one shoe at a time?

Laura M.

EMPLOYEE SINCE JULY 18 2005

Zappos Culture to me three and a half years later: fun and a little weird, interesting and really enjoyable. I love the fact that I have decided to move home probably six times a year and I am here in Vegas still. Not because I love the sun, the heat and the palm trees, but because I am at Zappos. This company has been a source of stability for me and my family. I appreciate the fact that I can get up before the sun is up and get home before my kids are out of school. It has been fun learning all the different personalities of my co-workers and, to top it off, to have two songs sung to me. That would never happen anywhere else. Well, not in corporate America.

Lauren A.

EMPLOYEE SINCE OCTOBER 22 2007

Zappos Culture makes me feel like the polka-dotted elephant on the Island of Misfit Toys from the Rankin/Bass "Rudolph the Red-Nosed Reindeer" television special. Except that instead of being stuck on that island because I'm too weird, Santa brought me to a place where we're all polka-dotted elephants. Polka-dotted elephants that have parades and karaoke.

Lauren C.

EMPLOYEE SINCE JUNE 19 2006

From day one of working here at Zappos, I was thrilled to be working for a company where the Ten Core Values align with my personal values. I am only more astonished each day how this company continues to grow and how I have grown right along with it. I truly feel this company has helped me take my life to the next level. I feel great being in a position to help others achieve their goals – to feel just as fantastic as I do about every aspect of my life. Each year the Zappos Culture means something a bit different for me, and this year it is all about personal and professional growth. I love that we have now rolled out our "Pipeline" classes so that the entire company can get a better understanding of the bigger picture of how our company is run. During these trying economic times, it is wonderful to have such an open and honest company providing more details about the inner workings of its organization.

Lauren P.

EMPLOYEE SINCE FEBRUARY 4 2006

Zappos Culture, to me, is loving what you do, building long lasting friendships and feeling like you belong. At Zappos, all of these things have happened to me. Working here, you don't have to feel like you don't belong – because you do, and everyone makes you feel welcome. I have been here at Zappos for three years; from the moment I walked into the building on my first day, it felt like home. I have built long-lasting friendships here and have had the pleasure of meeting and working with the most honest, compassionate and hardworking people in the world. I look forward to coming into work every day and working for this awesome company. The culture here is what has made Zappos so successful and why everyone loves to work here. I look forward to many more years here at Zappos and I feel so blessed to work for such an amazing company!

Lauren S.

EMPLOYEE SINCE JULY 29 2008

When I first came to Zappos, I had only heard about how wonderful the company was to work for, about how it was a young company but that it was the one company that had figured how to incorporate excellent customer service with caring about those that performed this task. I have to admit that I was more than a little skeptical but I was so intrigued/enchanted that I threw my proverbial hat into the ring ... I am extremely happy and humbled that I work for this wonderful company. I had come from a small corporation prior to this one and I thought that it would be impossible to get a sense of security, a sense of pride and family ... I have never felt so at home and above all, appreciated, here at Zappos. Zappos Culture to me is wild, anything goes, have as much fun as you can, a make- someone-laugh-out-loud kinda place ... it's making friends and then turning them into your family, it's laughing and taking time with those on the other end of the phone, and it's showing that in times where rudeness is the norm, there is a smile waiting to greet you, 24 hours a day, seven days a week.

Leilani G.

EMPLOYEE SINCE OCTOBER 23 2006

Zappos is not just a job ... it's not somewhere I come every day just for a paycheck. Zappos is much more than that. I love coming to work, being surrounded by such a diverse group of people, people that are all unique in their own way and that truly care about you, when you're up or you're down. Everyone is generally in a great mood (because they also love being here) We work hard, and play hard. We have fun around the office, and for a lot of people, including myself, coming to work here is an escape from any worries or hard times you may be having at home, or anywhere else. The culture here is like none other I've ever been around. It isn't fake or a front. Our core values are real. They inspire me to be the best employee I can be, and when I really stop and think about it, those core values overflow into my daily life, which in turn inspires me to be the best ME I can be.

Letha M.

EMPLOYEE SINCE NOVEMBER 12 2007

I am absolutely in LOVE with Zappos! I have been here a little over a year, and I still get up every morning with a smile on my face. I have met so many people that have come to be great friends. I feel truly lucky to be a part of such an awesome group of people.

Liane T.

EMPLOYEE SINCE OCTOBER 1 2007

I have never worked for a company that had such an awesome culture and core values that all employees live by. I feel very proud to work for Zappos where we all respect the same Ten Core Values. This is truly a humbling experience!! Zappos is the first place where I love coming to work and cannot wait to come back the next day. I come to work knowing that I get to see my extended family and laugh and have fun every day!!!!

Linda H.

EMPLOYEE SINCE JUNE 19 2006

Culture is the atmosphere and way of living for any given group. I believe culture is what a group decides will be the norm for their actions and beliefs. Our norm at Zappos is very, very unique. I love it so! The Ten Core Values that Zappos has shared with everyone are values that I already live by. (This is so not a lie. :-)) This is an aspect that I very much appreciate, because it gives a sense of unity between my employer and me.

Given that we are speaking of Zappos as a company I work for, I would like to say that the company, and how it is labeled, has changed for me over the years. It is no longer just my employer. Zappos is my family. I can see this sense of family when I hear anything involving the Zappos name or explain our culture to someone new. This is evident when I refer to Zappos as "us" or "we" and not "the company I work for" or "my job." My time here at Zappos is one of very few occasions in my life where I feel a sense of belonging and kinship.

With that said, being a part of this company has changed my life and its direction – because I am beginning to experience, more and more, a sense of belonging with the friends I've made within the company and other situations in my life. It feels as if Zappos was the actual reason for blessings in my life. Of course, I've got to thank the man upstairs, but it really, really does feel that way. This makes sense to me because of all of the encouragement I get from the leads, the management team, and most of all, Dr. Vik! What a great asset to the company he is! Whoa! That totally just sounded like Yoda! (Cheers to you, Scott K.!) Also, I find myself reporting good news every time I walk by his office. And even when there is bad news, I still have something to share. To be specific, these kinds of topics would include what my plan is to make it better for me, how that it became the reason why I learned something or just plain how I overcame that hardship. Growing up was so very hard and my childhood was not pleasant. So I am very lucky to find a family within my workplace. Thank you, Tony ... thank you, Zappos, for enriching my life.

Linda R.

EMPLOYEE SINCE DECEMBER 3 2007

Delivering WOW through Service is the heartbeat of Zappos. It's all about the WOW. What can I do to make my customer say, "WOW!" by the end of the call? How can I WOW you and make you feel special? Customer service – the reason I'm here.

Linda "Linder" S.

EMPLOYEE SINCE SEPTEMBER 1 2004

I don't think I ever thought about 'culture' until I worked here. Everyplace else is a job that you have to go to. This is a place that you GET to come to, and be with your friends, and do something that matters. It's about being connected in a whole different way, to your living and your life.

Loren B.

EMPLOYEE SINCE OCTOBER 1 2004

Culture '09: My time at Zappos has passed quickly and this will be my fifth Culture Book entry. In my past entries, I have looked back on my experience and tried to capture my feelings. This time, I thought I would look ahead to the future and in so doing, I realized that we have some tough times ahead of us. It occurred to me that it is our culture and set of shared values that will lead us successfully into the future. As other companies stumble and fall to the wayside, we will prevail. We will move forward strengthened, by the shared vision that the Ten Core Values give to everyone in the company.

Our success will be based on how well we maintain the culture we have built over the past ten years. In short, our culture is our heart, our soul and our will to not only survive, but to thrive in the tough times that lay ahead. I find comfort in knowing that as a company we are all on the same page as we start the next chapter in the book of Zappos.

Lori K.

EMPLOYEE SINCE MARCH 14 2005

To me, Zappos is not a job, it's an adventure! The culture here allows us to be creative, and if we aren't creative, we are encouraged to find our inner creativity. There is nothing staid or boring around here ... there are laughter and smiles wherever you go within the Zappos walls. We are a family, not just a bunch of people who happen to work together. Never in my life have I had a job like this and it makes me appreciate Zappos all the more.

Lorne S.

EMPLOYEE SINCE SEPTEMBER 18 2006

The Zappos Culture ... to me, it's about caring for other people. We look for ways to help others in their time of need. For example, I received a call from a lady that was ordering some boots for a family whose house had burnt down just before Christmas. They had lost everything. We sent that family our Culture Book that was signed by everybody here at Zappos. We also sent them a $100 gift certificate. It's a company that cares. The caller could not believe that a company would go out of its way to help this family. She stated we have her friends and family as customers for life. What a culture of caring. It works. This company would still care even if they never call us back. It comes down to the culture of caring.

Louie M.

EMPLOYEE SINCE AUGUST 7 2006

I write these things year after year and it seems to get harder and harder every time. It's hard to not say the same things that you did the year before, because I don't feel as if the company can get any better. I can say that this has been one of the toughest years for me to deal with while being at Zappos. We had a company-wide layoff, which was really rough on most of us. I had some really great friends who were let go. One thing that I can say is that although we are all going through tough economic times and companies are forced to make decisions like this, Zappos has proven how important everyone is to the company and made sure that everyone was properly taken care of. That being said, I feel that we are so much stronger because of it. We were forced to work even harder than ever before and come together to continue the success of the company. That shows how great our culture and relationships are. I really appreciate how much Zappos strives to look out for the best interest of each and every employee.

Luanne M.

EMPLOYEE SINCE MAY 7 2007

With the entire country going through hard times, you would expect that everyone would be affected. And we are. Even here at Zappos, we've been going through some changes. I think those changes will only make us stronger in the end. We are encouraged to continue to better ourselves, so that we can advance in a productive way. Personal, as well as professional, growth is encouraged. And through it all, we still have a lot of weirdness and craziness going on. The company has also helped me a great deal with a personal "journey" that I've been on this past year. I've been doing some major self-improvement, and Tony has allowed this to happen on-site, with Zappos subsidizing half of the expense. This has helped immensely! I might not have done it otherwise. How many companies do that?? I would say that the Zappos Culture means "family." Family is there to help you in good times as well as bad.

Lucas H.

EMPLOYEE SINCE JUNE 18 2007

The culture at Zappos is far different from that at other companies. Zappos Culture, to me, is all about living life to the fullest. This involves working hard and playing hard, which everyone does well here. Also, everyone stays on their game no matter how many crazy changes take place ... one team, same goals.

Mara K.

EMPLOYEE SINCE MAY 7 2005

Well ... I have been writing for the Culture book since 2005. I believe that our culture is growing with the company. Let me just thank Zappos for allowing me to continue to work for the greatest customer service company ever that also happens to sell merchandise: Shoes, Handbags, Apparel Ware, Electronics, Housewares, Bedding, etc.... This being said, I value our Ten Core Values and take them to heart. WOWing our customers with our service, Being weird and wacky, that is a fun one. Dressing up as a 1950s dancer — what company will allow you to come to work dressed crazy? We come to work in our pajamas and slippers. It is such a joy waking up at 4:00 am to go to work and have a great day, each and every day. This is because of our culture; each and every employee respects one another no matter the gender or age. If one of my teammates is not at his or her desk by five minutes before it's time to clock into our phones, I or others on our team will contact them to make sure they are okay. Moving forward, we have classes to discuss our history of Zappos, our culture, leadership and management. What company wants to expand their employees' knowledge and pay them for it? Keep up the great work! Thank you, Tony and Alfred, for everything! I LOVE ZAPPOS!

Marcela G.

EMPLOYEE SINCE JANUARY 22 2005

The Zappos Culture is a way of life that makes you a better person. It can be embraced both in and out side work. Every year, I learn new things that help my everyday life. I have learned to be more tolerant, and to be open-minded to change. Zappos becomes part of you. I'm extremely proud to belong to the Zappos family and have the opportunity to meet new "family members" all the time. Everyone here is different and has something to offer, that's what makes it special.

Margaret "Grace" G.

EMPLOYEE SINCE DECEMBER 3 2007

What I feel is Zappos Culture is the idea that it doesn't change from what you were told in training. I have worked for so many companies that state "It will be this way," and when you get to the floor you feel misled and a little depressed about it. I am able to tell friends and family about working here and feel great about what we stand for, even if it is hard sometimes. I like that we are as honest as you can be with each other, and that most people here care about what we do. We Rock!

Margie L.

EMPLOYEE SINCE DECEMBER 3 2007

Working at Zappos has been good for me. The Zappos atmosphere extends beyond the front door to the outside world. I find that I smile at people and say, "Hi!" more often because it is the norm at Zappos. So, not just employees and our customers who are benefiting from the Zappos Culture, but those we come in contact with in the world at large, as well. This is a good thing! Zappos challenges me, also, to do tasks that I never thought I would be doing, like live chat!

Margret H.

EMPLOYEE SINCE JULY 29 2008

Zappos Culture, to me, is FREEDOM. The freedom to be an individual. The freedom to think independently. The freedom to have fun at work. The freedom to do my job to the best of my ability. The freedom to grow. And most importantly, the freedom to WOW!

Maria E.

EMPLOYEE SINCE FEBRUARY 6 2006

What Zappos Culture means to me: fun and exciting new ways of learning and growing together as a team! Building relationships with friends and co-workers that we hope will last a lifetime, and not forgetting the ones left behind. Zappos is different in many ways ... bringing the "WOW" into every new year we face. What I love is being able to work in an atmosphere that we can call home. It's a place we not only work, but where we laugh and grow as people.

Marilyn G.

EMPLOYEE SINCE MAY 5 2008

What Zappos Culture means to me: family away from family. I have worked at many companies before, but this is the first time I felt like I have another family at work. I have lots of friends that I met here and now they are my friends away from work. The difference between here and other jobs is that people actually love their job here. They are happy to be here. I like how people are so friendly and sincere and how they help the customer. Thanks, my Zappos family.

Marina M.

EMPLOYEE SINCE OCTOBER 22 2007

Zappos Culture to me is Family. I have never worked somewhere that had such a family atmosphere. Everywhere you go, there is a smile to greet you, even though you do not know them. Someone is always holding a door open for you as well. You feel like everyone has your back. My co-workers are willing to listen and be a sounding board when times are tough. I feel better when I am at work.

Mario A.

EMPLOYEE SINCE JULY 5 2005

Zappos Culture is made up a diverse group of individuals. We all come together for the common goal of customer service and fashion. Zappos values the opinions and feelings of its employees and customers. I don't know of many companies that would actually make a Culture Book of their employees' honest feelings about their place of work. It lets you know that your company is listening to you and values your opinion. There are so many opportunities and different avenues within this company you can take and still be a part of the fashion industry, whether it's customer service, being a buyer, working in advertising, or building the website. This is truly a great place to work and I enjoy coming here every day.

Marissa G.

EMPLOYEE SINCE JUNE 18 2007

It has been a pleasure working for Zappos. I can proudly say that I have been with Zappos for almost two years and I have not been bored one day. This is my home away from home. Tony, our CEO is AWESOME, the best CEO I have ever met. Not because he spoils us (Tony, seriously, you spoil us), but because he is a very humble man and he cares a lot. He's very approachable and he doesn't act like a big shot. He is very down to earth and I admire him for being who he is. The environment that we have here at Zappos reflects our CEO. What other company has young children (from my first hand knowledge, 16, 17, and 18) advising that they admire Tony, our CEO, and want to follow in his footsteps and wanting to move to Las Vegas just to work for Tony because they emailed him and within a few hours it was actually him who emailed them back? They know our Ten Core Values and state that Zappos Core Values help them in their everyday lives. I also have to mention the benefits that I am very thankful to receive. Who would give their employees 10% of their annual pay, 100% medical benefits, pay co-payments, free lunch and beverages, gifts, parties, and 40% off purchases? Even 20% for family and friends? This is very expensive and it's more than generous. I like the fact that we have the free lunch and our benefits are wonderful, but the best part about Zappos is the Ten Core Values. They have naturally become a part of my everyday life. They're second nature. This is what makes Zappos strong. It's not a front for when we have tours or interviews. It's every day and it makes me feel really good to be a part of a company to where our customers would call in just to talk and give feedback on Tony, our representatives, how they want to work for Zappos and how genuine they know our customer service is. They tell me, "Thank goodness, real customer service is still alive." It feels great to be on the other end of the phone line when someone takes the time out just to call in and let you know these things. That lets me know that I am in the right place. I LOVE ZAPPOS!

Maritza R.

EMPLOYEE SINCE JULY 10 2006

Zappos Culture simply means being truly happy with your job and working environment. It means looking for ward to going into work each day. Yeah, I love Zappos ... doesn't everybody? Oh boy!

Mark C.

EMPLOYEE SINCE JULY 29 2008

Zappos Culture is all about being the unique individual that you really are. It shows us that you don't need to put a new face on when you're here, and I think that's how Zappos differentiates itself from other companies. Just because of the culture ... I love Zappos! :-)

Mark G.

EMPLOYEE SINCE APRIL 7 2008

Having spent decades in private and public enterprise, I can say unequivocally that the Zappos Culture and working environment is unique. From recruitment to training, to the real world-application of skills and values taught, Zappos is definitely an "out of the box" environment. Zappos' Ten Core Values create guidelines to assist employees in attaining success in the Zappos workplace, and corporate mentor Dr. Vik is always there to further assist employees in attaining their goals. My Zappos experience will follow me through the years!!

Marlene K.

EMPLOYEE SINCE JANUARY 1 2005

Zap·pos Cul·ture [zap-pohs] [kuhl-cher] noun 1. A group of unique individuals with a passion for all levels of service. 2. That which is creative and driven. 3. Simply amazing!

Marlene S.

EMPLOYEE SINCE OCTOBER 2 2006

I have been at Zappos over 2 years now, and in that time I've experienced a lot of change. Team changes, policy changes, building changes, personal changes, etc. The one thing that remains consistent throughout all the changes is the Zappos Culture. Our culture here is exuded throughout the work day and continues outside of work as well. It really changes your life for the better, both professionally and personally. Coming to work every day is like coming to my second home. It truly is a family atmosphere; after two years I still look forward to work every day. We even treat our customers like family and you feel that reward so often. I love Zappos and it's hard to imagine working for any other company, as Zappos is one of a kind. I am thrilled to still be a part of the Zappos family and look forward to the journey ahead.

Marquirita L.

EMPLOYEE SINCE APRIL 7 2008

Zappos Culture is unlike anything I've ever experienced with any employer. I remember the days of dreading going to work, even having to talk myself into going. The culture here at Zappos is amazing and infectious. You don't feel like you work for "the company", you feel like you're a part of it.

Martha C.

EMPLOYEE SINCE SEPTEMBER 1 2004

It's been almost five years and Zappos is still treating me like a VIP! In this bad economy, I'm not only blessed to have a job, but to have an AWESOME job is GREAT! I share stories about Zappos with anyone who will listen to me. It is a great place to work. What more can I say?

Martha P.

EMPLOYEE SINCE OCTOBER 24 2005

I feel at this point that every team member from NV to KY is a brick that this company is built with. We are all a piece of Zappos. Culture is the life of this living, breathing company. We are all in this together, and knowing that turns this company into a family.

Mary T.

EMPLOYEE SINCE FEBRUARY 20 2007

What Zappos means to me ... Zappos is my second family. It is a home away from home. The people here are amazing. Getting to know each and everyone of the Zapponians is exciting. Everyone here is so different and the way we all work together is amazing. I enjoy coming to work every day, and we all know that is something very rare these days. Compared to other companies, Zappos lets you be you ... you can actually show your creative side and still be accepted. The core values that we have don't only apply here at work but outside of the office. This place has really impacted my life. Tony, Alfred, Fred and the rest of the Zappos Family really have something going here. :-)

Maura S.

EMPLOYEE SINCE SEPTEMBER 2 2003

Zappos Culture embodies hard work, perseverance, tolerance, strength, fearlessness and patience. It certainly is the year of the Ox.

Max M.

EMPLOYEE SINCE AUGUST 20 2007

What is Zappos all about to me? Family, friends, good times, and being the best in everything! This last year has been a great year with its ups and downs. I've met some great new people, and have seen some great people go. All in all, Zappos is the best company ever! This year we are ranked at #23rd best company to work for by Fortune magazine. Which is pretty cool! We had a fun Vendor party at Rain in the Palms, with live penguins! Then we had a pretty fun Holiday party at Studio 54 in MGM. There is a lot more that happened during this last year, if you want an update, follow me on twitter: www.twitter.com/max_max.

Megan T.

EMPLOYEE SINCE OCT 1 2007

While I haven't been here long, I've really enjoyed my time here at Zappos. It's great to get up everyone morning and be excited about going to work! I'm very lucky to work for such a unique and special company with so many wonderful people. I feel like I hit the job jackpot!

Melissa C.

EMPLOYEE SINCE FEBRUARY 20 2007

Our Zappos Culture has made me a better employee, a better mother, a better friend, a better human.

Melissa Q.

EMPLOYEE SINCE MAY 5 2008

Zappos Culture is very important to me. Without a true culture, Zappos would be just like any other company out there. One of the biggest differences is that this culture allows me to be who I am. Here, you are encouraged to share your ideas or any possible concerns. Most companies try to suppress that. Zappos tries hard to take care of its employees and I really appreciate that.

Melody M.

EMPLOYEE SINCE NOVEMBER 12 2007

I feel that the culture of Zappos is equal to a roller coaster. It's really fun, but you have to be prepared for any sudden changes that might come. The ride is fun, because you are in it with friends and family. The change helps you to grow and become a stronger person.

Merenaite S.

EMPLOYEE SINCE JANUARY 7 2008

Working for Zappos has been a great experience for me. I am quiet, casual, and a shy person. Zappos has encouraged me to step outside of the box. The culture here is unlike any I've experienced. Zappos has a very positive upbeat atmosphere. I especially love the many opportunities that are open to us. I love the culture here because it's a culture that I am happy to display here and outside of work.

Michael A.

EMPLOYEE SINCE JUNE 2 2008

I just celebrated the 39th anniversary of my 21st birthday (you do the math) so I've worked many, many, many years in the retail and corporate world. I have never been in a place that is quite like Zappos, with the focus on customer service and company culture that applies to everyone. I like the feeling of helping customers resolve their problems or just simply place new orders and hearing their surprise when they find out how soon their order will arrive. None of my other jobs had that kind of customer focus; even though they used "customer service" in their mission statements, it was never like it is here. It's my pleasure to work at Zappos and hope that I can continue to contribute to the success of the company.

Michelle M.

EMPLOYEE SINCE OCTOBER 23 2006

No company is perfect. No management team has all the answers. Just as in any family, there are disagreements and bad days. The difference with this "work" environment is that we are more than just co-workers, we really are family. We cried when we lost people due to layoffs and we kept in touch with those who left. We celebrated huge milestones and no one department took all the credit – it was shared and accepted. Through it all, we kept strong and still believed in our values and our culture. No, not one company is perfect, but we do have many perfect days. Management may not have all the answers, but together, we always work to find them.

Michelle S.

EMPLOYEE SINCE JANUARY 7 2008

The culture at Zappos is what makes it such a remarkable place to work! It inspires me to better myself, explore new ideas and contribute my own, and have some fun doing it! It makes me get out of my comfort zone by expanding my thinking and the way I do things. Zappos is unique! I am encouraged to WOW my customers and make them feel special. I find myself calling other customer service centers and being disappointed that they cannot begin to compare to the service I am free to give at Zappos. The family atmosphere means that I will be greeted with smiles and good wishes when I pass others in the hall. You are never alone at Zappos! I am blessed that I have the opportunity to be a part of this outstanding company and look forward to what comes next!

Mike M.

EMPLOYEE SINCE OCTOBER 6 2008

What Zappos Culture has meant for me so far is that I feel as though I'm part of a work force that cares about me in more than just a corporate sense. The people here genuinely care about their fellow co-workers and seem to go out of their way to make everyone feel at home and like family. This culture is simply to do your best at your job while making the job a fun and friendly environment for your peers. My last jobs were pretty cut and dry when compared to here, in the sense that there was very little to establish camaraderie. The first thing I noticed here is that there is a strong sense of family and passion about the job. I remember coming in after three weeks of training, looking around and still hadn't run into anyone that was unhappy to be at his or her job and do their best for the company. The culture here is great and I am grateful to be a part of it.

Mike S.

EMPLOYEE SINCE NOVEMBER 7 2005

Zappos Culture is a living, breathing, organic thing. There are a few core values that glue it all together, such as resourcefulness (doing more with less) being humble, building community, embracing change and flexibility, doing all of this with a great positive attitude, and remembering to have fun, be unique and a little weird throughout the whole thing. The loose structure of ideals allows us an extremely positive environment that promotes new ideas, growth and learning. This environment empowers us to reach and discover new potentials that would not be possible in a strict, un-nurturing, or unfocused environment. Our culture is a strong, elastic foundation that holds us up and provides an infinite amount of possibilities for us to build upon.

Monique P.

EMPLOYEE SINCE OCTOBER 23 2006

When I think of Zappos, I think of family ... my extended family! We're here more than eight hours a day and great relationships are made here ... not just with our customers, but also with our peers. We sometimes see each other more than our own family, so we can't help but to care and look after one another here. It's not just a job; I've been here for over two years and I have love for my Zappos family with all my heart! We never have a dull day. We're always crazy, creative and fun! We always rock the house and I'm proud to be a member of this wonderful family!

Myra T.

EMPLOYEE SINCE MAY 29 2007

Our culture is about building relationships, learning to work as one and having fun. I think we all have one goal in mind, and that is to find happiness. Zappos believes in spreading that happiness by providing the best service possible. That's what life is all about. That's what Zappos gives. The very best!

N. Scott J.

EMPLOYEE SINCE JULY 29 2008

I LOVE THIS PLACE!!! The job, the benefits, the free lunch, but mostly the people! I've made so many great friends here. Just a few include (names have been changed to protect the guilty) Chibi Chibi, Polo, Mz. House, and of course the Card Dealer and Yoda! Love you guys, love Zappos, never change! Now if I can just get the company to move a little closer to my in-laws for my wife's sake ...

Nancy H.

EMPLOYEE SINCE NOVEMBER 12 2007

The Zappos Culture and Ten Core Values are so unique ... I do not know of any company whose core values could possibly come close. Not only are our Ten Core Values unique to the Zappos company, but each one of them can also be practiced in our personal and family lives outside of Zappos (well, almost each one - I'm 56 years old and am still trying to work on creating a little weirdness, but I do try to create the fun part!) Our Core Values have made me strive to not only be a better employee but also to be a better wife, mother and friend. Every day that I'm here at Zappos, I see our Core Values exemplified and every time I WOW a customer, I think I was able to deliver that WOW because of all the ways that our culture has WOWd me! Zappos truly is the BEST place to work and I am so lucky to work for such a GREAT company!

Natisha D.

EMPLOYEE SINCE AUGUST 7 2006

Working at Zappos has been an experience. It is special to me, because it represents my first career experience that offers opportunities or positive professional growth. I have never worked for a company that laid out such clear and concise requirements for moving up within the company. This company has been so open and honest, sharing information and wisdom about what it expects from its employees. This creates healthy relationships between managers and entry-level employees. As a result, it makes me want to work that much harder for such a wonderful company.

Nicholas B.

EMPLOYEE SINCE AUGUST 29 2005

Zappos Culture is definitely unique. It makes me happy to come in to work each day, seeing smiles wherever I go. Everyday I am WOWed by my co-workers. I'm just happy to be a part of this experience. Zappos is FTW!

Nicholas S.

EMPLOYEE SINCE NOVEMBER 13 2006

The Zappos Culture is about having a passion for growth and learning ... an open mind to change and an understanding for the differences in people.

Nikki S.

EMPLOYEE SINCE DECEMBER 3 2007

How crazy to think another year has passed already! We really do honor our core values! My favorite core value is #6 - Building Open and Honest Relationships with

Communication. I have recently sent many suggestions or concerns to management and the responses are quick and honest. I've been able to chat with upper management regarding concerns of mine from policy changes to things I think could be done differently. I honestly feel as though my opinions and suggestions are valued and appreciated. This company is truly more than I ever expected ... we are beyond great benefits, we are a family. I love most of the people I work with ;) I want to hang out with my co-workers because they are my friends and family. A lot has changed at Zappos this past year, from the layoffs to spending cutbacks. I thought that that would make a difference in the atmosphere ... we wouldn't have as much fun, we wouldn't be as happy (and spoiled). While we have changed, I believe all my friends, my Zappos family, has grown much stronger because of the hard economic times and cutbacks. I am truly grateful to be a part of Zappos.

Noel B.

EMPLOYEE SINCE JANUARY 29 2007

I love Zappos because it seems to understand the importance of building a community of caring people. This community acts like a family without most of the dysfunction. We really want people to succeed here, so we support, guide, encourage and train them to expand their opportunities by giving them the tools they need to grow and change. It can be a challenge trying to coordinate all of this while Zappos itself grows and changes. As long as we remain true to our culture and vision, as each individual succeeds in their own life, so does Zappos. It's a win/win situation. Now, imagine if the presidents, prime ministers, premiers and rulers of the world adopted this model! There would be no hunger, poverty, homelessness, illiteracy or epidemics. Everyone would also be really well dressed with cool discounts. Now that may sound like a utopian, socialistic ideal, but here at Zappos, we do all of this and still prosper. So, what's wrong with making sure that everyone succeeds? Not a thing!!!

Ozzy S.

EMPLOYEE SINCE SEPTEMBER 6 2005

Our culture goes well beyond what anyone expects when they first come to Zappos. It may be surprising to find out that you can be yourself without having to worry about what others think of you, but that is exactly what it is. You become part of the family as soon as you come in through the front doors. After working here for several years and watching our family get larger and better, I have realized that our culture is contagious and it will be hard for anyone to try to contain it.

Pam G.

EMPLOYEE SINCE JANUARY 28 2008

What is Zappos Culture to me? Hmmm ... I would have to say it is the antithesis of the corporate world. I have worked in various businesses in my lifetime, and too often I've been told that I cannot cross-train or transfer to another department because I was indispensable, too valuable, where I was. Then shortly afterward, I would find a new job where I could grow and the former boss would learn that no one is indispensable. At Zappos, that attitude is not to be found. Quite the opposite! I have been "booted off" a specialty team because it was time for me to learn a new skill set and broaden my horizons. AWESOME! I can learn more about the company by actually learning different skills in different areas, and am encouraged to do so! Not only do I not have to be stifled in the corporate mindset, I do not have to worry about business attire. Jeans and a t-top are standard fare and wholly acceptable. I can wear sneakers or Birkenstocks and no one will frown at them. I can even have streaks of blue/green in my hair! WOW! I can really be myself! And speaking of being myself – Core Value #3, "Create fun and a little weirdness," is my favorite, because I can be my weird self and not be shunned. All I can say is that working at Zappos this past year has been the best experience of my life! I can help people (which I love to do), be comfortable, and be myself. Thank you, Tony Hseih!

Pam T.

EMPLOYEE SINCE OCTOBER 1 2003

The Zappos Culture still continues to astonish me after being with the company over five years. But what's more exciting is thinking about what the Zappos Culture will be like five or ten-plus years from now. On a serious note, it's everyone's responsibility to continue cultivating and protecting our culture, and to remain focused on delivering outstanding customer service. This commitment is what differentiates Zappos from any other company and I feel privileged to be here. But on a lighter note, what other company would actually have a "Don't Ever Click Here" link on the front page of their website that leads you to being Rick Roll'd!

Patrice C.

EMPLOYEE SINCE APRIL 2 2007

It is truly a pleasure working at Zappos and being part of the diversified Zappos family. There is always a positive feeling here from your friends and team members. The opportunity for growth is always available and encouraged! Thanks, Zappos!

Patricia N.

EMPLOYEE SINCE OCTOBER 23 2006

I have enjoyed my job at Zappos. Being able to have fun and be a little weird makes my day at Zappos always something to look forward to. I have learned that embracing change can be a positive thing, just by sometimes looking outside of the box. I love my job and the people I work with because we are family.

Patricia S.

EMPLOYEE SINCE FEBRUARY 20 2007

I am thrilled to be a part of our wonderful family here at Zappos! And having Tony as the head of our family is awesome! He is very inspiring, and I love the fact he sits right along with the rest of us, instead of closing himself up in an office. Tony also takes phone calls from customers – just like the rest of us! And he empowers us with the ability to really WOW our customers! I have worked for several companies, but this is truly the first place where I look forward to coming to work! You never know what you are going to see here! The parades are always fun! I love having the opportunity to chat with people when they call in! It's really fun to share stories with people from different places!

Pedro D.

EMPLOYEE SINCE FEBRUARY 20 2007

Zappos Culture ... This is the third one I've written ... Nothing has really changed about how I love our Zappos Culture. Friends are still here to nurse me to recovery after a Zappos Party. I'm still swimming in Tony's pool every Fourth of July ... rocking out there on New Year's, too. Still as crazy as ever! One of the few things that has changed is the core value of Building a Positive Family and Team Spirit. This year, for me, has been one of the best. I've lost so much in my personal life ... I lost probably the most important person in my life – BUT I gained so many friends from the loss! My family bond here at Zappos has been strengthened to an incalculable amount. The way my Zappos family has treated me has me smiling every Monday morning at 8 a.m. I'd say 95% of all my friends HATE going to work. They complain EVERY DAY about how lame their jobs are ... How dead-end their jobs are ... how bored they are ... how upset they are. So I take them to my work functions. What are best friends for?

I love coming into work. Being a member of the R-desk is incredible. I come into work and sit amongst friends and laugh from 8 to 5, Monday through Friday. I could never imagine myself being anywhere else. Zappos rocks because of our culture!

Peri G.

EMPLOYEE SINCE AUGUST 28 2006

There are many words that come to mind when I think about the culture of Zappos. The one word that sticks out the most would be the word "family." When I researched the word "family" on Wikipedia, here is what I found: "Family denotes a group of people <http://en.wikipedia.org/wiki/People> affiliated by consanguinity, affinity or co-residence. Although the concept of consanguinity originally referred to relations by "blood," some anthropologists <http://en.wikipedia.org/wiki/Cultural_anthropology> have argued that one must understand the notion of "blood" metaphorically, and that many societies understand 'family' through other concepts rather than through genetic distance <http://en.wikipedia.org/wiki/Genetic_distance> ." While some of us here at Zappos are bound by blood, literally, all of us have a metaphorical blood that runs through us to help create a strong family atmosphere. That metaphorical blood is otherwise known as the culture of our company. Our Zappos Culture is something that each and every employee lives and breathes every single day, and it allows us to live and deliver WOW in every aspect of our lives. It is incredibly unique, and something that only we, as a family, can share. There isn't another company out there that has a culture like ours, and I am proud to be a part of the Zappos family!

Porsha P.

EMPLOYEE SINCE JANUARY 7 2008

I look at the people in my life and I know life is good! I have a feeling of peace and the sun shines down on me. I have this amazing freedom to show my true colors!

Priscilla G.

EMPLOYEE SINCE JANUARY 8 2007

Our culture here at Zappos is like no other! Zappos Culture is being able to be yourself and not be judged while at work. It is about having fun and loving what you are supposed to do. I don't think anyone could compare what job they have to ours here! I love coming to work feeling so comfortable and knowing I will have a good day. I can just brush off what is going on outside of work and keep a smile on all day!

I have been here for over two years now, and not once have I been disappointed being a part of the Zappos team. I can do nothing – be nothing –but appreciative to Tony and the rest of my Zappos friends because they make my day here at work! It's definitely a second home for me and I wouldn't want to be anywhere else right now! It is hard for many to say they love what they do on a daily basis, but I can say it all day and truly mean it =)

Quintaye P.

EMPLOYEE SINCE NOV 12 2007

I can honestly say that after three years, I still look forward to coming to work every day – which says a lot about this company. Very few people can say that about their job (at least the ones I know anyway). Being part of the Zappos Culture means you are privileged to have the opportunity to be here and be part of a such diverse group of people that are from all backgrounds. You are encouraged to succeed not only professionally but also personally and the opportunities are endless. What else can I say? Zappos is the best. Looking forward to the many exciting years to come here at Zappos!

Rachael B.

EMPLOYEE SINCE JANUARY 30 2005

I love that each day I come into work at Zappos, I get to learn and experience something new. I get to be surrounded by fantastic, driven people who find meaning in their work. I love that I get to be a part of everything that Zappos is and help others see how they can continue to learn and grow. Thanks to everyone at Zappos for helping our culture grow stronger year after year :)

Rachel R.

EMPLOYEE SINCE MAY 29 2007

Zappos is the kind of company that loves you even in your sweat pants, and forgives you when you're grumpy and hung over ... But most importantly, Zappos is the kind of company where a small-town girl can finally realize her life-long dream of growing a luxurious beard ... and still not be the weirdest person in the room.

Reandra D.

EMPLOYEE SINCE MARCH 10 2008

OMG, I cannot believe I finally get a chance to write in the Culture Book about my Zappos experience. This has started as the ride of a lifetime, and it is still going! So, I started to pursue my career at Zappos back in 2006. Unfortunately, due to a series of unfortunate typing events I did not end up getting the job until two years later, on March 3, 2008. From that date on, I knew that my previous tries just meant that it wasn't my time (yet). Now I have been at Zappos for almost a year and I love every bit of it. To this day, I am still overwhelmed by the Zappos Culture. It's like the culture is the law of Zappos, and everyone follows it. Everyone is nice and cheerful and so full of life. You always have someone you can go to if you need a hug, a smile, or just someone to vent to (Dr. Vik). I love my work more and more every day (I said work, because it doesn't feel like a job). Zappos has always been great to me and to my family. My five-year-old even decided that she no longer wants a party at Chuck E. Cheese, she just asked if she could have her birthday party at Zappos! How amazing is that!

Rebeka F.
EMPLOYEE SINCE OCTOBER 2 2006

What does the Zappos Culture mean to me? It means coming to work and having fun with my teammates. The culture means I can come to work and be me, not just another butt in a seat. I really appreciate the people I have met and now can call my friends. The culture makes it easy to say that your team is really your family away from home.

Rena D.
EMPLOYEE SINCE OCTOBER 16 2004

The culture at Zappos is so unique. I don't think you will find the kind of culture that Zappos has anywhere else! The people I work with are just not co-workers or associates. They are my family! I look forward to coming to work each day ... just to be around the other half of my family. Working here for the last four years, I have made the best of friends. The more the company grows, the bigger my family gets. We truly work as one team with one dream. I think about the tours that come through and see the amazement in people's faces ... they can't believe we are truly this happy ... all the time. All I can say is I love the company I work for, and am happy to be here working with my family.

Renea W.
EMPLOYEE SINCE JANUARY 8 2007

Although we've all been through some hardships over the last year, Zappos has managed to stay focused and upbeat. It's nice to know that a company can pull through any tough situation, still maintain a positive attitude and continue to have high hopes for the future.

It has been a true pleasure working for such a wonderful company these past two years!

Renee N.

EMPLOYEE SINCE NOVEMBER 16 2004

To me, the Zappos Culture means togetherness. I'm still amazed at the strong bond and family unity we have and continue to build, through thick and thin. I'm really proud to be a part of the Zappos family where everyone is appreciated, supported, and encouraged to learn and grow. I love being able to come into an environment where I can be myself. Four years ago, Zappos had me at hello!

Ricki M.

EMPLOYEE SINCE AUGUST 16 2004

The Zappos Culture can almost be summed up in one word: concern. Nearly without exception, the Ten Core Values add up to concern. Concern for our customers, concern for our co-workers and concern for our vendors. When that concern is genuine, the momentum it generates for the company and the individuals involved are life-altering, as the past ten years of history have shown. As we all strive to demonstrate that genuine concern into the future, the growth of this company and the life-altering experiences of those involved can only continue to snowball and enhance the lives of everyone involved in the Zappos experience.

Rita S.

EMPLOYEE SINCE OCTOBER 23 2006

Our culture creates strength and a strong connection within our family, our community and the world. Our culture has a positive ripple effect on every aspect of life that it touches and makes the world a better place to live as long as we keep it simple and pure. We should be very proud in our own humble way.

Rob S.

EMPLOYEE SINCE MAY 2 2004

Our Zappos Culture is like the Force from Star Wars. It binds us together and is everywhere and everything for Zappos. Our company almost certainly wouldn't have grown to what it is today without a strong culture to support it along the way. Business is business in a lot of ways, but a strong culture can enable you to accomplish great things even during the toughest times. It distinguishes you from the status quo and gives you the most strategic competitive advantage in the market. How do you stop a group of crazy people that are hell bent on accomplishing the same goals?! I don't know and don't have an interest in finding out. I've grown up at Zappos in a lot of ways and I'm proud that this company has impacted my growth as a person and professional. I'm also blessed to be able to leave a mark on the ever-evolving culture and brand that drives our business. Stay Classy, Zappos!

Robert M.

EMPLOYEE SINCE NOVEMBER 13 2006

It has been a little over two years that I have worked for Zappos.com and I have really nothing bad to say about this place. Every day I come into the office I feel like I am coming to my second home. I feel that I can be myself here and that is very refreshing. At previous jobs I felt I had to act a certain way, but working for Zappos, I can be my crazy self and let my hair down once in a while. =0)

Robin G.

EMPLOYEE SINCE AUGUST 7 2006

Another year has gone by and I still have the best job that anyone can have! I can't believe that I am just as excited about my job now as I was almost three years ago. The only difference is that the people that I had just met then are good friends now. We have cried, laughed and grown in the last couple of years. There have been babies born and parents that have died ... we have shared all aspects of life. Zappos is not just a job, it is a slice of life!

Robin P.

EMPLOYEE SINCE APRIL 25 2005

Being a part of the Zappos family has allowed me the opportunity to grow personally, professionally, and spiritually. My co-workers are my extended family. We support each other through adversity and encourage each other to reach our greatest potential. We share our dreams and our sorrows. We essentially do life together, while at the same time, focusing on our goal of strengthening the brand of Zappos as a household name that offers incomparable, world class, customer service.

Rose R.

EMPLOYEE SINCE AUGUST 13 2006

What is Zappos Culture? I think to be chosen "Company of the Year" by the City of Henderson and to be ranked 23rd of the "100 Best Companies To Work For" for by Fortune Magazine says it all. It is indeed a place where employees feel secure and important. It is a place where customers feel special because they get the best customer service no other company can provide. I have worked at Zappos for over two years and have enjoyed being a part of a great company. Zappos Culture is very unique and will not be found in any other company. We have an opportunity to grow with the company. I feel like Zappos is my home away from home. My co-workers are my friends and we support and help each other. We are empowered to make decisions that we feel will make our customer's happy. I'm glad to be a part of this fantastic company.

Ruby A.

EMPLOYEE SINCE JULY 29 2008

First of all, I have never worked with a company that believed in Culture. Working for Zappos is the best thing I have ever done. I have always worked for CORPORATE companies. Since I have been working for Zappos, I no longer have headaches, dread going to work or hate talking with customers. Thanks, Zappos, for the relief!!!

Ryan E.

EMPLOYEE SINCE MAY 5 2008

The culture at Zappos is different from any company I've ever worked for. It is fun and a little weird! :) I love working somewhere where, every day, I'm going to do something totally different than the day before ... and the people are all amazing. I love Zappos!

Ryan I.

EMPLOYEE SINCE SEPTEMBER 10 2007

I have successfully completed my one-year stay at Zappos since the last time I wrote my thoughts on Zappos Culture. To be honest, not much has changed. I still feel strongly about Culture and its importance to Zappos. I like the feeling of coming into the office every morning and not feeling like it's work. I get to work with great people on a day-to day basis and see their sense of culture. Like I've said before, it's a melting pot of different forms of culture here. Culture comes in multiple forms here, whether it be potlucks and trying out a different dish from someone's own personal culture or just seeing their neat decorations on their desk to express themselves. I can't think of a better place than Zappos for such an experience!

Sarah H.

EMPLOYEE SINCE DECEMBER 3 2007

Zappos is my home! I couldn't wish to be working for a better company. This company is so much fun and we don't just say that we are a family here, we ACT like one big weird kooky family! I have definitely found the job that I plan to make into my career! I heart Zappos!!

Scott K.

EMPLOYEE SINCE AUGUST 16 2004

Zappos Culture has been and will continue to be about the smiles. Although Zappos has been through some rough waters in 2008, I really feel that everybody has pulled together and stayed positive, even at our darkest hour with the layoffs in November. I'm constantly WOWed that while the rest of the country may be in complete turmoil, I can still come into the office and count on my co-workers for a laugh or smile ... this makes me very happy. We're a self-contained, special little world, full of joy and wackiness. It may sound like a cheap rip-off from the movie "As Good as it Gets," but Zappos puts a smile on my face and "makes me want to be a better man!"

Sean M.

EMPLOYEE SINCE JUNE 5 2006

When I started working here in June 2006, I had planned on leaving Las Vegas as quick as humanly possible. However, by the time I completed my training here at Zappos, I was starting to rethink that move. Is it possible that I found someplace to work where I would be valued? Was it possible that I found someplace to work where work didn't feel like work? Almost three years later I can honestly say YES! To both questions! The people, the Culture and the customers make this the best place I have ever worked in my life and I can honestly say that I plan to be here now as long as I possibly can. Zappos has been an incredible gift in many ways and I am very humbled to have the opportunities that I have here.

Sean Paul E.

EMPLOYEE SINCE JUNE 2 2008

Well, what can I say about our culture and core values? These two main things are what make our employees help the incredible place of Zappos' progress. As for me, the core values have helped me not just progress through Zappos, but through my new residency here in Las Vegas, NV. Just like my baby boy Maverick, I too am growing, but within the great place of Zappos.

Shannon C.

EMPLOYEE SINCE APRIL 7 2008

Culture to me means having constant comrades amongst your co-workers. In our effort to build a positive team and family environment, I have made the most amazing friends that I am honored to work alongside with every day. It is a pleasure to be with people that have your best interests at heart and encourage you to grow in your personal and professional life.

Shannon M.

EMPLOYEE SINCE AUGUST 20 2007

I've been here almost two years now. I have learned so much from working at this company. I have learned the real meaning behind the values and vision that the founders and CEO have for our company. I enjoy watching us grow and every day I'm growing with the company. I look forward to moving up the Pipeline! :-) It's amazing because I mention Zappos and everyone knows about it. My oldest son, DeAngelo, told me that he's going to one day take Tony's job from him because he wants to be the CEO and Tony is his mentor! WAY TO GO, ZAPPOS!

Shannon R.

EMPLOYEE SINCE JANUARY 29 2007

The Core Value near and dear to my heart is, "Pursue Growth and Learning." Here at Zappos, we are encouraged, and given ever so many opportunities, to explore this Core Value. While serving at Zappos, I have been able to learn new skills by participating on a variety of teams, encompassing both the Customer Loyalty Team and the Human Resources Department. But the very best part of all is getting to know and appreciate the many individuals with whom I have worked here at Zappos! They have all been fantastic, distinctive, fun-loving people that have truly enriched my life!

Sharon R.

EMPLOYEE SINCE MARCH 12 2007

Zappos Culture, to me, is a flexible and creative atmosphere that allows people to be who they are. Their special personalities and talents make our work atmosphere fun and interesting– with never a dull moment! Zappos Culture is grown in a very positive and reinforcing wealth of embracing growth and change, to constantly build and reinforce an even better, stronger, and more positive culture for the future! It's a grand thing to go to and from work every day with a smile on my face! Thank you, Zappos, for being so unique and fulfilling in so many wonderful ways!

Shauna S.

EMPLOYEE SINCE OCTOBER 6 2008

Zappos Culture to me means that we stand out from any other company. I love how Zappos doesn't put a label on anything. You can be yourself, dress how you want and act goofy anytime you want. What other company would let you have a parade just for hitting a goal? Zappos does!! This company is by far the best to me.

Shauntenea B.

EMPLOYEE SINCE OCTOBER 1 2007

Zappos Culture means, to me, a group of individuals from different walks of life, come together to form this one big melting pot. It also has another form as a family, people that are truly sincere and care about your well-being. Zappos is one BIG village of AWESOME people.

Shavone T.

EMPLOYEE SINCE SEPTEMBER 18 2006

I've been here two and a half years and I'm still loving it. I'm grateful to work in such a wonderful place full of wonderful people. Hopefully I can stay awhile and enjoy the ride!!

Sheena G.

EMPLOYEE SINCE JULY 29 2008

The culture here at Zappos is something that I have never experienced before! The Ten Core Values truly do resonate in the everyday operations, so there is never a dull workday. Not a day goes by that I am not encouraged to grow and learn, be a little fun and weird, and try to WOW everyone I come across, whether it is a customer, a co-worker, or even a stranger on the street. Things are definitely done the right way here and I am amazed every single day. Working here is an adventure and I hope to continue that adventure for years to come.

Shunjerra R.

EMPLOYEE SINCE APRIL 7 2008

The best part of Zappos Culture is that on my first day I was not given a 200-page novel on the dress code, like what I have received from other companies. I have worked for other companies that make it a point to regulate your clothes, shoes, jewelry, tattoos etc. I like that Zappos does not think that your personal style plays a part in your ability to do your job.

Stacey G.

EMPLOYEE SINCE JULY 9 2007

Zappos Culture sneaks up on when you are not even looking. Sometimes you are not aware that you are following or living by the culture. Just one day you are out shopping and start helping others, and the people you are helping ask, "Do you work here?" and you answer, "No." All I can say is sometimes that is a really amazing feeling.

Stacey H.

EMPLOYEE SINCE DECEMBER 16 2004

I feel what makes Zappos Culture different can be summed up in one word: freedom. We are able to be ourselves, because that is what makes the company great. Our ideas and opinions are actually heard. The freedom to be zany and serious – at the same time – is one of the main things that I like about the Zappos Culture.

Stacy H.

EMPLOYEE SINCE JUNE 19 2006

I count Zappos as a huge blessing in my life. Our culture is a way of life and it has become a part of who I am. I don't think I will ever find a place like it. Zappos is so much fun and every person is just as important as the next. To express my love for Zappos, I have written a haiku:

Zappos is the best
We laugh, sing, eat cake, and WOW
Live and Deliver

Stephanie B.

EMPLOYEE SINCE APRIL 2 2007

Zappos is AWESOME! I love working for a company that lets me be myself :) Our culture is like nothing else out there and I appreciate every second that I'm here. The company really takes pride in the service that we have to offer and working here has made me spread the good service outside of work as well. I follow the Core Values in my everyday life and it is great! Woot Woot!

Stephanie C.

EMPLOYEE SINCE JUNE 18 2007

Zappos Culture is unlike any other. I could try to tell you how amazing my job is, but this culture is something that you truly have to experience. I am very fortunate that I get to experience the amazing positivity that is the Zappos Culture. I work with the most amazing people and that is what maintains our culture. I have a family that I can talk to about anything, that will drive me to be better and that truly wants us to succeed. I am extremely proud when I get to tell ANYONE that I work for Zappos. I know that they may not understand my excitement when I say that, but one day they will. I am sorry that I don't have anything better to describe what Zappos Culture means to me. It is simply amazing.

Stephanie H.

EMPLOYEE SINCE SEPTEMBER 18 2006

Another year, and it's gone by so fast. I feel like I just wrote one of these weeks ago. It has been another amazing year and yet again, it wasn't like any other year. It seems the longer I am here, the faster it goes and the less it feels like a job. Every weekday I wake up and go into Zappos, only to have a good time, help people and enjoy every minute of it. I think my favorite part about working here is that I can still be me. It is really like a family every time. Even when changes are made, desks are moved, everyone can be so friendly. I catch myself outside of the Zappos environment being overly nice, happy and all around cheery. I also notice more when I feel people aren't as Zappos-ish. I feel if every company were more like our family, everyone would be a happier place.

Stephanie W.

EMPLOYEE SINCE NOVEMBER 16 2004

Zappos Culture means being able to be yourself and be embraced for that individualism, yet still be a part of a team. It's about learning to adapt to change. Zappos encourages us to grow and learn all that we can, which drives determination in each and every one of us. I am passionate about my job here because I feel truly blessed to be a part of the Zappos team. It's the best place I have ever had the privilege to work.

Susan J.

EMPLOYEE SINCE FEBRUARY 20 2007

*C**ULTURE BOOK*
Working at Zappos has been an amazing LIFE experience. The Ten Core Values that we practice everyday are simple but profound. I am truly grateful for the experience.

Susana P.

EMPLOYEE SINCE OCTOBER 22 2007

There are many aspects to Zappos Culture. The main thing for me is that I don't dread coming to work. I have made so many friends here, friends that I will probably have the rest of my life! You can't say that anywhere else. Every day is a new experience, something new and exciting. Whether it be random outbursts of Disney songs or a parade, there is never a dull moment. Zappos is full of fun and weird people who work hard. It has definitely earned its place as one of the best companies to work for.

Tam T.

EMPLOYEE SINCE OCTOBER 2 2006

Our culture separates us from other companies, and makes us unique in so many ways. We are encouraged to be ourselves, and embrace each other's differences. Each employee is treated as family from day one. I am proud to say that my feelings for this company have not changed since the first day I started work here. Zappos is definitely the greatest company I have ever worked for!

Tamra J.

EMPLOYEE SINCE JUNE 2 2008

I came to Zappos in mid-2008 and I immediately fell in love with the environment. I love how everyone is happy and smiling. As I continued to grow in the company, I realized how awesome it is that people in other departments are friends. I always avoided the people in other departments because I thought they felt as if they were too good to be my friends. Little did I know that I was only hurting myself. Zappos Culture is not only alive in my work life; it has also spread to my personal life. I find myself holding doors open for people, letting cars merge in and I'm just in a better mood. I have realized how smiles truly are contagious!

Tanai M.

EMPLOYEE SINCE JANUARY 7 2008

Starting work at Zappos has changed my life in so many ways. It has made me appreciate the small things and all the company has to offer. Since being here I have become so passionate about my work and progressing within the company. I love to be at work now, whereas before at other jobs, I would dread going in. Outside of work it has made me change the way I look at things and the way I treat others. I hope to be here for many years to come.

Tara M.

EMPLOYEE SINCE MARCH 10 2008

I have worked at Zappos for over a year now and have found it to be nothing short of amazing. Having the opportunity to work here and be a part of the culture has truly been a blessing. I love the feeling of being able to come to work and share who I am with everyone around me. I did not know at all what to expect when I started working here. I was used to the casino business where you had to follow specific dress codes, could not be eccentric and show no piercings or tattoos of any kind. This was not me. I am full of energy, pretty tatted and love piercings. I love how Zappos allows my true colors to shine through; they help me to not only succeed in the company, but also with myself, in a personal way. Zappos is basically the place to find your pathway. Zappos has become my second home full of many people that truly are my family.

Tasha G.

EMPLOYEE SINCE OCTOBER 10 2005

Zappos is not just a job to me it's my family! Over the past three years that I have been with the company, I have created some long-lasting relationships with people that I will never forget. I love that our Culture is so distinct from other companies. I have never worked for a company that encourages you to excel in your current position and then gives you all of the tools that you need to be promoted within the company. I am definitely proud to say that I work for Zappos!!

Teresa P.

EMPLOYEE SINCE MAY 5 2008

Let me start out by saying I love working at Zappos!! I never have trouble waking up to start my day here. Everyone is so full of life and could brighten your worst day! It was hard to believe at first, but once you get sucked into the culture you find yourself not only applying it here at work but also outside of work. I think before working here, I was one of those very snooty retail workers that didn't seem very approachable. Since being here, I smile at random people in stores, and I find myself wishing anyone a good day. I love it here and don't want any other job other than Zappos! Keep up the WOW!

Terri A.

EMPLOYEE SINCE NOVEMBER 6 2004

To me, Zappos Culture means many things ... the ability to embrace and appreciate each other's differences ... coming to work knowing that at some point during your workday, you will find yourself laughing hysterically because a co-worker did or said something really goofy ... or on some days, feeling completely comfortable being that goofy co-worker.

Thomas S.

EMPLOYEE SINCE JANUARY 28 2008

It is very comforting to work at a company with a culture based on a strong foundation of constructive core values. In 2008, we saw the world's financial system implode, in part, because it was a dishonest culture with a foundation based on destructive core values. It's an awesome feeling to know what your own core values are and to know that you are surrounded by others who have that same guidance, not only in their decision-making and behavior in the workplace, but outside the workplace.

Thomas T.

EMPLOYEE SINCE JANUARY 29 2007

Zappos is awesome!!! I am blessed to be employed by a company that supports growth, learning, success and individuality. Zappos has become a home away from home. I come to work knowing that it will be a great day. I love the people I work with and I love the opportunities that Zappos offers. I have worked here for nearly three years and it has been a fantastic roller coaster of fun and excitement. There is never a dull moment. I love ZAPPOS!!!

Tiffany L.

EMPLOYEE SINCE MAY 23 2005

Zappos Culture: family, fun, always a surprise! A place where magic truly happens!

Tom S.

EMPLOYEE SINCE DECEMBER 3 2007

Zappos Culture is an environment that, most of the time is quite fun and relaxed. You can be yourself and don't need to act happy. It's a place where growth is really encouraged all the time. Zappos is different than others with the company-paid employee snifters, relaxed environment, various parades, happy hours and awesome parties. You work while having fun at the same time. I like Zappos due to its uniqueness. I've never worked at a place where you can have so much fun. Zappos is always looking for ways to better itself and make it a great place to work.

Travis B.

EMPLOYEE SINCE OCTOBER 6 2008

The service that Zappos provides for our customers is unheard of! I have rarely ever received service from any other company even close to the service that Zappos provides to our internal and external customers on a daily basis. The magic behind this service is our culture and the passion we have for our jobs. I feel the reason that Zappos employees are passionate about their jobs and care about our customers is because we have a sense of pride for the company that we work for. This has a lot to do with the way Zappos treats its employees. Employees know that Zappos cares about them and treat them well by providing them with excellent benefits and perks. Zappos also communicates virtually everything with us about the business so we get the big picture and realize the impact that we have on it as a whole.

Travis S.

EMPLOYEE SINCE OCTOBER 6 2008

I started at Zappos just recently, beginning with the training class of October 2008. Since then I have noticed the many improvements I have made personally in my everyday life outside of work. Whether it's the people, the core values that we're taught, or even the general attitudes of every employee I run into; Zappos has honestly helped me become a better person. My attitude is better towards meeting new people and with everyone here always so happy, you can't possibly leave work in a bad mood. I feel very lucky to have found a job at my young age that I can enjoy every day.

Tree S.

EMPLOYEE SINCE JULY 31 2007

Zappos Culture has changed the way I live my life. I try to WOW everyone, no matter where I am. My leads have always encouraged me to learn new skills, not just to help the company, but also to improve myself. We are like a family here, and that makes our customers part of our family. It is a pleasure to come to work, and I know that it shows in the way we treat our customers. I am blessed to work for a company that encourages me to be myself, a bit different and in a way, a little weird. We have made a lot of changes this past year, a lot that were hard for Tony to make, but we all know that they were to make us stronger, and they have. Zappos ROCKS!

Troy C.

EMPLOYEE SINCE MAY 29 2007

Being here at Zappos for two years now, I am still no less blown away by the unique and wonderful culture we have here. We truly are more of a family than a group of people who just show up to work, ignore each other and then go home. We look out for each other. We celebrate each other's successes. We laugh together, cry together, drink together and grieve together. It all comes down to the Ten Core Values that guide us in everything we do. It is what got us through the rough days at the end of 2008. Without those Core Values and our Culture, Zappos would have pulled itself apart. Walt Disney once said, "If everyone tells me I am doing things the wrong way, then I know I am on the right track!" That could be Zappos' unofficial motto!

Vanessa L^a.

EMPLOYEE SINCE MAY 7 2007

My poem for Zappos:
I moved to Vegas with stars in my eyes
and worked for places that told me nothing but lies.
In a moment when I almost turned around,
I found Zappos and never again did I frown!
Parades, parties are incredible things,
but it's the family spirit here that gives me wings!!
All I can say is, I found the place I want to always stay.
Something new and exciting happens every single day!

What I've learned here: Zappos is a place where negativity is as unwelcome as the flu. It's a place where acceptance reigns over judgment. It's a place to become the best YOU that you can be. It's a place to find yourself. I know I did.

Vanessa L^e.

EMPLOYEE SINCE APRIL 7 2008

WOW. That's all I can say. Working here at Zappos has been, and still is, an AMAZING experience! I love the culture! It seemed waaay too good to be true at first, but after a while it started to sink in and I'm so grateful that I came to work here (and that it's true)! I've made so many close friends and have had so much fun working here! At my last job I dreaded waking up and going to work. I haven't had that happen to me once while working here! I actually look forward to working! Which is a new thing for me! lol. I love the family atmosphere and even though we're supposed to be humble, it can be pretty hard. I love it when people ask me where I work. I always say "Zappos" with a huge smile. It's like a cult – but a good cult that I don't mind being sucked into. I can't wait to see what the future holds for me and this awesome company! =D

Veronica J.

EMPLOYEE SINCE JUNE 27 2005

It's easy to almost take for granted the environment that we cultivate at Zappos. It just struck me again today, for the nth time, how much family I really have here (in the non-blood-related sense, although my sister now works here as well!) My birthday was last week and I had taken off a few extra days to celebrate. You always expect to come back to a few hundred (at least!) emails when returning from a vacation or long weekend, but I never expected to come back to so many emails just wishing me a happy birthday, from people I talk to regularly, people I've met at least a couple times before, and even people whose names I barely knew. All of them conveyed a simple wish, but that so many people took time out of their day to wish it for me reminded me how much I appreciate my family here.

There's no question that many people I've met during my nearly 4 years at Zappos have definitely become my extended family. There are certain ways to recognize family (according to various email forwards we've all received at some point); some are humorous, others more poignant.

When you fall down, family makes sure you're okay, and then laughs out loud at how silly you looked (so you can laugh with them, of course). When you look great, family makes sure to let you know; when you look horrible, family makes sure to let you know that, too! When you do well, family helps you celebrate your successes. When you have a setback, family is there to ease your worries, give you constructive feedback, give you a kick in the ass and tell you to get back out there and knock 'em dead because they know that you can.

My Zappos family has done all of this for me, and more, and those that know me also know that I have done and would do the same for them in a heartbeat. (Someone please fall down soon, I've been dying to laugh all day! but please don't get hurt or I'll feel bad.)

Vincent V.

EMPLOYEE SINCE JULY 29 2008

"Culture is the integrated pattern of human knowledge, belief, and behavior that depends upon the capacity for learning and transmitting knowledge to succeeding generations."

(Merriam-Webster Dictionary). Before I came to Zappos, I heard good and amazing things about this (our) company. When I was lucky enough to come and experience Zappos in person, as an employee, the welcoming and kindness of everyone I came across shocked me. Before Zappos, I have never felt so welcome at a company that I have worked for. The culture here is awesome. We have a very relaxed atmosphere, and at the same time, we work with a sense of urgency. After all, we are Powered by Service. Being able to come to work in "street clothes" has my day starting and ending very comfortably :-) . Our culture here for learning and development is outstanding. I love that we have classes here to help us along our adventure through Zappos and through our lives as well. I am very excited to be a part of this Zappos family, experience, and culture. As the definition of culture states above, to learn and transmit knowledge to succeeding generations, I vow to deliver WOW to everyone here at Zappos, the newcomers, our customers and you. Thanks for reading my input and our Culture Book! Zappos is truly awesome!!!

Viola H.

EMPLOYEE SINCE JANUARY 8 2007

It is a well-known fact, both within Zappos and in the public, that we have a set of Ten Core Values here at Zappos. To me, these Core Values help to create our Zappos Culture. Recently, some of our family members had to be let go, due to the economy. Well, our CEO, Tony, showed all of us how our Core Values work to create our culture. First, he sent us all an email explaining why this action took place and let us know how it affected him. This was his way of Building Open and Honest Relationships With Communication. By telling all of us how he felt (and you could feel the emotion he felt through his words) he helped to Build a Positive Team and Family Spirit. Now, all of us will need to learn to Do More With Less. We will become better employees as each of us Pursues Growth and Learning in order to help fill in any gaps that might have been created due to the layoffs. Each of us is willing to Embrace and Drive Change in order to make this happen. But not everything that happened last year was bad news. Zappos was named number 23 in the Fortune Magazine's "100 Best Companies To Work For" (we even made the cover!). We hit $1 billion, yes, $1 billion in gross merchandise sales! Did this go to our heads? NO! Instead, it made each of us more Passionate and Determined to continue to Deliver WOW Through Service. Did Tony change who he is because of these things? Not at all! He still comes to work in his Zappos T-shirt and jeans. And because our Leader is Humble, we are Humble and Proud to be Employees of Zappos!

William B.

EMPLOYEE SINCE JULY 31 2007

WOW, where do I start? First, I think it is appropriate that I start this entry off with a "WOW," because that is what we are all about. I have been consistently WOWed since I started here. I could go into the benefits, the pay, the family atmosphere, the freedom, the fun, and so on and so forth, but instead, I will provide a short and simple paragraph that encompasses all that I feel and have experienced at this company. Zappos has changed my life. No other company I have worked for in the past has ever done that, no matter what the pay, position, or the benefits. I have absolutely NO desire to ever work anywhere else. Our lives are so short, every year passes quicker than the last, and I sincerely hope that every one of those years, up until the day of my retirement – all 30 of them – is spent at Zappos.

Yhaira Y.

EMPLOYEE SINCE OCTOBER 6 2008

My first week here, I thought, "O.m.gosh! This company is run and employed by ex-cheerleaders and former Disneyland employees!"...Don't get me wrong, I was thrilled to be working in such a positive and upbeat environment. Tickled, actually =) but I thought, "Can people really be this happy every day?? Maybe it's something in the water??" I mean, I'm a pretty happy person, but even I have those days where I wake up a sniveling, woolly-haired cranky beast! But no one here seemed to EVER have a bad day!

A couple weeks later, I found myself – bullhorn in hand – leading a military-style parade ... as though it were the most common thing in the world! And I realized, those days still happen every now and then ... but the people around me make all the difference in the world! I may come to work with the "I don't wanna smile at ANYONE today" attitude ... but it is simply wiped clean from my mind as soon I walk in and am greeted with smiles and waves. It's crazy, really! Like the "Twilight Zone" ... but in a good way. =)

Zachary Z.

EMPLOYEE SINCE JANUARY 28 2008

The culture here at Zappos means many things to me. First and foremost, it means being myself. I am not told to cut my hair, remove my hat and piercings and be just another employee with no individuality. I can be fun and weird here, not just with the co-workers I sit around, but also with every one I come across. It's playing games after work every week with people from here only to see more joining in every week thereafter. The Zappos Culture to me is an uncanny synergy where work and family blend into one ... where being yourself is embraced and not ignored for the sake of the bottom line.

Zerina "Z" P.

EMPLOYEE SINCE MARCH 10 2008

Zappos has been an experience like none other. Never in my widest dreams did I ever dream of such a wonderful place to work. I never feel as if I'm coming to "work." I look at it as going to my second home! I love being part of the future of Zappos. Hey, I work at Zappos, that sounds good!

There's a lot of reasons why Zappo[...] reason to play hard.

B-1. Certainly never a shortage of reminders around the office of what one can do after work.

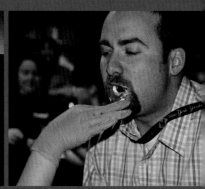

ians work hard. It gives all the more

B-2. The Cupcake Conteset asks the question everyone wants to know...
how many cupcakes can you stuff in a human stomach in one sitting?

B-3. Our annual Zappos picnic. Chances are you'll be exhausted from playing so hard, full from eating so much and...very, very wet.

If only we'd stop trying to be happy we'd have a pretty good time.

EDITH WHARTON

II.

**CORPORATE
HELP DESK
LEGAL
HUMAN RESOURCES**

FIG II-1. A few central beliefs of Zappos' Recruiting Team. Candidates that don't swear by (1) business in the front, (2) parties in the back and (3) mullets (most importantly), need not apply.

FIG II-2. Tours of Zappos are somehow becoming a part of The Vegas Experience. We're not sure how it happened, but if we're on the same list as the Bellagio Fountain and the Liberace Museum, we'll take it. (To schedule your own tour, email tours@zappos.com. Really, come on by!)

Alane C.

EMPLOYEE SINCE NOVEMBER 1 2006

Working at Zappos has been an adventure, to be sure. This last year I was able to be creative at my job by getting together with two of my wonderful co-workers and forming the Zappettes. Liz, Kathy and I started singing "Happy Birthday" to people and evolved into a singing trio that brings happiness to others through music. We sang on videos, for company events – we even did holiday songs for the "hold" music during the holidays. We are currently working on an original song to let people know we sell clothing as well as shoes. Zappos is a great place to work. Working here allows me to do my job in the legal department and also work together with others, using our talents to spread cheer and sunshine all over the place. So – be adventurous, creative and open-minded, and whistle while you work ... or sing!

Alfred L.

EMPLOYEE SINCE DECEMBER 16 2004

2008 was quite the roller coaster. One might even have thought that Charles Dickens was referring to 2008 when he wrote, "It was the best of times, it was the worst of times..." After coming off a great 2007, we began 2008 very hopeful about the future. In fact, all the highly respected economists were also predicting that the second half of 2007 was going to be better than the first half. Boy were they wrong.

One of our happiest moments in 2008 (and in Zappos history) was meeting at our all-hands meeting on February 29 (in Las Vegas) and March 1 (in Louisville) to tell everyone that we had made our 2007 operating profit goal, and our Board of Directors had approved paying out a profit sharing bonus for the first time in Zappos history. It just didn't seem like it was going to get better than that.

In the second half, we faced the meltdown of our financial system and the toughest economic environment Zappos has ever faced. We had to make some tough decisions and had to ask some of our friends to leave the Zappos family. I thought that day was going to be one of our saddest moments in 2008 and in Zappos history. Even though it was sad, it also turned out to be one of our proudest moments. We all rallied together to help and support each other in a really tough time. We then moved forward and turned a very tough situation into an opportunity to continue to build our relationships with each other and with our customers. Our rallying together allowed us to reach $1B in gross sales in 2008 and to make the Fortune 100 Best Companies to Work For in one of the worst retail environments in our lifetimes!

What amazes me about our culture is how it helps us pull together and weather the ups and downs that allow us to come out stronger.

Altovise M.

EMPLOYEE SINCE OCTOBER 9 2006

Let's see, I have been here now for two years and three months and I still love coming to work. It just amazes me how much my fellow workers live and breathe the Zappos Culture. I'm happy that I work at Zappos because people here embrace and drive the culture so much, it makes you look at things differently, both work-related things and in your personal life. Whenever I have a situation come up, I'm happy to know I can think about the culture that we have and try to use it to determine my outcome, whatever the situation may be.

Amanda K.

EMPLOYEE SINCE JUNE 2 2007

To me, the Zappos Culture is like having a really big extended family, a group of people who truly care about what is going on in your life. The culture was brought to life for me when I had a loss in my family; not only was I given time off from work, but Zappos sent flowers to my family to show care and concern during a difficult time. The Zappos Culture reached out to my entire family and it was great that they could experience the Zappos Culture firsthand.

Andrea W.

EMPLOYEE SINCE JUNE 4 2007

The culture at Zappos is absolutely amazing! It is awesome that each department can rely on other departments (something I have never experienced before). I love the fact that outside companies want to emulate what we have perfected.

Andrew K.

EMPLOYEE SINCE JANUARY 29 2007

Argh. Why is it so hard for me to put this into words? I guess I think about the culture more in terms of a set of feelings, so here's a stab at qualifying them: Passionate, not just for challenging myself in how I approach my "work," but also for Zappos' service-driven philosophy. Genuinely caring about candidates, vendors and employees. Excited by group discussions and ideas shared while reading books from the Zappos Library, and taking Pipeline classes. Endlessly amused by the antics of my teammates. Respectful of the

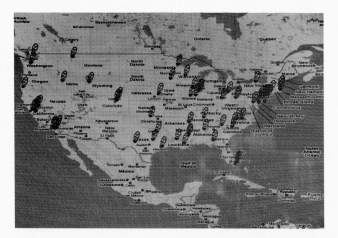

FIG II-3A. In the main lobby of Zappos, a monitor reveals real-time purchases across the country.

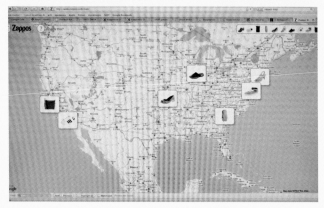

FIG II-3B. On April 6, 2009, Zappos unveiled www.zappos.com/ map, showing all products purchased in real-time. Unverified reports indicated that national productivity levels dropped by 54% on April 7th.

responsibility we all share in keeping it all going. And thankful that such thoughts are even encouraged to be shared.

Anne F.

EMPLOYEE SINCE JANUARY 28 2008

When I started working at Zappos a year ago, I never knew a company like this existed. What I mean by that is, a company that believes in its employees and in treating its employees with respect. I have always been made to feel important and to feel as if I play an essential role in the growth of our company. I have also made many close friends while working here. My husband (who also works at Zappos) and I have no siblings, so we have quite small families. This being said, I feel that the friends I have made here at Zappos are my brothers and sisters. Some of us hang out together almost every weekend! I LOVE ZAPPOS!!!

Fɪɢ II-4. Gathered together from the cosmic reaches of the universe, here in the Hall of Justice League are the most powerful forces of good ever assembled...Superman, Wonder Woman, The Wonder Twins, space monkey Gleek and The Zappos Legal Team...dedicated to truth, justice and peace for all mankind (especially Zappos employees, customers and partners).

Brandis P.

EMPLOYEE SINCE MARCH 22 2005

Working in the Recruiting Department at Zappos is like an ongoing "Saturday Night Live" skit. So there are basically two things I love most in life:

1. Whiskers on kittens
2. Working for Zappos

Cheryl Anne F.

EMPLOYEE SINCE AUGUST 28 2006

Failed Zappos advertising ideas within the past year:
1) I've got great news! I've saved thousands of dollars in business clothes and suits by working at Zappos!
2) Zappos: What can chartreuse toile do for you?
3) Air conditioning vent filters: $15.00
Year's supply of sunscreen: $ 250.00

Money dropped into slot machines (one quarter at a time): $357.75
Surviving the Vegas heat to work at Zappos: Priceless

Christa F.

EMPLOYEE SINCE DECEMBER 20 2004

Sappy but true Culture Entry

Working for Zappos has enriched my life in so many ways. Our Ten Core Values go beyond our business and into our lives. As a result, over the years, I have experienced more personal growth and peace than I could have ever imagined would stem from my job and into my life. I still vividly remember making the decision to change careers and come to Zappos and how nervous and unsure I was at the time. Choosing to come work at Zappos has been one of the very best choices of my life.

Humorous but equally true Culture Entry

Here is how I would define my experience of the Zappos Culture every day:

- Broken Tagalog conversations.
- Shorts, no matter what the weather.
- Deep, intellectual and passionate discussion of Twilight. Yes, I am Team Edward!
- Fighting over who gets to go to the speaking engagements about Zappos – okay, fine, you can go!!
- Very lengthy emails with Cliff Notes for folks with short attention spans.
- Exclamations of "Ouch" and lots of daily ruckus because evidently, that immovable part of the desk is a surprise every day.
- Shanty Towns.
- Food area with required greeting to the hostess before you can enter.
- Amazing renditions of the Tootsie Roll.
- Kings with very confusing rules.
- The most affectionate and yet highly inappropriate expressions of admiration, respect, and love.
- "I wish you weren't a liar."
- Knowing every SNL skit backwards and forwards despite having never seen most of them.
- Odd nicknames, like being called "little boss" by the tiniest person in the WORLD.
- iPods so your co-workers can "concentrate" when really, they just like to make you yell.
- Random adoption conversations.
- Obsession with tchotchkes.
- New Kids on the Block and Hello Kitty – really? Yep, really.
- Team building or buy the team something? It's not a bribe.
- Mullets – the perfect analogy for Zappos Recruiting and Zappos in general – **_Business in the front and a party in the back!_**

Christian J.

EMPLOYEE SINCE OCTOBER 26 2008

I feel like we are all in the middle of a big storm in the ocean and I consider Zappos to be a beautiful island where people are always looking out for one another. At Zappos, we are like a family. I know, deep in my heart, that we will survive and remain stronger together.

David T.

EMPLOYEE SINCE AUGUST 18 2008

I have always heard that the grass isn't always greener on the other side. Well I am here to tell you that in this case it is. Ever since my first day here I have felt no less then family. A lot of companies try to instill that concept into each of their employees. Not one company I have ever worked for has ever achieved it at this level. The Ten Core Values that are taught to you here carry over into everyday life. The two that really stand out for me are "Build a positive team and family spirit." There isn't a time I can walk down the hall without everyone I walk by saying hi or even holding the door open for me. I find myself holding doors outside of work for people that are in such a hurry in life. The core values have shown me how to look at life in a different light. Take a step back and make sure that you are treating people in the same way you want to be treated. The second core value is to "Be Humble." No matter how successful you get, always remember where you came from and how you got here. It took everyone helping each other to rise to this level. With all Ten Core Values in place, life is just better.

David V.

EMPLOYEE SINCE JULY 1 2005

Culture comes in all forms, and has to do with the behaviors and beliefs, characteristic of a particular group ... and in great cultures, it embodies excellence within. The Zappos Culture fosters excellence found within life and living. It provides individuality, freedom and also includes "Doing the right thing" as its tenet. And the most amazing thing about the Zappos Culture is that it positively affects the group at work and at home, while easily spreading to others, not currently within the Zappos Culture, affecting others positively, as well. "Do the right thing, and the right things happen" sums up our Zappos Culture.

Dorsey T.

EMPLOYEE SINCE FEBRUARY 12 2007

My story is very simple and sweet. There isn't a day that goes by that I regret giving up my stressful corporate job, where no one cared about you, to work for Zappos.

Every day I come in I'm greeted by my extended family, where people actually care if you are there or not and they actual know your name. I try not to take days off of work because every day is fun and unique here, you never know who you might meet.

Dory D.

EMPLOYEE SINCE MAY 9 2001

Zappos has and always will be a positive influence and learning experience. I have watched us grow from 75 employees to being Fortune's #23rd best company to work for. We have gone through many changes, some good times and not-so- good times, but we always come out as a positive influence in people's lives. This last year has been a huge learning experience for me and showed me that we most certainly never know what direction life is going to take us, but whatever direction that may be, the Zappos family always takes care of its own. The Zappos Culture has been here since day one and it means that we will always look out for each other. I am still amazed at the humility, compassion and determination of those who have been here since the beginning, and those that are no longer with us. I will always appreciate our humble beginnings and hope that all people who come aboard understand the sacrifices and hard work it took us to get here, and the sacrifices and hard work it will take to push us above and beyond. After almost eight years I am still very thankful that Zappos gave me the opportunity to be a part of this wonderful journey.

Eduardo D.

EMPLOYEE SINCE MARCH 10 2008

I am very grateful for the opportunity of working here at Zappos.com. It is a very good company and its rhythm of work is very good in comparison to what I had. Thanks to you I am a part of the group at work and that makes me very happy and calm working here. Thanks.

Eric V.

EMPLOYEE SINCE APRIL 3 2006

It's work! Our culture doesn't only exist in the best of times but rather our culture defines us under the most trying of circumstances. I'm incredibly thankful and proud to be part of the Zappos family!!

Erica J.

EMPLOYEE SINCE DECEMBER 12 2007

It makes me sad to hear people say they hate their job or the company they work for, because we spend the majority of our time at work, more than we do at home with our family and friends. Working at Zappos, I feel fortunate that I actually like coming to work every day and that the people I work with are my friends, not just co-workers. To me, the Zappos Culture allows you to have a healthy balance of work life and personal life. Here's to another year of working harder and playing harder … (raise glass here and toast!).

Heaven T.

EMPLOYEE SINCE JULY 5 2006

I can't believe another year has passed already! It seems like just last week I was typing away for the last Culture Book entry. Zappos. A unique name for a unique company. I have met the most light-hearted, energetic, humorous people while working here. It truly is a place that you could just be yourself and enjoy the company around you. Here, hula-hooping with vendors and breaking out into random dance moves are encouraged. I know that working here will be an experience that I will always treasure, and I am thankful for that. Zappos feels like a home away from home and I look forward to the future that it holds! You go, Zappos! We're all here, standing by your side!

Hollie D.

EMPLOYEE SINCE JUNE 12 2006

Zoo, **A**daptability, **P**eople, **P**ersonality, **O**ptions, **S**ummer Vacation Caring, **O**ff-the-Wall, **M**aking a Difference.

Jamie N.

EMPLOYEE SINCE DECEMBER 13 2004

After four years with Zappos, the thing I love the most is that it just keeps getting better. Every day brings with it new and exciting challenges. There is never a dull moment at work, and that is not just because of the work we do, but also because of the people we are lucky enough to be surrounded by.

Jerald T.

EMPLOYEE SINCE JULY 1 2005

I am the luckiest man in the world! I can't believe I get to get up every day, with the anticipation of going to a place where I can thrive and prosper. I am so thankful that Tony, Fred, Nick and Alfred saw the vision of what has become the greatest show on earth. There are so many times during the day I laugh with joy and amusement of what the company and my co-workers do. If there truly is a heaven, I hope it is a continuation of Zappos.

Jo C.

EMPLOYEE SINCE MARCH 10 2008

Zappos is not a job to me; it's a way of life. I get to come into work every day and see the shiny happy faces of my co-workers, who are more than that to me. I get to come to a place every day that encourages me to be myself, that nurtures growth. We work hard, we play hard and we love what we do!! I'm not just a number here and I've never felt like I wasn't appreciated. Being at Zappos is being a part of something bigger than myself ... a ton of people working together towards the same common goal. I am here because I believe in what Zappos is doing ... trying to change the world one customer at a time :)

Josh F.

EMPLOYEE SINCE APRIL 16 2007

This has been a year of change for me here at Zappos. To all the people that have helped me along the way – thank you. With all the support and positivity Zappos offers, I feel I have grown as a person and I'm very grateful for that. In closing I want to say to all our fallen Zappos brothers and sisters that you are all in our hearts and minds. We are all grateful for all of your hard work and the good times we shared.

Josie D.

EMPLOYEE SINCE JULY 3 2006

It's exciting to be involved with such a young, progressive, and ever-evolving company. The development and changes I have seen in the few years I have been here are amazing. I can't wait to see what the future holds for us. I am very proud and fortunate to be a member of the Zappos family.

Kacee N.

EMPLOYEE SINCE SEPTEMBER 24 2006

Zappos is an amazing place to work. It's not just a job, it's like a second home. It's also nice to be around people who are more outgoing then yourself. I wake up every day wanting to go to work. It's just a crazy, fun, always-something-new-going-on type of place to be. I love you guys!! Woot Zappos!

Keith G.

EMPLOYEE SINCE JANUARY 1 2005

I have been working with Zappos for eight years. I have seen many changes in the company. One thing that is consistent is the company's efforts to keep and improve its culture. This was one of the worst years that Zappos has gone through. We had to tighten costs, close the outlet stores, lay off 8% of the employees, cut back on the catered lunches and charge a small fee for vending, which is donated to Nevada Childhood Cancer. We experienced some positive things as well, like increasing department efficiency, reaching $1 billion in sales, making 23rd on the Forbes "Top 100 Companies to Work For" list. When you walk around Zappos, all the employees still have the greatest attitudes and continue to smile. They still WOW the customers. People pull together, to do what they can to help the company get through these tough times. This is what makes Zappos a great place to work.

Lisa M.

EMPLOYEE SINCE NOVEMBER 8 2004

I have been here four years and the Zappos Culture has changed in many ways. However, there are certain constants in the culture. It is these constants that are the driving force of

Zappos. Every employee is passionate about the company, the culture and the customers.

Liz G.

EMPLOYEE SINCE NOVEMBER 6 2006

Within all the chaos that is life at Zappos, there is an amazing support system. I know that no matter what comes my way, I will have people to back me up, to take part of the load, to provide a shoulder to lean on or a joke to make me laugh. It is the family atmosphere that makes me glad to come to work each day. I count myself lucky to be one of the people who are given the chance to call Zappos home.

Lynn H.

EMPLOYEE SINCE MARCH 24 2008

Picture this – I'm sitting at my desk in the Benefits Department, with a bag of fresh popcorn from the Help Desk, listening to our trainers in TLD talk about the classes they taught today (and laughing). My HR co-workers are busy at their computers, some with headphones hooked to iPods, and I can hear a ping-pong game going on in the lunchroom. This is bliss. Working at Zappos sometimes feels like a miracle to me. I've never worked harder, and had more fun doing it, ever.

Maria U.

EMPLOYEE SINCE MARCH 19 2008

For me, Zappos is one of the best companies to work for. We have opportunities, good relationships with friendly people and always greet each other with a smile.

Martha A.

EMPLOYEE SINCE MARCH 19 2008

I think it is ZAPPOS growing as a company that has given me the opportunity to project myself as a person and a worker. I feel that ZAPPOS is a large family of which I am a part.

Mary D.

EMPLOYEE SINCE NOVEMBER 28 2007

I'm so thankful and proud to be a part of the Zappos Culture. Without a doubt, I feel like I'm back on campus. The culture energy explodes throughout the day and you can feel it, see it and hear it from everyone that comes your way. It's a family, it's a way of life and I'm lovin' it.

Melissa R.

EMPLOYEE SINCE JANUARY 1 2005

When I think about the Zappos Culture, I think about the many inspiring people and experiences. I am so fortunate to have been involved with the growth of Zappos from the beginning ... a time when we did not have the Ten Core Values on paper, but when they were practiced day in and day out and became the foundation for our amazing culture today. I have witnessed and been a part of dreams coming true for this company, especially this past year and for that, I am very grateful. I recently took a sabbatical and was able to reflect on my time with Zappos. The culture is one in a million and for me personally, one of the greatest experiences of my life that I know will not happen again!

Michelle S.

EMPLOYEE SINCE MAY 24 2006

It's an unbelievable, chaotic experience. What is blue today could be green tomorrow and that's okay. Really. It's okay because once you realize and embrace the chaos, it revolutionizes how you do things. Welcome to Zappos and "turn on, tune in, drop out."

Millie C.

EMPLOYEE SINCE JUNE 1 2006

Zappos is its own universe. Real-world rules and limitations are not applicable. Instead, we govern Zappos using one principle: strive to always and consistently be unusual, unique and extraordinary.

Missy R.

EMPLOYEE SINCE JANUARY 1 2005

I have been with the company since 2004, and still, to this day, it amazes me. The Zappos Culture is a wonderful entity itself, which has created a family vibe that cannot be broken. It is such a great place to work, where you can be yourself by letting your spirit shine. I love coming to work each day knowing to expect the unexpected.

Pam C.

EMPLOYEE SINCE OCTOBER 2 2006

Culture is what we live by, to give our lives meaning and to make a difference to those around us. I came here from Silicon Valley, where there was no culture in the work place. So when I started working for Zappos, it truly defined culture shock! The culture we have at Zappos is what separates us from other companies, and I am so happy to be part of it!

Patti C.

EMPLOYEE SINCE MAY 9 2005

I've been in the work force for quite a few years and I have never experienced anything like Zappos. Nor do I think I ever will again. Working here is like working with your family, because we are a family. Not only do we strive to WOW our customers, everyone works to WOW each other. The Ten Core Values that we have are carried over into our personal lives. In a word, Zappos is WOW!

Rachael P.

EMPLOYEE SINCE SEPTEMBER 8 2008

To me, Zappos is much more than just a job. I've only been with Zappos for about five or six months, so I'm a fairly new employee. Having said that, it is amazing what an impact the Zappos Culture has had on my life, both in and outside of work. My favorite core value would definitely be "Pursue Growth and Learning." I find myself more motivated and determined than ever to do so. There is an infinite amount of knowledge that you can gain here at Zappos and there are opportunities to grow every day ... not to mention how welcoming and friendly everyone is. It almost just makes you want to take a step back and just observe it. It becomes even more apparent when you're outside of work and someone doesn't hold the door for you or smile at you as you walk past them. It just makes you appreciate Zappos that much more. I'm proud to be at Zappos and I look forward to continuing to grow here.

Rebecca L.

EMPLOYEE SINCE JUNE 25 2007

Working at Zappos is like going to college, with classes, clubs and other extracurricular activities. ;) The best part, though, is the close friendships I have with other Zapponians. Recently, I was talking on the phone with a friend from pre-Las Vegas days. Upon hearing that my significant other was often away for work, he asked what I did all by myself. I was taken aback, until I realized he assumed that I wouldn't have any friends here (I'm a relatively recent transplant to the city). Zappos definitely fosters close connections between its employees – I don't think I have ever made as many close, real friends at a company as I have here.

Rebecca R.

EMPLOYEE SINCE NOVEMBER 12 2007

We have incredible core values as a model to live by, and using those as my benchmark, I'm a better person through my efforts to live them. I can't think of anyone else at any other company who can say they think they are becoming a better person by going to work – I feel incredibly lucky to truly believe that about how Zappos Culture affects me.

Renna C.

EMPLOYEE SINCE JULY 9 2007

The Zappos Culture is a way of life that enables us to embrace the company's core values. Zappos gives us the freedom to be ourselves and create our own path within such a driven company. I believe that because of our culture, our employees work harder, smarter, and are more efficient than companies that do not embrace a non-traditional way of operating. Simply put, Zappos is one of the BEST places to work!

Richard H.

EMPLOYEE SINCE JANUARY 1 2005

In the early days, when Zappos was still an infant, I recall that I had a dream on the night that Tony proclaimed that the company would exceed one billion dollars annual gross merchandise sales by the year 2010. Earlier on that day, there was a mix of excitement, euphoria and skepticism in the small office that housed all the employees and some of the shoes that the company owned. Despite the astronomical growth the company was experiencing, many still considered it as simply a brilliant PR/marketing stunt.

My dream, which I shared with Tony and others the next day, was so puzzling that it actually woke me up in the middle of the night. In my half awake-half asleep state, I could still vividly see the huge sign that said, "From A to Z" in my dream. What did that mean? Did it mean that for Zappos to reach the one billion dollar goal, it would have to carry merchandise ranging from A to Z? Or did it mean that the company must have employees who can master the skills from A to Z to make it happen? After some more soul searching, I finally came to the conclusion that the phrase really meant to say, "From Amazon to Zappos." That is it! For Zappos to reach its one billion dollar goal, the company must advance what Amazon pioneered a decade ago to the next level in Web 2.0 – and transform everything, such as company philosophy and culture, from how Amazon did it to how Zappos does it. By doing so, the customers will naturally flow from Amazon to Zappos as well.

Well, as Tony may tell you, Zappos is very different from Amazon and we should probably never try to compare the two. Amazon is all about the lowest possible prices, and Zappos is all about the best services in the world. Yes, services, that's the way I live the Zappos Culture, both internally and externally. Nothing could be more joyful than helping others do what they want to do, not just passively waiting for requests, but pro-actively looking for opportunities. Amazing things happen when one is nice and kind to people. More often that not, what goes around, comes around. Indeed, I find the Zappos Culture so powerful that I try to practice it both inside and outside the company, 24 hours a day. Yes, even in my dream, in which some night I may find a new meaning again for that magic phrase, "From A to Z."

Rosa R.

EMPLOYEE SINCE MARCH 19 2008

In the time that I have worked at this great company Zappos, I learned what companionship, loyalty and opportunity mean. I now see more positively from another point of view and know that, in this world, everything is possible if we put all of our efforts in.

Rosalind S.

EMPLOYEE SINCE JUNE 6 2005

This is a great time of the year for me; I love putting together my entry for the culture book!!! This year is 2009 and I'm still learning and growing!!! I've been through some changes and I have welcomed them with open arms. :) Change is good; it keeps me on my toes and reminds me that yesterday can never be today. Flow with it or you'll be left in the past. I didn't know how to start this year's culture book entry so I thought "the dictionary" and here is one of the many definitions from www.dictionary.com: "Culture – The predominating attitudes and behavior that characterize the functioning of a group or organization." After I read it, I said, is this Zappos? Yeah, but we are so much more!!! So I came up with an acronym. :)

Community
United
Long
Term and
Undisputedly
Recognized
Everywhere

Now, the definition of these words put all together definitely describes the Zappos Culture!!! I love being a part of this amazing company!!! We are led by example and the driving force of our amazing workplace is our fabulous employees. We're all able to share our ideas and make this the most ideal place to work on earth. I think there are some pretty awesome folks here. ;) If you've heard all the stories about us and still don't believe it, stop by and see for yourself. I'll be happy to welcome you myself!!!! And it is the happiest place to work!!!!!

Saffet O.

EMPLOYEE SINCE AUGUST 25 2008

What is it about our culture? Being a relative newcomer to the company, coming in to such an environment was most certainly an eye-opener for me. However, as I discovered more and more about the company, its people, and its values, there was one characteristic that could be seen in all who work here: passion for what they do.

In so many other companies, I've seen individuals stumble in to work in the morning and stumble out at night without much care for their jobs, impacting not only their own day-to-day work, but also the morale and work of others around them. At Zappos, it is a fantastic experience to see those around us with enthusiasm, energy, and a commitment to perform to the best of their abilities. It's this unique trait that spreads throughout the company, infects everyone, encourages all to succeed, allows employees to bond, and ultimately creates a happy workplace ... a rare phenomenon indeed. If the old adage that "if you do what you love, you'll never work a day in your life," is true, then very few ever truly work at Zappos.

Sean K.

EMPLOYEE SINCE MAY 8 2006

My Culture Book entry for this year is about Family. Here is a quote: "The most important things in life are your friends, family, health, good humor and a positive attitude towards life. If you have these then you have everything!" – (Author Unknown) This quote truly reflects Zappos. When I come to "work," I'm coming to an environment where I'm not working with co-workers, but instead, with friends. These friends are my family. We take care of business and each other. Together, we are all trying to accomplish the same goal and make a positive impact in the world.

Tomas M.

EMPLOYEE SINCE MARCH 19 2008

I feel that this big company Zappos has given me the opportunity to integrate as a worker and become a part of a chain. I feel like a link that helps out, as we all work together in harmony.

William A.

EMPLOYEE SINCE FEBRUARY 25 2008

Zappos is a stress-free place to work. It gives you the confidence to do your job. The feeling is nice. You want to give your best to show the respect back. It is a joy to work for Zappos. The culture becomes you.

Zack D.

EMPLOYEE SINCE APRIL 3 2006

This is year three of a fun ride. To hear that Zappos.com is #23 on Fortune's 100 Best Companies to Work for has me in awe. When I first came aboard I had no idea that within three years I would be working for one of the best companies in the United States. All I can say is WOW. God is good...

Zappos.co

RIVIERA

LARRY GATLIN
GATLIN BROS

MILLER

welcomes you to

Fig C-2. The Mike Tyson Conference Room. No guarantees you'll still have your ear after the meeting, but you might get Robin Givens in exchange.

m

CIRCUS CIRCUS
HOTEL·CASINO

LAS VEGAS STRIP

CIRC
AM TO M
MS A

TRAVELODGE

SOUVENIR

DINERS·CART·BLANC
AMER·EX·B·S·A·MAS
SHOW·RESER···IN·ROOM

DISCOUN
LIQUO

VACANCY
COLOR TV

BAILEYS $14.9
KESSLER 750 54

#1Auto Care

09
19

Deppy

he Strip

Fig C-1. Walking around the Zappos headquarters is like taking a mini-tour of Las Vegas. If it weren't for the 700 people actually working in Nevada (and 700 in Kentucky), you might not even realize there's a billion dollar company being run within these walls.

Fig C-3. The Penn & Teller Conference Room. It's been heard that Penn, the vocal one, told Larry King that their success is due to the fact they have never been close friends. As usual, Teller could not comment.

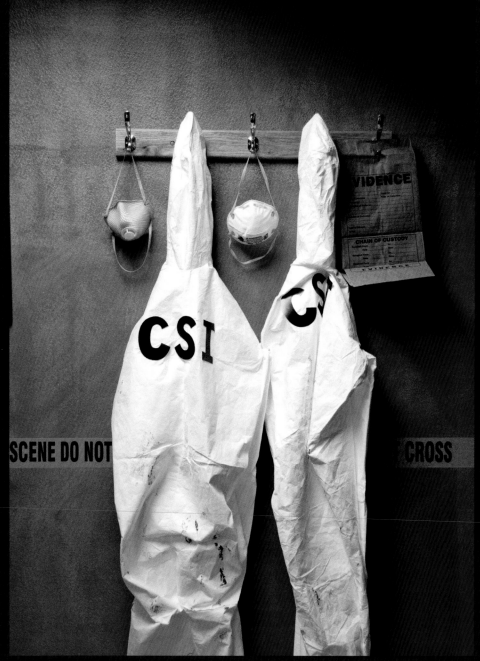

Fɪɢ C-4. Since things that happen in Vegas also stay in Vegas, we can't really tell you what happened in this particular conference room.

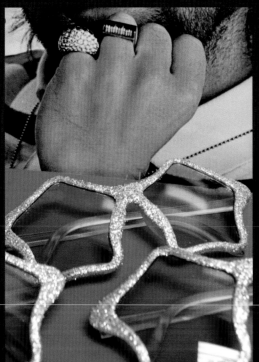

Fig C-5. From the Elton John Room (since Reginald Kenneth Dwight Conference Room—his birth name—wouldn't be quite as catchy). We have a collection of Elton John-inspired sunglasses, with the hope he'll come put one on, one day. For some unknown reason, this hasn't happened yet.

Fig C-6. Zappos would not be complete without a room dedicated to Ol' Blue Eyes, Frank Sinatra. Oh, if that conference room could talk....it probably wouldn't say much since Sinatra never sat in there. BUT, thanks to a gift from Capitol Records, you can sit in the room and listen to him croon away, all day.

IT IS ONLY POSSIBLE TO LIVE
HAPPILY EVER AFTER ON A DAY TO
DAY BASIS.

MARGARET BONNANO

III.

FINANCE

Fig III-1. Monopoly meets Zappos in this version of the classic board game. Except, instead of owning Park Place, you can take a ride on the Clarks® Express, become the "Master of Wow", discover a cure for boredom and create a little fun along with way. We might as well rename it Zonopoly.

Amanda N.

EMPLOYEE SINCE JULY 10 2006

The Zappos company culture is an extremely engaging, caring one that fosters a desire to provide the very best customer service. This is shown not only in how we deliver packages to consumers but how we care about each other. This goes beyond customers, to employees, to investors, to vendors, and to partners. It's the few extra minutes taken that make a difference in someone else's life – whether it is giving or receiving a simple "Hello," a "Thank you," or "How can I help?"

Amy B.

EMPLOYEE SINCE MARCH 19 2007

Zappos Culture means that my co-workers are my friends, and that work is a fun place to spend my day.

Audrea H.

EMPLOYEE SINCE SEPTEMBER 10 2007

I've been with Zappos for a little over a year and have experienced our Core Values in our culture daily. Zappos, to me, is passionate, caring co-workers, a frat house work environment, grand celebrations, parades, nerf gun wars, TLD enrichment classes, holiday festivities, a trusted organization, my giant spider, YouTube, dedicated management, tours, blogs, work (yes, we all have a JOB to do), and binding friendships! It's just a great feeling to tell someone you work for Zappos. I have a sense of pride to be associated with Zappos, and be able to contribute to such a great company and culture.

Berna B.

EMPLOYEE SINCE APRIL 30 2007

Zappos Culture is very unique and lots of fun. We are always thinking of how we can WOW our fellow employees, and especially our customers. In my 25 years here in the U.S., this is the only company that I have worked with that is really down to earth and very people-oriented. That is the reason why we are the 23rd best company to work with in the Fortune 100. I know we can still go up the ladder in the year to come. Zappos always thinks outside the box. We always go an extra mile to please everyone. That is why our Ten Core Values are very important to us. I am very lucky that I am part of this Zappos Culture. Zappos is one of the best – if not the best – company that I work with. I will continually do my best to keep Zappos Culture in place so we can be the first. Always keep our Zappy smile.

Brenda B.

EMPLOYEE SINCE FEBRUARY 4 2008

I remember the first All Hands Meeting that I attended for Zappos. It was the first time that I had the opportunity to see Zappos in FULL force, and I can remember how proud and honored I felt to have been chosen to work here. It was the first time that I was able to witness, for myself, the close family bond that Zappos had built with its employees and I remember the great sense of relief I felt, knowing that this would be my new home. I was amazed (still am:) at what Zappos has been able to accomplish with its culture and GREAT employer/employee relationships. I can truly say that I feel like the FAMED Charlie of Willie Wonka and the Chocolate Factory. I KNOW that I have FOUND the golden ticket!!

Core Value#3
"Create a little FUN & Weirdness"

Chrissie Y.

EMPLOYEE SINCE DECEMBER 10 2007

Friendly, smile and excited!!!

Claudia T.

EMPLOYEE SINCE NOVEMBER 12 2007

Being able to grow professionally and personally as the company grows itself.

Cynthia T.

EMPLOYEE SINCE APRIL 28 2008

I still feel as though I am dreaming! To not get that yucky "Sunday" feeling where you dread Mondays is something new to me. I actually cannot wait to get here and I cannot wait to do my work and please other people. Zappos makes me want to do the best I can with everything I do. I have never been in an environment that made me feel that way. Thank you!

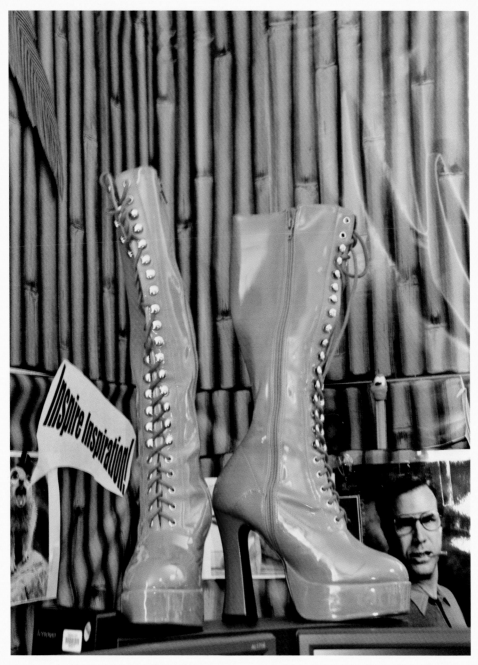

Fɪɢ III-2. Red boots you normally wouldn't associate with CEOs and CFOs, but these particular ones were worn by Alfred and Tony during a video shoot for HR. They were dressed up as nurses, while dancing to Thriller. Bets still being taken whether they bought some for home use.

Daniel S.

EMPLOYEE SINCE JUNE 18 2007

Our culture is all about the people that work for Zappos. I have never worked for or seen another company with such passionate, positive and fun people that enjoy what they do 24 hours/day, 7 days a week. Zappos is really more of a lifestyle than just a typical job. And I mean that in a good way!

Deborah P.

EMPLOYEE SINCE NOVEMBER 27 2006

For me our culture is a wonderful blending of all that makes each of us unique and special. It is a place where each of us has the opportunity to show off what we are capable of today as well as the opportunity to grow and learn so that we can be even better tomorrow. We collectively make Zappos and ourselves successful. Because of our culture ... we know no bounds! For me this is refreshing and vitalizing;) Thanks, Zappos!!

Debra J.

EMPLOYEE SINCE SEPTEMBER 10 2007

This will be my second entry for the Culture Book. It got me to thinking about what impresses me this year versus last year. Everything was so new last year. The impact was pretty big on me. Everything was new and powerful. Now, with a full year under my belt, I find that Zappos still WOWs me. As a company, Zappos still loves to evolve and not stay with the status quo. I love to be challenged and yet I also love to do what I am currently doing in my job with accounts payable. The WOW factor at Zappos gives me the option of learning new things by taking the classes that are now offered internally and still staying in my position. So while I continue to learn and expand my horizons, I can do my job and be ready for the day my inner drive says it is time to try the next challenging job Zappos has to offer. I LOVE THIS PLACE!!

Eric K.

EMPLOYEE SINCE FEBRUARY 4 2008

Growth and learning. With chocolate milk.

Ericka D.

EMPLOYEE SINCE NOVEMBER 12 2007

Culture at Zappos is what makes Zappos so special. Thanks to the different cultural events and activities, I've had the opportunity to know my co-workers better. I really enjoy working at Zappos.

Frank Z.

EMPLOYEE SINCE FEBRUARY 20 2007

In my view, the most interesting thing about Zappos Culture is really in its simplicity. This culture is what happens when motivated, creative, intelligent people are allowed to really let their ideas and vision run wild. It provides a venue for all of us to achieve common goals through the culture. There's a camaraderie ... a sense that we all do our jobs as well as we can, because we know everyone else is doing the same. And most importantly, we always find new ways to make work fun and a little weird.

Jeanette T.

EMPLOYEE SINCE NOVEMBER 19 2007

My very favorite Core Value is "Pursue Growth and Learning." All the companies I have worked for have given you the opportunity to go back to school, and they will pay a percentage, but here at Zappos they provide a guideline for each position, and if you are interested in another position, there are classes, books and tests you can take to get you prepared for the position – if one becomes available. Now, that is a company that cares about the growth of each employee.

Jeneen M.

EMPLOYEE SINCE NOVEMBER 13 2006

I am thankful each day to work with people I respect and have fun with, in an environment where I can freely express myself. I am honored to be part of a movement of energized, talented employees who are building a successful business and an epic brand, while increasing the happiness level of the world.

Jessica V.

EMPLOYEE SINCE OCTOBER 13 2009

Zappos means being yourself. I can be myself and better yet, I'm not alone in that spirit. And that's what makes this place the best place to work – that we can be ourselves. I'm happy every day that I'm here ... happy to be a fellow Zapponian in all the sense of the word.

Jimmy A.

EMPLOYEE SINCE NOVEMBER 28 2005

Zappos Culture is the reason I wake up on the right side of the bed every weekday.

Jimmy C.

EMPLOYEE SINCE NOVEMBER 12 2003

Zappos Culture centers on punctuating hard work with a lot of fun. Whether it's setting up Halloween haunted houses right on the cusp of monthly close to launching ping pong attacks against each other in between budget meetings, we know to balance the stressful moments with good-natured hijinks.

John P.

EMPLOYEE SINCE AUGUST 20 2007

This year our culture took on a special meaning. 2008 was a very difficult year for all retailers, with many closing down. In times like these, the bottom line normally trumps culture in many companies. However, we pulled together as a family to get through the difficulties. We realized that now is the most important time to keep our culture alive, and to continue relying on our core values to guide our daily actions.

Katie W.

EMPLOYEE SINCE JANUARY 8 2007

2008 was certainly a very tough year. I can't even count how many times I heard the word "financial" and "crisis" in the same sentence! We definitely were not immune to it either. It's sometimes easy to forget how serious things are in the world when you're in the Zappos bubble. When we were forced to do the layoffs in November, it affected every single one of us. We lost members of our family ... not just co-workers. That is what Zappos has meant more to me than anything in the two years I've been here ... family. I never thought I would feel that way about a job. As heartbreaking as the layoffs were, they brought us closer together and more focused on the Ten Core Values than ever before. Everyone is trying to help. I think the core value of the year should be "Build a Positive Team and Family Spirit" because we are surviving something very serious and coming out better and stronger.

Keith C.

EMPLOYEE SINCE JUNE 30 2008

I've been at Zappos about seven months. The culture here is driven by the employees. It's a living, changing thing kept in check by our Ten Core Values. You can't have a Zappos Culture without 100% commitment from the people. Everyone I'm in contact with lives and breathes the core values ... especially the open and honest way we communicate with each other. I'm WOWed every day, so I can't wait for tomorrow.

Lakshan F.

EMPLOYEE SINCE FEBRUARY 1 2008

The Zappos way of life brings people together and turns a work day into so much more.

Maja L.

EMPLOYEE SINCE FEBRUARY 11 2008

Zappos Culture means having a big smile on my face Monday through Friday ... ;-)

Meg M.

EMPLOYEE SINCE APRIL 23 2007

I can make a difference! Whatever issue I choose to approach on any day, I am motivated by knowing I should take action because," I can make a difference!" Improving a process, providing accurate data to management, brightening a staff member's day, fostering better relationships with vendors, buyers, banks ... I do it because I can make a difference. The management and fellow employees here at Zappos empower each individual to make a difference; the result is a constantly improving company with very few limits.

Michael H.

EMPLOYEE SINCE MARCH 31 2008

I have to admit I was intimidated by the culture when I first started. I was worried I wouldn't fit in, because I am not the most outgoing person, but Zappos Culture embraces individuality. The culture is also about being customer-centric. It is about being considerate of all our stakeholders: co-workers, suppliers, community, investors, and the list goes on.

Mike A.

EMPLOYEE SINCE FEBRUARY 6 2006

This past week we were named to Fortune's "100 Best Companies to Work For" as we debuted at #23 in the rankings. The fact that we were recognized says a lot about how our unique culture is becoming visible to the outside world. Our culture does not just magically happen. It is the result of many dedicated people striving for the same goal – to provide the absolute best customer service experience. If we keep that overall goal in mind, the various rankings and accolades will ultimately take care of themselves. Delivering great service is what we do, and as long as we keep that commitment, the future will continue to be very bright.

Miriam M.

EMPLOYEE SINCE OCTOBER 82007

Zappos Culture is MP3 players and jeans. It's the coolest work environment I've ever been exposed to and I think it makes me a more productive employee. Knowing I can put on my headphones and drown out the world when I have a deadline makes it so much easier for me to succeed. And wearing jeans every day makes me so comfortable.

Pati V.

EMPLOYEE SINCE MARCH 3 2007

WOW!! What a place to work! Where else can you go to work, have fun and get paid to do it? We are awesome!! I went on a trip to Utah recently to see my grandkids and stopped to get gas in a town called Beaver. As I went to pay for my gas, the clerk saw my Zappos jacket and asked me if I worked there. When I told her, "Yes," all she did was rave about how awesome our service is. I, in turn got her email address and when I came back from vacation I emailed her a discount coupon. Her service was also awesome.

Patrick S.

EMPLOYEE SINCE NOVEMBER 14 2001

Wear whatever you want and free Perrier, what more could you ask for?!

Rachel M.

EMPLOYEE SINCE JULY 9 2007

One of the greatest things about Zappos is that Zappos has figured out this simple formula: If you treat your employees right, your employees will treat your customers right. I love working for a company that is truly about providing top-notch customer service. The customer service attitude reverberates company-wide, in how we treat our customers and each other, and it is key to our continuing success.

Ran G.

EMPLOYEE SINCE FEBRUARY 23 2009

The Zappos Culture is an awesome environment. I am able to be myself and wear the things I like to wear to work every day. I love it. It makes me feel proud to be part of a company with great culture.

Rich E.

EMPLOYEE SINCE APRIL 7 2008

Since I have been a Zapponian for almost a year, it is really exciting for me to be given the opportunity to share with you what the culture at Zappos means to me. Essentially, it is a sense of community when I come in contact with folks from my own department and in other areas. Whether I'm passing in the hallways and sharing a friendly "Hello," gathering documentation, or figuring out solutions to problems, I can see that we all share values of respect for each other and passion for performing at our best. The culture allows me to grow in my profession and as a person. My managers really care about my professional goals and about things like what did I do last weekend. This has built trust and loyalty ... I can seek advice and even feel confident enough to ask questions when I feel lost – without ever being made to feel stupid. In turn, my managers have given me projects where I get to use my ideas and skills for completing the tasks. I enjoy the time I spend with my fellow Zapponians, both in and out of the office, and I feel fortunate to work with them. We share stories about things like a cool restaurant one of us went to, and even share our skills like how to perform a v-lookup function in Excel. Zappos is a wonderful place to work, learn, grow and have fun and I do it all with a big smile on my face!

Roxane Z.

EMPLOYEE SINCE JANUARY 18 2005

Another great year at Zappos has passed so quickly. Working at Zappos these past years have been a very rewarding experience to me. I have learned a lot throughout these years. There have been up times and down times for both my professional and my personal life. My Zappos co-workers have shared and helped me through these times. I really do feel that I have a second family here at Zappos.

Sandra A.

EMPLOYEE SINCE APRIL 19 2004

After being here about five years, I love that I can still say "Zappos Rocks!"

Sandra H.

EMPLOYEE SINCE JULY 14 2008

Zappos in brief: TALKS THE TALK, WALKS THE WALK in style, with outstanding customer service, Ten Core Values and amazing employees. I love it here!

Scott S.

EMPLOYEE SINCE JUNE 16 2008

So far this year has been a whirlwind!! This has been my first year with Zappos and I am floored by how much this company differs from most organizations. During the short duration of my employment with Zappos, I have felt more accepted and encouraged than any combination of years at previous jobs. The culture lives here and is truly alive in the Ten Core Values. Most organizations create a vision, mission, and values that are preached and then put away in a filing cabinet. Not Zappos! Every day we are asked to live and breathe these core values and I am finding that they are spilling out into my life outside of work. The culture here encourages people to express themselves, make mistakes and learn, and become the very best person you can be. While no place is perfect, Zappos is the closest I have ever seen.

Tim K.

EMPLOYEE SINCE AUGUST 18 2008

Wow!! I have only been here for six months but the culture at Zappos is amazing. It feels like I have been part of the Zappos family for years, everyone is so accepting, easy to talk to, and great to work with. Even though I have only been here less than a year it is hard to imagine life without my Zappos family.

Victoria B.

EMPLOYEE SINCE AUGUST 13 2007

To me, the Zappos Culture is a blueprint for how to approach life in general. I also appreciate how everyone can voice opinions without fear of being shut down. What a concept to actually value and respect everyone, and not just give lip service. Thanks for making this such a wonderful company to work for.

Zolidays

Happy
Zappoween

A-1. Even though Zapponians see each other every day, we find every ~~excuse~~ justified business reason to get together outside of work. Especially when there's a Zoliday.

BOO!

St. Patty's Pinch Patrol

Zoliday Party 2008

THE BEST VITAMIN TO BE A
HAPPY PERSON IS B1.

INSIGHTFULLY CORNY
ANONYMOUS PERSON

IV.

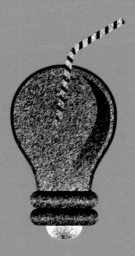

MARKETING
CREATIVE SERVICES
USER EXPERIENCE

Aaron M.

EMPLOYEE SINCE MAY 27 2008

I came to Zappos from a very buttoned up, hierarchical office environment where everyone's goal was to get the next title, the office, etc. The Zappos Culture is unlike anything I've seen. Employees are genuinely nice and happy about being at work. During the interview process at Zappos, I figured it was all part of the recruiting effort. I kept expecting to hear at least one person open up and let me know that it was just another job and that there was nothing really special. That never happened. After I decided to join, I still thought that the "truth" would come out. I was sure that I'd find that people were just here for a paycheck like those at so many other companies. It never happened. It's the little things that stand out. It's the smiles when you walk down the hall, the doors that are held open as you approach and the true passion for seeing Zappos succeed. It's the people that go to work every day not worried about their promotion, but only worried about promoting the Zappos cause. This isn't to say that everyone is happy every day. There are plenty of frustrations. However, when people are not happy with work, it's because they only want the company to succeed. This may lead to disagreements as everyone wants to do what they feel is best for the company, but it's comforting to know that it's all out of honest efforts for the betterment of Zappos.

Adam M.

EMPLOYEE SINCE NOVEMBER 10 2008

Zappos is a business, and businesses must regularly make tough decisions. Zappos is the first company I've been a part of that really thinks about the well-being of its employees before making such decisions. Because Zappos thinks so highly of its employees, we think highly of Zappos. And in return for Zappos' genuine regard for all of us, we work as hard as we can each day to make Zappos even better.

April S.

EMPLOYEE SINCE JUNE 23 2008

Working here at Zappos has taught me just how important culture is, not only at work, but in life as well. We are a family that continues to look out for each other. There is always someone eager to lend a hand or a shoulder to lean on. I can't imagine my life without Zappos or a world without its values.

Fig IV-1. Nemo likes to hang out in the Fish Market conference room. But if it happens that you don't see him there, try the Hotel Montmartre in LA. Apparently that's where all the cool fish (and cats) go.

FIG IV-2. Members of our Marketing team. Hey, if you were this happy at work every day, you'd want to get hung up in the hallways too.

FIG IV-3. Someone in our User Experience team used to go to Bob's Big Boy every day on his way home in Kentucky. Why the mustache? Because the Content team had a Magnum PI parade and slapped one on. Confused? Just come visit, we'll explain.

FIG IV-4. A mannequin in the Creative department. Speaks for itself, we think.

Ashley F.

EMPLOYEE SINCE JULY 9 2007

My love for Zappos has grown exponentially in the last year thanks to the culture. The way that everyone embraces the Core Values has been, and will continue to be, the driver of our success. Great culture and happy people!

Brian K.

EMPLOYEE SINCE APRIL 14 2003

This is a tough one for me. I have now been here for about six years and I have been fortunate enough to see what we currently call Zappos Culture evolve into what it is today. That being the case, I believe the culture is whatever you perceive it to be, or whatever you want it to be. I suppose that is the beauty of it. It is an intangible thing that I cannot describe, and as soon as I attempt to I think the meaning will dissipate – for me, at least! It is something that makes many people happy. If the culture makes the masses happy then that is enough to make me believe there is something powerful about it. But what is it about it? I don't know, and that is a good thing!

Brett H.

EMPLOYEE SINCE APRIL 26 2004

Zappos Culture to me is the fact that five years later, I still look forward to work every day of the week. I've been given managers and leaders who actually care about my job, my life, my little place in the world. But not every day is the best day of my life ... and some days are harder than others. But I know that I have a family waiting for me at work that will be there if I need them. I'm very close with my momma, and she is very far away from me, and she is relieved every day knowing that I have a second family in Vegas. And the greatest part about my five years at this place relates right back to my mom. She is so proud that I work at a place that treats its employees and customers like human beings. Not all companies can say that ... in fact, a depressing amount can't. And anything I've done that makes my momma proud is probably one of the best moves I've ever made in my life. Deciding to work for Zappos was the best decision I've ever made.

Darrin S.

EMPLOYEE SINCE OCTOBER 18 2004

I suppose I could sum it up like this. You know you've stumbled upon a great culture when the line between home and work life becomes blurred.

Donavon R.

EMPLOYEE SINCE JANUARY 29 2007

I can't believe how much my life has changed over the past 2 years that I have been with Zappos. When I first came to the company, I was not too thrilled with being here. What drew me in was the culture ... the fact that this place seemed to actually live out the Ten Core Values. I joined the company with a good bit of hesitation and skepticism. Two years later, I can't believe how much I have personally grown from my time here. I have grown professionally, as I have learned what it is like to LEAD, not just manage, and I have grown personally, as I have learned what living the culture is all about. Never did I ever imagine that a company would be as concerned, if not more concerned, with the individuals in the company as its bottom line. It is refreshing to come to work and know that I am making a difference and having an impact in my department. It is even more rewarding to know that my part, no matter how small it may be, is adding to the story that is and that will continue to be Zappos.

Holly O.

EMPLOYEE SINCE FEBRUARY 5 2007

One thing I love about Zappos is there are so many friendly people here! It truly makes for a better workday, and a positive experience.

Jason C.

EMPLOYEE SINCE SEPTEMBER 24 2007

To me, Zappos Culture is about an entire company of individuals, who are not only allowed, but also encouraged to be themselves, working together to make the group stronger as a whole. When you have a company that is so honest and open about everything that goes on, whether it is in good or difficult times, it makes everyone feel as though they are truly part of a great organization – unlike most others. Because our

Fig IV-5. Warning. The affection experienced between Zappos people is infectious.

Fig IV-6. This tree stands in Creative and conforms to every holiday season. In this instance, the Creative Tree is paying homage to the Easter bunny and his peeps.

culture brings us so close, we have an entire company of people who love being here, and who would do anything they can to help make the company successful.

Jeff G.

EMPLOYEE SINCE AUGUST 28 2006

There's only one word that comes to mind when I think of our Zappos Culture: "UNIQUE." I'm thankful for having the privilege to work for such a unique company, and look forward to its future!

Words of advice for my fellow Zapponians: "All that we are is the result of what we have thought." -Buddha

John F.

EMPLOYEE SINCE NOVEMBER 17 2004

As a former soldier, now a veteran, freedom rings in my soul. At Zappos we have so much freedom – refreshing, isn't it? A big part of the Zappos Culture directly comes from the freedoms allowed to us as employees. Reflecting on this, an old adage comes to mind … 'The tighter you grip sand in your hand, the more spills out. If you loosen your grip and open your palm, the more sand you can hold." The same goes for people. The harder the grip you have on people, the more they want to get away from you. The looser your grip on them, the more freedom you give them, the more people stay around.

Krista A.

EMPLOYEE SINCE JULY 16 2007

Best Place to Work Ever

… Singing in the halls · Finding a company You Have Lots in Common With · Exciting Challenges and rewarding work …. 2008 – Reported Here First: The *Best* fun in the *World!*
Zappos.com/ - *999k* - Cached - Similar pages -

Lively Staff
Fun Holiday Parties
Hurricane Linda
Superior (Customer Loyalty)

Style (More on Mandles)
Genius Capabilities
Spliffs
What happens in Vegas

More results from Zappos.com »

Kristopher K.

EMPLOYEE SINCE JUNE 19 2006

If Zappos Culture were a woman, I would take her out to dinner and pay for her meal, even with no coupon.

If Zappos Culture were a man, we would adorn ourselves in professional football jerseys and high-five each other in a bar ... constantly.

Oh, what great times we have shared ...

Libby H.

EMPLOYEE SINCE OCTOBER 8 2007

Thomas Carlyle once said, "Culture is the process by which a person becomes all they were created capable of being." Working at Zappos is simply that, an amazing opportunity to grow, build and explore your passion(s) with co-workers who are more like cousins than colleagues! How many people do you know can say they learn something new each and every day? And more importantly, when was the last time you played catch in your work parking lot to brainstorm ideas? Or had a parade come though your cubicle and add a little flavor to your latest conference call? That's Zappos and that's why I love it here.

Lynn S.

EMPLOYEE SINCE SEPTEMBER 10 2007

You know when you're drinking soda and someone says something so surprising or funny that you accidentally shoot soda out your nose? Yeah, the Zappos Culture is like that.

Melissa L.

EMPLOYEE SINCE AUGUST 4 2008

I was just going out for a beer in San Francisco and I ended up moving to Vegas. The Zappos Culture is magnetic. I just couldn't help but be drawn to it. To me, the Zappos fun and zany culture is what sold me on the idea of moving from the city I love to a place I never thought I'd call home. But, it really is nice to be a part of something this great. To me, culture is everything, and as an Inside Zappos Blogger, it is my job to be obsessed with our culture and to show the world what the employees here at Zappos are really all about. I am so proud to be a part of Zappos and to play such a great role in highlighting all that is Zappos Culture.

Michelle T.

EMPLOYEE SINCE SEPTEMBER 5 2007

The culture to me is like the Golden Rule times ten, where the culture is really defined by our Ten Core Values. They are more than just ten statements that live on my badge. They are more than the ten statements that are being incorporated into our creative and marketing campaigns. They are more than the ten statements that we learned in CLT. For me, the Ten Core Values have infiltrated every aspect of my life, making me a better me.

Mig P.

EMPLOYEE SINCE MARCH 24 2008

I feel lucky to work here at Zappos. Based on my experiences and opinion, I feel that the Zappos Culture is about collaborating with talented people from different backgrounds and disciplines who come together for a common purpose of making customers happy by providing excellent service. I think brightening up someone's day is the objective. In order to accomplish our mission, it requires everyone to be on the same page and contribute their ideas to take things to the next level. It also requires us to take risks and do things we are maybe not familiar with in order to learn and grow. People make the difference, they also make the culture. Any company can sell merchandise, but it takes a special group of individuals to make customers happy in any way possible, big or small.

Nate L.

EMPLOYEE SINCE JULY 14 2008

I send daily reports to Tony in rap form, and not only is it okay, it is encouraged! Here is an excerpt from a little ditty called Keyword Paradise:
As I search through the index of the crawler that's Google
I take a look at my life and realize its kinda futile
'Cause I've been trackin' and reportin' so long that
Even my mama thinks that my mind is gone
But I ain't never crossed a keyword that didn't deserve it
Maybe treated like a punk, you know that's unheard of
You better watch how you moving, and where you ranking

Or you and your homies will start to be tanking
I really hate to trip, but I gotta lope
As they croak I see myself in the pistol smoke, fool
I'm the kinda G that Zapponians wanna be
I'm on my knees like a nerd
Sayin' prayers for those keywords
I'm an educated fool, with keywords on my mind
Got 22 on my list and others on the side
I'm a loped-out intern, google-whacking gangsta
And my Search Team is down, so don't arouse my anger, fool
First pages ain't nothing but a heartbeat away
I'm livin' life do-or-die, ah, what can I say?
It's on page three now, will I live to see it number four?
The way things are goin', I don't know
Been spending most my time
Living in the Keyword Paradise
It's gettin' hard to find things to rhyme
Living in the Keyword Paradise

Ned F.

EMPLOYEE SINCE DECEMBER 5 2001

There are many reasons to appreciate working within the Zappos Culture. Over this past year, I've most appreciated the opportunity to grow and develop professionally within the organization. Thank you, Zappos! I also appreciate the fact that I can share with my fellow co-workers the wonders and joy of wearing mandals on a daily basis.

Patrick W.

EMPLOYEE SINCE MARCH 2 2003

Zappos Culture, to me, means that no matter where you come from or how much money you make, you have the ability to impress people in other ways. For instance, bringing your own utensils from home instead of using a new plastic fork every day and throwing it away is very admirable. Riding your bike to work is extremely hip here; anywhere else I've worked, it would have been cooler to drive a sports car. You don't have to wear expensive shoes to work every day, but if you do, nobody will think you're trying to overdo it either. On the flip side of that, you're not looked down on for using plastic forks, or driving a sports car to work, and definitely not for wearing nice shoes. I guess what I'm trying to say is that our Zappos Culture has a lot to do with accepting, tolerating and appreciating each other's differences. That, my friends, is what I like most about our Company.

Phil S.

EMPLOYEE SINCE DECEMBER 11 2006

The Zappos Culture is unrivaled and we're all very fortunate to be able to contribute to it. Our passion and drive is evident in our work, and it gives us the confidence do better with each step forward. I'm proud to say I work at Zappos and hope to contribute many more years to its success.

Rafael M.

EMPLOYEE SINCE JULY 7 2008

I work at Zappos pretty much thanks to a previous number of this book, so writing this entry is really exciting! I was working at another company and I saw Tony's presentation, "Top Ten Lessons Learned in E-Commerce," while I was at a conference. I was so impressed about the strong Zappos Culture and the company's commitment to customer service that when they announced they had copies of the Culture Book, I was the first one talking to my co-workers about getting one. The rest is the beginning of my Zappos history. Working here has been fun. I feel that I have grown a lot as a professional and as a person. It is really exciting to be part of a company that strives to serve each and every one of its customers. This is not an easy task, and I am really happy of being part of the process of achieving this ultimate goal. As Zappos works towards the outside to provide great service, the company also works towards its employees. Working here makes me feel like I am part of a great team of people that values what each brings to the table as an individual. I hope these first seven months at Zappos are only the beginning of a great life experience of many years.

Robert A.

EMPLOYEE SINCE SEPTEMBER 4 2007

Zappos Culture to me is Happy People Providing Awesome Customer Service with a Little Weirdness!

Sara M.

EMPLOYEE SINCE MAY 6 2008

Zappos Culture reflects real world diversity more than the standard expectations and behavior found in business, allowing us to be more comfortable as ourselves and opening the thought process for creativity and innovation.

Sean C.

EMPLOYEE SINCE NOVEMBER 5 2007

Zappos is not a job...it's my home away from home.

Stacy E.

EMPLOYEE SINCE SEPTEMBER 4 2007

I have learned, grown, changed and adapted over the past year all because of Zappos and the incredible people I work with. I'm looking forward to another year with a company that uniquely and diligently pushes me to new levels ... often levels within myself I never knew existed ...

Tiffany G.

EMPLOYEE SINCE APRIL 28 2008

Zappos is family to me. From day one, I felt like I belonged here. Moving 2000 miles away from home wasn't an easy thing to do, but working at Zappos made me feel like I went from one family to the next without missing a beat. And, trust me, you don't get that feeling everywhere you go or every place you work.

C an you tell there's always a di
Zappos? That's right. It smel

BIG BROTHER

IS WATCHING
YOU

Luckily, we're not big brother.
We just wanna get to know you better!

Join the team & family spirit!
Put your twitter name in your profile!

tinct scent when you walk around like team spirit.

Don't be Shy...

Just say Hi

From the committee for Cell-Free Hallways at Zappos.com

"Drop the phone and just say Hi"

E-1. From Bald Blue and Tattooed Day to Spirit Week, there's never a shortage of team spirit. Smell it now?

Y OU CANNOT ALWAYS HAVE HAPPINESS,
BUT YOU CAN ALWAYS GIVE HAPPINESS.

ANOTHER ONE OF THOSE
WISE ANONYMOUS PEOPLE

V.

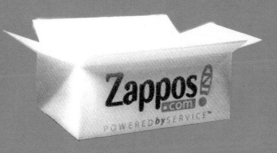

MERCHANDISING
CONTENT

Fig v-1. ECCO boots worn for last year's 8000 Meter Challenge, that's now resting in Merchandising. They're still comfortable and don't smell, but if you don't believe us, you're welcome to check yourself.

Fig v-2. Zapponians in this department find themselves reading magazines and surfing the interweb much of the day. But sssshh. Don't tell management.

Fig v-3. One of our Core Values is to ' Be Humble'. But if you've got chest hair like this, you might as well flaunt it.

Aaron T.

EMPLOYEE SINCE OCTOBER 5 2005

The Zappos Culture is no joke, it's the real deal. It's the glue that's held us together throughout the years, and it's what makes us still feel like a tightly knit family, even though we've grown to having so many people in the company. I'm proud to be a part of a company that encourages me to be myself, make my own decisions, and gives me plenty of opportunity to grow along with ALL of my co-workers, regardless of department or position. It's truly something you read about!! -- no pun intended :)

Alana P.

EMPLOYEE SINCE AUGUST 21 2006

What I value most about working for this company is that I can be myself. I'm rewarded for thinking outside the box and taking chances. The passion and dedication this company encompasses is contagious and I feel fortunate to be a part of it.

Alesha G.

EMPLOYEE SINCE SEPTEMBER 14 2004

To me, Zappos has become so much more than my job; it has become my family. And I think this is because of the culture we have here. Employees value their relationships with each other as if each co-worker was one of their family and has been a part of their life forever. I can count on anyone, at any time, for support with work and with personal life. I have definitely been through my share of personal things in the last year and still have a lot ahead of me. But I know, without a doubt, that I have the support of my team and Zappos in all that I will go through. I can't imagine being anywhere else at this point in my life. I am so proud to work for a company that truly cares about its employees, and to work for a company whose employees truly care about each other.

Alex D.

EMPLOYEE SINCE NOVEMBER 23 2005

I feel extremely proud to work for a company that values its identity as much as Zappos does. In three and a half years here, I've watched our company grow immensely. Although there have been many changes along the way, our company culture has remained intact and seems to be strengthened each day. To me, I think this is exemplified in the fact that I wake up every morning excited to go to work. I've had the opportunity to work in three different departments at this company and in every position I've had, I have always genuinely believed in the goals we've sought to achieve. I also believe that everyone else here at Zappos shares this view. I think it's this collective enthusiasm and passion for our company that drives and fortifies the Zappos Culture.

Alison C.

EMPLOYEE SINCE SEPTEMBER 21 2008

When I came to Zappos, I knew that it would be a different kind of a place ... over the years I had read about this up and coming footwear website, I had heard about the great culture that it had and its huge focus on customer service. It didn't quite seem possible that a retail company like this could exist. My experience working for other retailers has been, for the most part, the complete opposite. I have seen a lot of "what not to do" over the years, working for some big corporations with "profit (at all costs)- focused" (not "people-focused") managers. What drew me to Zappos was a glimmer of hope that this might be a company that is truly different from other retail companies. And guess what? It is! Zappos is a place where "working as a team" is more than just a buzz word. . . it is actually something that people do (and do well!). A place where you enjoy working and laugh more than you cry (and yes, there are companies out there that cause you to do the opposite). A place where employees are passionate about what they do, and in every job, at every level, they understand how their position and their performance can make a difference in the company. A place where communication, growth and learning are important, ongoing focuses and where the company takes time to celebrate individual and team successes. A place where challenges are faced head-on and opportunities are addressed proactively. A place where everyone works hard and plays harder ... and loves what they do! Every person here takes an active role in the company's success. I have been so incredibly impressed at how this company truly lives its Core Values ... they are not just there as "feel good" words, there is an active expectation behind them that they are not to be followed, but to be lived.

Amanda W.

EMPLOYEE SINCE DECEMBER 24 2007

The Zappos Culture is defined on a daily basis ... during any common day at Zappos (based on the Ten Core Values!).

1. I am WOWed daily by the generosity from co-workers, vendors, and friends.
2. No two days are the same. I am constantly adapting to new ideas, processes, problems and beliefs.
3. Every day has a touch of craziness and flair! It's kinda fun and kinda random at the same time!

FIG V-4A. At the awards ceremony, Zapponians like to spend time getting closer, but sometimes sweat beads on the forehead can be unpleasant. (Don't worry, they kissed and made up afterwards.)

FIG V-4B. At the ceremony, Magnum PI awards are handed out for excellence in content writing.

FIG V-4C. As well as Trifecta Awards, when a Zapponian hits his/her sales, inventory and mark-down plans for the entire year.

4. Adventures are hidden behind every corner ... like Ellis Island, Karaoke and the Hoover Dam!
5. I have learned that it doesn't matter how educated you are, there are lessons to be learned every day.
6. Verbal conversations are only the beginning of communication. Parades are another form of communication that I never thought I'd experience at an office job!
7. I've become part of a family.
8. Not only have I grown, but I've become more efficient – even outside of work.
9. It's so easy love what we do, and want to do it better every day. I look back to when I started, and every day I've wanted more.
10. My work here at Zappos is only as good as my team. I have an AMAZING team. I can't help but be proud of working here.

Amara S.

EMPLOYEE SINCE SEPTEMBER 12 2005

Working at Zappos is such an amazing journey. The culture is unparalleled. I have never had the privilege of working for such a company before. Zappos encourages creativity and spontaneity from all employees at all levels. It is so refreshing to work for a company so unique and driven. I have forged so many great relationships and have grown exponentially. I will always treasure the experiences I've had at Zappos. It is truly one of a kind.

Amber O.

EMPLOYEE SINCE OCTOBER 11 2005

When I first started at Zappos, I was fresh out of high school, and my only professional experience was watching young kids. I remember wanting nothing more to fit in to this "business world," but I quickly realized that Zappos was much less corporate than I had thought. Three years and some change later, Zappos' fun and zany culture has helped me come out of my shell and develop my personality. I'm definitely not the same person I was when I started, and I'm very grateful for that. Every day is something new, and I look forward to recapping about the random nothingness that was talked about the day before. It's so much fun to see everybody's personalities displayed prominently next to their computers, and I'm glad my love for the Beatles and horror movies has been accepted. I work with the best people possible and am flattered to be part of something great. I mean, we are Oprah approved ;)

Amber T.

EMPLOYEE SINCE JUNE 11 2005

One of the things that most stands out to me from our Zappos Culture over this last year is our Core Value #2, Embrace and Drive Change. There have definitely been many changes, both exciting and challenging. 2008 was the most challenging year I have experienced since I have been in the online retail industry. Most of us can say 2008 was the worst we have seen in the general economy in our lifetimes. With regard to how we do business, we have had to reinvent the wheel and, on many levels, get back to the basics. People have come and gone, and the ones who are lucky to remain have pulled together more than ever through tough times in anticipation of the better times ahead.

Even when we are struggling, it is comforting to know that I work with people who are like family to me and I am able to lean on them. When we are celebrating, I have the fondest of memories with people I will never forget and laughter to fill the years. Since my first day here, I have always felt it a blessing to work for what I truly believe is the best company out there on so many levels.

The more things change, the more they stay the same. The best is yet to come!!!

Amy V.

EMPLOYEE SINCE OCTOBER 8 2007

When I came to Las Vegas, I knew that there was no place else I would rather work than Zappos. Even at that time, I had no idea what an amazing company this was. Unlike other places I've worked at, Zappos promotes cooperation over competition. Everyone's ideas are heard and respected. There is so much emphasis on personal and professional growth that, in the short time I've been here, I already feel that I am a better person for having experienced the Zappos way. I am proud of the company I work for, and I am very grateful to be here.

Anastasia P.

EMPLOYEE SINCE APRIL 23 2007

Top Ten Reasons I Love Working @ Zappos (In No Particular Order):
1. Surrounded by Heelarious® co-workers who embrace my craaazy, sassy, and quirky mannerisms.
2. I'm finally encouraged to grow by management. I'm not treated or spoken to like an inferior just because I don't know the answers to every question & issue that comes

across my desk/Outlook inbox.

3. An awesome window seat (it was a real treat the day it snowed).
4. Flexible work hours.
5. Sparking, Twittering, and The Spoke(n) Word.
6. A laidback, wookie-hating, Phish-loving, and patient boss who's capable of BBQing an entire farm in one weekend afternoon.
7. Every day I learn something new.
8. Cute guys are never in short supply. ;)
9. Silly team outings.
10. I love that I'm no longer the only Simpsons fanatic in the workplace.

Andréa L.

EMPLOYEE SINCE JULY 30 2007

When I started at Zappos (almost two years ago) I knew I had come across something special. I'm so thankful I get to come to work and enjoy what I do and whom I work with. We are family. I can count on my co-workers to learn from, to party with and to laugh with. Zappos has changed me personally and I hope to stay here for a very long time. Did I mention we have free ice cream?

Andrew N.

EMPLOYEE SINCE MAY 29 2007

I haven't written an essay since college, and I'm pretty sure I've forgotten how. So instead, I'm just going to list my favorite byproducts of the Zappos Culture.

1. A workplace full of warm, friendly and thoughtful people.
2. A fun, vibrant and positive energy that radiates throughout the company.
3. A shared feeling of purpose and contribution to company goals and the community.
4. Being able to actually enjoy coming to work.

Andy H.

EMPLOYEE SINCE JUNE 10 2002

I remember I was six years old the first time I was told about Halloween. "So let me get this straight. I get to dress up as Luke Skywalker (awesome) carry a light saber (awesomer) and then get free candy from everyone (awesomest)?! Wait, free candy?!? Could this really be true?" It was one of those moments in life when I literally fell out of my seat because something so wonderful, so amazing and something I've always dreamed of could come true. I think a happy dance followed soon after.

Fast forward 20 years. I'm told about this company that has this amazing culture where service is at the heart of everything they do. Free shipping, Free returns for 365 days, 24/7 customer support, huge selection of footwear, apparel, watches, electronics, and more! And this is just for the customers! Now imagine for the employees: free lunches, life coach, holiday party, crazy parades, wacky events, amazing people to work with … the list goes on! And for the vendors: free shuttle from the airport, vendor party, enthusiastic buyers, and more! So you can imagine my disbelief when I was told about this company. I again fell out of my seat.

This company does exist. Zappos is this company and will always be this company. It is the amazing Zappos Culture that makes it what it is today. I do my happy dance at my desk everyday and still continue to fall out of my seat.

Angela C.

EMPLOYEE SINCE MARCH 6 2006

I have been with Zappos almost 3 years now and it is hard for me to remember how my life was before I worked here. Zappos has become that familiar friend whom you just 'click' with. It's the kind of place that you feel really privileged and honored to work at (even before we made Fortune's list). So, it really is not a challenge for me to get up every morning and come give Zappos my all. After all, that's what friends do :)

Anji C.

EMPLOYEE SINCE NOVEMBER 7 2005

Zappos has a culture that is chock-full of fun, values, and inspiration. I suppose the average person, employed elsewhere, simply experiences everyday life as waking up and tending to their job as a chore or duty. Working at Zappos is the exact opposite. You are filled with an energy and environment that allows you to experience both personal and professional enrichment. I feel like I won the career lotto; working at Zappos, I can continue to strive towards success and share in those of others as well.

Anna F.

EMPLOYEE SINCE APRIL 4 2005

Zappos Culture is the foundation of everything we do at Zappos. It is a common ground, an understanding, and a set of core principles that all customers and vendors have come to expect from our company. Not only is our culture a part of the big picture of our company it's also something that we, as employees, believe and practice on daily basis. It makes work both fun and challenging and inspires us to do our best for the best company to work for every day. One of the important aspects of Zappos Culture is about balance. We work hard and play hard. The balance of professional and personal life as well as growth is encouraged.

At Zappos, we are empowered to do and be the best we can be. How wonderful!!

Anne P.

EMPLOYEE SINCE JULY 29 2008

To me, Zappos Culture means that you can be yourself in a building full of different people. I think we are united not just by our similarities, but by our acceptance of everyone's right to be unique.

Anonymous.

We have been through some very difficult times in the past year, but continue to build our culture in all directions. We continue to grow and build our success through culture by focusing on service in all aspects of the company from the vendor, employee, and customer levels. Economically, the world has changed drastically and only the strongest will remain standing – Zappos has proven to be one of them. It is the culture of this company which has provided the strength for this company to move forward, and bring happiness to those all around us. We have fun, and we think outside the box to maintain this growth and success. And through great relationships that have been formed through both the good and bad times, we are one big family. We will continue to focus on this unique culture of ours in a meaningful manner. In short, we are and create the Zappos Culture.

Anonymous.

What I love most about our culture is that as a whole, it makes coming to work something I look forward to rather than something I dread or just don't feel excited about. I know that I can be myself here and that everything – from my sense of humor to my ideas to learning from mistakes – is appreciated, instead of being frowned upon, as it was at certain previous jobs. Also, personalities are bound to clash from time to time in a place with so many employees, but I feel that our culture really holds everyone together as a family.

Anonymous.

A Haiku for Zappos:

Simple caring thoughts
Zappos delivers with love
great happiness grows

There is truly nothing better than to work for a company that not only treats you like a valued member of the team but a member of the family. To be a part of something that strives to make the world a better place is something that stays with you forever.

Anonymous.

Many of us live away from our families and don't yet have families of our own. That is why I feel that Zappos is so great. The family atmosphere, combined with kindness and respect for one another, is something very seldom seen in the work place. I feel very fortunate to have found this very amazing company.

Anonymous.

It is the greatest thing to see our culture making a difference. Our mission has always been to deliver the best possible service, but I really see our purpose as being a positive example of the way business is done and beyond. It's a very humbling feeling to know that you are a part of something that is channeling positive change in the world. How awesome is it to see examples of our culture beyond our doors!?! I was watching the speeches that President Obama and Secretary of State Hillary Clinton gave when she was welcomed to the State Department. They spoke of transparency, culture, growth, and learning and creating a family environment, I was simply amazed. I couldn't say whether or not we have set an example that has reached the halls of Washington, but what a great feeling to know that is the direction the world is heading.

This environment has been the catalyst to progress in my life. I have reached above and beyond what I have ever believed myself to be capable of. I think back to my first day here, so excited and grateful to have been chosen to be a part of this incredible place. The Zappos Culture has not only brought out the best in me, but it has helped make the best even better.

One of my favorite questions to ask new friends is what they want out of life, and most people say they just want to be happy. It really made me define what happiness means to me and to seek that out. To me, it is genuine contentment, I have everything I need and I am satisfied with what I have. I spent years looking for this in the wrong places. I never actually understood what I needed in my life to achieve this. I almost feel as if I have stumbled upon the key to it here at Zappos. I'm not saying coming here every day to do your job will make you a happy person. It really is embracing everything that our culture has to offer. Whatever it is you may be lacking in your personal life, you can find it here and it encourages you to make the positive changes in your personal life to keep that feeling alive, even when you leave.

I wish for all of us here to have the deeply profound impact in their life that the culture here has made on me. Our culture has changed me, shaped me, and created a desire to want something better for myself and those around me.

Anonymous.

Let me just give you a couple of quick examples of why I love this company and our culture:

I just heard Jerry T. (The Zappos Mayor) say, "You want to take my dog for a walk?" and by dog, he means his dog hand puppet, which, by the way, does have a Zappos name badge. I bet if I looked it up, he'd have a site manager picture as well. His name is Harley, not to be confused with Jerry's real dog Harley. When he and his wife Pam got Harley his name was Marley. Since Jerry has always wanted a Harley (Davidson that is ... don't think that's a good idea, Jer, but it's never too late to rock n roll), they decided to re-name Marley as Harley just so he could say, "Hey, you want to see my Harley?"

Take Chris P., a.k.a "CP," for example ... here's a quick little list of some of the things he keeps at his desk:

- Gigantic blowup microphone
- Cow print hats, with horns
- Children's blowup waist floatie, in the shape of a duck
- Another children's floatie with strawberry shortcake print
- Three wigs... I'm sure you could find more if you really looked
- 100-piece chalk set with plastic tote for ease of carrying

Okay, you get the picture. He just came over by my desk to deliver a picture of him in a doctor's mask kissing another buyer on the cheek (totally acceptable and yes, we're all that close) at one of our fabulous Happy Hours. Do you want to know what he was wearing when he dropped the picture off? A referee jersey, a curly black wig, a pair of huge sunglasses with sparkles on them, and a baseball cap. All things you can find at his desk.

May I remind you of my last Culture Book entry? I used CP as a culture example in there as well... I believe it had something to do with him in a Super Toilet Paper Man outfit, running around toilet-papering people's desks. Why? Ummm ... because that's just a great example of our culture and the fact that it's okay to just be yourself. Core value #3: Create Fun and a Little Weirdness. Here's to you, Chris and Jerry, for being great examples of Zappos Culture! I hear Kermit the Frog singing in the office somewhere ... gotta go. Peace!

I heart Zappos, my blood runs Zappos blue!

Anonymous.

The culture promotes a family environment that not only keeps me looking forward to coming to work every day but it also has allowed me to form lasting friendships. I feel lucky to have found such a unique company.

Anthony A.

EMPLOYEE SINCE AUGUST 20 2007

Zappos, as a company, continues to define the meaning of its culture. I don't believe I ever thought so much about culture and what it has meant to me until the first day I walked through the front doors of Zappos, a year and a half ago.

I define the culture at Zappos as a reminder to always challenge yourself and to go above and beyond the status quo. Even on the hardest of days, which we all have, I really do try to see things from a more positive perspective than what I've been used to in the past.

Core Value #2: Embrace and Drive Change, has resonated so strongly with me in the past few months; it has reminded me that change of any kind is something to embrace, and that I do have a big part in how that change affects me. Zappos Culture has been a very positive influence in my life, and I'm very thankful for this experience.

Ash S.

EMPLOYEE SINCE NOVEMBER 7 2005

I helped my team make a department instructional video that included bathroom humor and have suffered no consequences to my career here so far. In a different video, we pretended to be swearing by having normal dialogue being bleeped out. In future videos, we hope to poke fun at co-workers and managers. Does making fun of people, swearing, and farting contribute to company culture? I can't answer that but the fact we feel comfortable about demonstrating a serious subject in a funny way probably wouldn't fly somewhere else. Not taking ourselves too seriously is an important part of the Zappos Culture, even though we're the best company in the world ever.

Ashley M.

EMPLOYEE SINCE NOVEMBER 12 2007

Imagine waking up each morning and being happy to go into work. Yep, I'm serious. It's awesome.

Barbara B.

EMPLOYEE SINCE MARCH 21 2006

Working at Zappos means expecting the unexpected, in a good way. I love coming into work and not knowing what the day will bring, whether it is "What tour is coming through today?" or "What activity will be happening next?" It makes things exciting and interesting. I have enjoyed every minute spent working here. It's the best place that I have ever worked and it definitely feels like my home away from home! I love Zappos!

Bernadette T.

EMPLOYEE SINCE AUGUST 20 2007

What is the Zappos Culture? Whether you visit the website, the office, the warehouse, watch the commercials, or talk with any of the friendly Zapponians, you'll experience the Zappos Culture. By definition, culture is a set of ideas, beliefs, or ways of life passed down from generation to generation. As for me, I believe if I can positively impact everyone I come into contact with, more people will have a better day, and, like dominos, those people can make someone else's day and so on. In the long run, I know if I do good things for others, then my team, our department, Zappos and even the world is better off. From the very first day I stepped into the Zappos office, it was like getting a whiff of freshly baked banana-nut bread with a side of pickles. Yeah, definitely weird but entirely enticing, and it was different, all right. I've NEVER worked in an environment that was so warm, welcoming, energized, and wacky (in a good way – think Dr. Seuss, The Cat in the Hat, and stop thinking about the pickles already!). Seriously, even after being with the company for nearly two years, I'm still surrounded by awesome people who are equally driven and inspired by the same or similar beliefs. Sure, when you're at work, you can't help but spread the same mentality, but everyone here at Zappos chooses to focus on the Core Values every day, whether they are in the office or out and about. The vivacity of the Zappos Culture is alive and vigorous and this makes Zappos the best place I've ever worked. Of course, the zany atmosphere, strong camaraderie, and off-the-wall goofiness, add to it – they are like sprinkles on my double-fudge brownie sundae. And, I can't wait to be a part of the sweet future that's in store for us.

Bill J.

EMPLOYEE SINCE NOVEMBER 15 2004

Working at Zappos.com has been a great experience for me over the past four years. I'm constantly challenged to learn more, communicate new ideas and help cultivate our culture. I've accomplished things that I never thought possible because of the support of my associates, and the never-ending push to embrace and drive change. Walking down the aisle to my desk every day gives me a sense of pride that I've never experienced at any other job.

Braden M.

EMPLOYEE SINCE MAY 22 2006

WOW. This was a crazy year. The housing market was in the toilet, stocks were way down, retailers closed their doors, and large companies went bankrupt. Despite all of the hardship, Zappos' numbers were up. Not because we worked like crazy, which we did, but because we were all so stoked to be part of the Zappos Culture. Our passion for our culture and the best work environment imaginable helped perpetuate Zappos into a very great position for 2009. I have worked for Zappos for three years, and through all the growth and all of the changes, the only thing that remains the same is our wonderful culture. I am more excited to be part of Zappos now than ever. Cheers to all for more of the same :)

Brian W.

EMPLOYEE SINCE OCTOBER 15 2007

A great man once said, "I went to a restaurant that serves breakfast at any time. So I ordered "French Toast during the Renaissance" ... That pretty much sums up how I feel about Zappos. Except for the whole restaurant and French toast bit ...

Brooke J.

EMPLOYEE SINCE MARCH 28 2005

In times when all you hear about are layoffs and grim times in the economy, it is really exciting to be part of a company that is planning for an increase. I really feel as if I am an integral part of moving the needle for Zappos. I feel like I am part of the company's success and part of a family. The culture is just refreshing compared to most work atmospheres. Everyone is trying to pull his or her weight for the love of the company and to make sure the person sitting on either side of him or her still has a job. We all pull together to help each other out. We all care for one another. It is great to come to a job where you know your co-workers want to see you succeed. Zappos grows people personally and professionally. I can't think of any other place that offers so many great benefits to their employees and has such a pleasant work environment.

Bruce R.

EMPLOYEE SINCE DECEMBER 11 2006

Over the years, as we endure the ups and downs, the highs and lows, say hello to new friends and goodbye to old, the constant is that we care. We care enough not to take it all for granted, enough to take what we do seriously with passion and determination, but not to take ourselves too seriously. Caring is the bond and what allows the culture to endure.

Cameron G.

EMPLOYEE SINCE SEPTEMBER 12 2005

"Pursue growth and learning," that core value really seems to sum it up for me. Zappos would not be the company it is today without so many people who strive every day to make a difference. Zappos is the collaborative effort of everyone involved, and only through growth and learning can we become better than the day before.

Carla L.

EMPLOYEE SINCE DECEMBER 4 2006

I am SO thankful and lucky to be working at Zappos. The culture continues to live strong and it is embedded in all Zapponians. Because of this, we are able to weather any storm and overcome any obstacle. Especially with 2008 being as tough as it was in the retail industry, Zappos still remains strong. We couldn't have done it without every employee embracing our Ten Core Values like never before. In this last year, I feel like our relationships with our customers, vendors and co-workers have grown stronger than ever. The greatest part is how everyone works as a unified team for the common good of all. Even though 2008 was a tough year for everyone, we still were able to enjoy ourselves at the office and participate in some silliness and day-to-day fun. Our team still tried to get each other with whoopee cushions, parades still came through the office, we came up with fun ways to greet the tours, and we found little ways to thank our fellow employees. Tough times can mean tough measures, but at least at Zappos, a little fun and weirdness is still part of the deal :)

Caron O.

EMPLOYEE SINCE MARCH 26 2007

I have been pleasantly surprised at how well Zappos is weathering the current economic storm. There is no doubt in my mind that the culture at Zappos is the reason for this ... We are a family and we stick together, in good times and in bad times! You listen to the news and all you hear is doom and gloom, but walk into Zappos and there is a prevailing sense of optimism. How refreshing!

Cassandra "Casey" L.

EMPLOYEE SINCE MAY 19 2008

What is Zappos Culture to me? It's what makes my co-workers my family away from home. It's what makes me want to jump out of bed and come to work each and every day. It's what has me prepared for the unexpected at every turn. Without our culture, Zappos would be another sea of cubicles, not an amazing place to work that is exciting, educational and character building. Our Culture is what makes Zappos amazing, strong and outlasting.

Cat S.

EMPLOYEE SINCE JANUARY 7 2008

The last year has been a huge growing and learning experience for me, both inside and outside of Zappos. Being a part of the Zappos community has taught me a lot about myself and has encouraged and pushed me to achieve things I might not have previously thought possible. The Zappos Culture has become a way of life for me, and what may have been crazy and weird to me a year ago has now become a normal part of my daily Zappos life. Our culture here is like nothing I have ever experienced, but it's also this culture that makes my day and helps me appreciate how great life is here at Zappos. It's always funny to try and explain the way our world works here to other people because it has really turned into something of a phenomenon, which stokes me out on it even more. Our culture is definitely one of a kind and is something I am proud to be part of each time I talk to someone about Zappos. I head a comment about one of our Fortune magazine pictures in relation to everyone in the photo having a good time and looking like we were at a New Year's Eve party; this is how I feel almost every day here and I wouldn't ask for anything else (well, no hangover).

Catherine 'Catie' S.

EMPLOYEE SINCE APRIL 7 2008

Zappos Culture is the reason why I chose Zappos. I came from a company where culture is a very important value, and I made sure upon leaving the company that I looked for a company with a similar culture. What I got at Zappos way surpassed my expectations. I am beyond thrilled to be at Zappos. We support not only a flawless culture but encourage growth – not just company growth but personal growth. With the career opportunities that Zappos encourages and the attitudes of all my fellow co-workers, Zappos is a place where I plan to succeed and grow. I believe in Zappos Culture, I'm proud to be part of it and look forward to more amazing years here.

Cathy T.

EMPLOYEE SINCE JULY 9 2007

It's like being in Disneyland all the time (the happiest place on earth)!! Some days it's like riding the "Pirates of the Caribbean" and some days, it's like being on the Matterhorn; we also have all the Disney characters here too ~ :) I'm so lucky and grateful to work for such a wonderful company and be amongst the same characters as myself … I'm definitely part of something special. I come to work and I'm inspired to find ways to improve my skills … lucky me

Chanele H.

EMPLOYEE SINCE JANUARY 29 2007

I've been working at Zappos for just over two years and I'm still just as excited as I was the day that I came in to interview for a job here. How many people in their twenties are able to say that about their job? How many people of any age are able to say that about their job? We are definitely in the minority. I have so much fun every day and I am constantly surprised and proud when I see a parade, a camera crew, or someone walking through the halls wearing a giant milkshake costume. I feel honored that I have the chance to be part of a wonderful company who is changing the world, one pair of shoes (or clothing, handbags, accessories, cosmetics, housewares, etc.) at a time.

Chris P.

EMPLOYEE SINCE MAY 17 2004

The Zappos Culture never ceases to amaze me. Year after year, I see new faces that carry the same ambition and passion for the business that our early leaders set forth. It's great to see that so many people at Zappos that have embraced our culture and made it better and better - even after growing as much as we have over the past few years. Our people have taught me so much about everything that revolves around our Ten Core Values and I'm truly lucky to be part of such a great brand.

Claire S.

EMPLOYEE SINCE JUNE 25 2007

It's difficult to express what the Zappos Culture is because we live it every day. But, if this past year here at Zappos has taught me anything, the lesson is simply this – when you are passionate and determined, good things will come to you. It has been my personal experience that working hard and playing hard have really become the same exercise in that all of our efforts channel into the same goal: to build a wonderful company. So, even the work can feel like play when you are surrounded by positive and progressive minds. I feel blessed to work among creative and vivacious people, who inspire me daily. I couldn't imagine a world without Zappos, because it has added so very much to mine.

Clay D.

EMPLOYEE SINCE JUNE 19 2006

Zappos' fast growth and prosperity probably wouldn't have been possible without our special culture that motivates employees and business partners. Hopefully, the same culture will help us through these historically tough economic times. Through creative thinking (instead of running scared) and continued optimism, Zappos will not only survive these tough times, but will become an even smarter and stronger company when the economy gets better. That's the value in having a strong company culture. Thanks, Zappos!

Dana B.

EMPLOYEE SINCE JANUARY 15 2005

Zappos Culture is a strong, powerful atmosphere; a phenomenal force that drives us to be better people, better employees, and empowers people to continually strive for something better. We are a fantastic bunch of people brought together by our passion and love of what we do. Sadly, many companies don't have any culture at all, or don't make the effort to create one. Often people don't think that far, or even realize that it's an option, because they are so used to what is considered a "common workplace." Zappos founders brought their fun, energetic idea of what a motivating workplace should be and created an environment that uplifts people. Our culture is a very fun, uplifting environment that makes you happy to get out of bed each day. When the culture makes you excited, it makes your time feel more fulfilling, the rewards are greater, and you're empowered to continue growing. It's outstanding to be a part of something so wonderful!

Danielle T.

EMPLOYEE SINCE JULY 9 2007

This is my second Culture Book entry. Since the last entry (i.e. last year), I have seen a lot of changes and I now work on a different team, writing solely for clothes. Why am I telling you this? Well, at Zappos I have had, and will continue to have, the opportunity to pursue my personal passions and grow professionally at the same time. I really feel like anything is possible at Zappos. "Embrace and Drive Change" is one of our Ten Core Values. I used to see change as something to fear and combat, but after seeing that change can bring such great things, I get excited to hear about all the twists and turns in the Zappos' journey. Change is actually good! Plus, after almost two years, I still love coming to work and adore the people here. I work hard and can get stressed at certain points, but I always have a great time. I spent the majority of my twenties working at jobs I hated and it infected my whole life with negativity. I live in such a positive place because of Zappos. I applied to

Zappos because my last job denied my request for a raise and I was so mad! I saw my old boss recently and I thanked him for not giving me that raise. It was one of the best things that happened in my life. Thank you!

David C.

EMPLOYEE SINCE MARCH 20 2006

Zappos Culture. In the three years I have been at Zappos, the culture has continued to evolve and change without losing any of its message or impact. Despite the changing economy and challenging times, Zappos Culture remains a constant that continues to bring optimism and enthusiasm for what the future brings. Our culture is what will bring us to the next level.

Dee C.

EMPLOYEE SINCE OCTOBER 1 2007

When I saw the "It's That Time Again" email for the new 2009 Culture Book ... I had to pull out my 2008 Culture Book to reflect back. At the time, I was three months on the job. I spoke about what an awesome experience it had been and how the company and everyone within had WOWed me. I had to admit that I had started working numerous hours on my laptop and how I enjoyed it, because I loved what I was doing. Now that I am a year and three months on the job, I had to sit back and see how I felt today. I still love my job and my co-workers. I have a great boss and director that really support me and want to see me succeed. I love Zappos and where we are and what we have all learned this past year. When I walk in through the office doors, I am dazzled by smiling faces and by warm greetings. I couldn't ask for anything more. What a great year it has been ... but 2009 is going to be even better! So, to quote my own entry in the 2008 book, "Drink the punch! You won't regret it!" I really mean it! I know because I am still drunk from it!!!

Dena M.

EMPLOYEE SINCE SEPTEMBER 25 2006

Well, this is my third Culture Book entry, so here goes ... I think it is pretty remarkable that with the way the economy has been over the last six months to a year, and the retail industry in particular, our company has been able to come out ahead. We were not totally immune to it, but I think the culture here is what helped us make it through and I believe the team and family spirit here is stronger than ever. So what has this past year at Zappos taught me? Well, not anything that I didn't know before, but I definitely cherish the culture and environment we have here more. Every day I see something that makes it even more special and more worthwhile. I realize more and more every day that I am not just building a career here, but also building lifelong friendships and relationships. And I've learned that at Zappos, there is definitely truth to the saying "We may not have it all together ... But together, we can have it all." :) With any luck, I'll be here for many more years to come.

Eddielynn T.

EMPLOYEE SINCE JANUARY 29 2007

What do I think about the Zappos Culture? ... All I can say is that I've never worked at another place quite like Zappos. The Zappos Culture and environment is very unique. I enjoy and look forward to coming to work every day because I LOVE what I do here and I LOVE my Zappos family. So for me, the culture is our family and team bond, which I have never really experienced anywhere else, which is truly amazing ...

Eileen L.

EMPLOYEE SINCE JANUARY 16 2002

The Zappos Culture is a place where you can bring your passion to life. It's a place where you take calculated risks in order to gain market share ... go big or go home, as we like to say. We focus on the company as a whole and decide what is the best path to take. We are a family that works together and plays together. We're truly interested in the lives of the team that we work with. The lines are blurred between what is work and what is play, since we are doing what we love. You are free to speak your mind. The only constant thing at Zappos is change. The weirder you are, the better you fit in. Our motto is service in all aspects of the company and that's what keeps us growing and humble. Zappos Culture to me means "Family!" Through good times, sad times and bad times, we have all been there for each other, when someone has needed somebody to laugh with, a shoulder to cry on or even someone to just listen to them. One of our fellow employees is always there to lift your spirits up!! On my first day of training, I was so overwhelmed with the type of assistance we were able to offer the customers (being able to build a RAPPORT!!!). I have been to many call centers where there was always a script to read to the customers and a time limit. It always made them feel like they were being rushed and told the same thing over and over again, with no resolution in the end.

Elisa C.

EMPLOYEE SINCE SEPTEMBER 11 2006

Well, this year has been challenging, but you can see where building a positive team and family spirit plays a part in the company. The end of '08' was frustrating and hard, it was a time for everybody to grow and share ideas. I did learn a lot (and continue to learn) and it was neat to see how the company pulled through and is still doing really well. Can't wait to see where 2009 takes us!

Emaile H.

EMPLOYEE SINCE JULY 31 2006

I was asked, "What does our culture here at Zappos mean to me?" Well, I can say that I'm still WOWed regularly after two years of being here! 2008 proved to be one of the most challenging times since I've been here, but never have I seen a company pull together as a family to weather the storm the way we all did. Sure, it was tough, but we all made the best of a difficult situation. We all continued to help one another and kept things "fun and a little weird" to keep things in the Zappos spirit! Hard times can easily tear groups apart, but I watched as this family grew closer and bonded more. Everyone put their heads together to work through the situations that we, as a company, faced. It is because of this greatness that we were able to achieve our billion-dollar goal in 2008, instead of 2010 as originally assumed. I'm grateful to be amongst such great people and can only look forward to more great times and great accomplishments along the way!!! =)

Eric Y.

EMPLOYEE SINCE SEPTEMBER 18 2006

The Zappos Culture, to me, lies beyond the walls of Zappos and within each of us. A perk in being an AB is traveling. I love going to market and walking into an appointment and lighting up a showroom with the Zappos Culture rays that surround each of us. The greetings are charismatic because people are fascinated with Zappos and want to know what's brewing over here. The positive energy and vibrant spirit that we each embody by embracing the Ten Core Values is looked upon very highly in the industry. Our culture is contagious, and the fact that people are genuinely interested and intrigued is humbling. Each story we tell, each meeting we have, each laugh we share – our culture continues to shine!

Erica W.

EMPLOYEE SINCE NOVEMBER 20 2004

The Zappos Culture and everything it stands for has changed many lives, including mine. I love being a part of making a difference in this world and that is what the Zappos Culture truly means to me. The people that make up the Zappos family are people that care, who are trustworthy and honest. We not only care about our co-workers, but we care about everyone that comes into contact with us. I look forward to many more challenging yet wonderful years as a part of the Zappos family.

Eric H.

EMPLOYEE SINCE DECEMBER 3 2007

I'm more than elated to say that this is my 2nd culture book entry and for that I am very grateful and also very pleased. This past year that I have worked for Zappos has undoubtedly been one of the best years of my life. I've had the opportunity to experience so many new and exciting things – I will always cherish these memories. I think that's what Zappos Culture is all about, new and exciting things ... giving people the chance to experience things that they normally would never have the opportunity to. Whether it's a vendor party or history class or even a parade, I know I've never worked for a company that does that on a regular basis before. These things boost morale and really follow our Ten Core Values. Create fun and a little weirdness, Zappos! Here's to a wonderful and exciting year!

Fred M.

EMPLOYEE SINCE AUGUST 1 1999

There once was a best place to work
Whose culture seemed almost berserk
It was friendly and fun
Delivered WOW by the ton
At Zappos, joy is a perk

Galen H.

EMPLOYEE SINCE JANUARY 5 2004

Zappos Culture to me is a way of life. In the simplest terms, it is an attitude of "Work hard and play hard." It is an avenue for individual expression and individual growth. It is a platform for openness. We all strive to make this one of the greatest companies in history and we are allowed to do whatever it takes in order to achieve that. This includes allowing us to take the current culture and add to it through all of our diverse personalities. I am proud to be a part of our culture.

Graham M.

EMPLOYEE SINCE AUGUST 14 2006

In 2008, I watched as the Zappos Culture took its first hit in the three years since I started. I watched as the economy dropped, and people started losing their homes, and companies started going out of business. I watched as our culture had its heart broken for the first time. We said some painful goodbyes, we faced uncertain outcomes, we reached a crossroads, and we chose a path. The path we chose was not an easy one. We saw things in ourselves that we didn't like, and we made as many wrong choices as right. But we persevered. We fought on. And as 2009 came upon us, we began to see the rainbow through the rain. 2008 was a tough one, and I personally raged against more than I embraced, but when the smoke cleared, I found myself more proud than I have ever been to be a part of this company.

Hannah E.

EMPLOYEE SINCE MARCH 20 2006

What does Zappos Culture mean to ME? The longer I've been at Zappos, the more the answer to that question evolves to mean so much more than just our Ten Core Values. There's something intangible about Zappos Culture, something that's hard to quantify in surveys or polls, something that other companies are constantly coveting. When I see the tours from different companies go by every day, it constantly reminds me that we have something truly special here at Zappos, enough to make other businesses and companies notice! To me, the true meaning of our Zappos Culture is most evident after unfortunate events take place, the death of one of our team members, the company-wide layoffs, the not-so-favorable economy ... I think the true measure of a culture's solidarity and family spirit really shines through during the rough times more so than in good. It is then that we can really take the opportunity to put these Ten Core Values into practice, and be the better for it in the end. Although 2008 was far from a perfect year, I think Zappos Culture is all about continuing to strive to be better in every way possible, to become better and stronger than we were the prior year, to innovate beyond what we started, not just once in a while, but every day. This is the very reason why Zappos is such a great place to work and to call home.

Heather T.

EMPLOYEE SINCE NOVEMBER 29 2005

Zappos Culture, to me, means friends and family. It's a place where I can come and be myself. It's a place where my ideas are heard and my work is appreciated. Zappos is more than just a place where I go to work; it's a place I go to work with really caring, friendly people.

Hilary L.

EMPLOYEE SINCE FEBRUARY 21 2006

Zappos Culture to me is building a positive team and family spirit. I enjoy coming to work because of the relationships that I have here. Every day I learn something new from a friend, not just a co-worker.

Holly E.

EMPLOYEE SINCE JUNE 13 2005

When Zappos says, "Create a family and team spirit," it is not joking. It's funny how you really don't realize all the things you go through with your co-workers/team until hard times come around, and they all help you pull out of it. I recently was told some bad news and needed to go through some medical adventures. When I found out, I didn't want to tell people, as I didn't want the sympathy. As time went on, and I didn't have many people at home to talk to or friends that happened to be never there when you need them (I'm sure everyone has a few of those) ... my Zappos family was there for me. I consider myself very lucky to be a part of such a big family. When hard times come your way, your Zappos family is always there to help and support.

Hongyee H.

EMPLOYEE SINCE NOVEMBER 19 2007

2008 has been a rough time for my family and I, but the one thing that kept me going is Zappos. There isn't a word to describe how much my Zappos family has done for me and I thank them every day for it. I'm so thankful for everything my team has done for me, and I'm grateful to be part of the family.

Jacqueline M.

EMPLOYEE SINCE OCTOBER 8 2007

Zappos Culture is only found at Zappos! Others can learn about it, and witness it firsthand. They can even try to duplicate it. But the only place that this phenomenon can be found to such an extensive degree is at Zappos! Our Zappos Culture is what makes this company such a great place to work, and I'm happy to be a part of it!

Jarett A.

EMPLOYEE SINCE JUNE 9 2008

After coming from a standard and corporate strict buying office, Zappos is truly a breath of fresh air! It's wackily funnier times every day, goals built from the bottom up and the top down, and it consistently upholds unconventional, out-of-the-box approaches to all aspects of the business. The Zappos Culture is unique, welcoming, and a rollercoaster extravaganza!

Jason M.

EMPLOYEE SINCE JANUARY 22 2008

How did I ever end up in Vegas? Well, let's see ... It all started when I was living on the east coast and a job offer in San Francisco fell through (December 2007). I randomly found an ad on Craigslist from Zappos; it needed a Product Information Coordinator. What the heck is a Product Information Coordinator? I applied. Long story short, I sold everything that wouldn't fit in my rusty 1994 Nissan Altima, and headed to the City of Sin. I originally planned for it to be a three-day road trip, but I was on a roll and ended up driving 32 hours in two days. I arrived in Vegas super late on a Thursday evening, found a place to live on Friday and started working at Zappos on Tuesday (Monday was a holiday). It has now been a little over a year since I started working at this great company and it's been quite the adventure. I went from Product Information Coordinator to Senior Product Information Coordinator to Lead Video Content Coordinator and was even featured in a Fortune Magazine centerfold. Zappos made me famous! Okay, it wasn't really a centerfold, but it was a pretty big picture. Just don't be surprised when I leave Zappos to pursue a modeling career. Just kidding! I am not letting it go to my head because I am remaining humble (Zappos Core Value #10). So, I will stop talking about how there was a big picture of me in the February 2009 '100 Best Companies To Work For' issue of Fortune Magazine. (Cough) Page 54. (Cough) Okay, but seriously ... I love working at Zappos and can't picture myself anywhere else. Sure, I miss Florida's humidity, surfing at Cocoa Beach and all of my friends in Orlando, but my Zappos family has made living in Las Vegas pretty rad.

Jay de G.

EMPLOYEE SINCE AUGUST 20 2007

My interpretation of Zappos Culture is going out of your way to acknowledge, please, or help anyone you come in contact with. Basically, to come out of your comfort zone, and see what transpires. Whether it may be a fellow worker or guest, the simplest actions sometimes can leave a lasting impression. In this day and age, especially during these tough times, we tend to get too caught up with our work and we lose focus. I'm so grateful to be part of a company that truly lives, breathes and maintains the Zappos Values and where the employees are genuinely upbeat and positive. It makes coming to work fun, but a bit challenging, because you see it all around you and you want to test yourself to see if you're on their level. For me it's not just a job, it's a livelihood.

Jeanne M.

EMPLOYEE SINCE FEBRUARY 28 2006

What does Zappos Culture mean to me? EVERYTHING! Our culture is what makes me feel thankful every day that I have the privilege of coming into Zappos to spend my day with my co-workers, who are truly my best friends and my extended family. There is a vibe in the office that can't be forced or manufactured, it's truly in our DNA. Every vendor partner I work with can't help but comment on it when they are in our building – saying how fortunate we are to be in a place full of such optimism, vision and creativity. The respect we show to each other and toward those brands we work with is infectious. Though it's currently a difficult environment for many retailers, our passion for our brand and our colleagues will be a key factor in driving our continued success. It was incredibly gratifying this year to have that recognized by Fortune magazine's "Top 100 Companies To Work For" list! We have tremendous opportunities in the months ahead. I am excited and proud to be part of a company that will embrace our culture as we continue to evolve and grow.

Jeff B.

EMPLOYEE SINCE NOVEMBER 16 2006

Culture is what brought us through the end of the year in 2008. Although everyone had hardships, our culture brought us to the end of the year stronger than ever. This past year, more than ever, culture has taken an ever-more important role in this company. We kept going strong even during a struggling economy and even through the dreadful layoffs. Those unfortunate mishaps tested our culture. We could have crumbled and failed, but we succeeded as a company because of our Zappos Culture. It kept us determined to get back up after the falls and to keep trucking along, inch after inch, to not only achieve our goal, but to keep the morale up through the end of the year. I believe we succeeded on both ends. Culture this past year has become more important to me. It keeps us going as a team of employees that love their job and are determined to keep it that way.

Jenn M.

EMPLOYEE SINCE DECEMBER 4 2006

Zappos continues to exude immense opportunity and inspiration through our passion to influence one another. This influence extends to our customers, partners, and the overall business community. Our purpose is the reason I'm nowhere else.

Jennifer G.

EMPLOYEE SINCE FEBRUARY 19 2008

Zappos Culture, to me, is an environment that breeds creativity and individuality and encourages growth. Zappos is different from other companies because you are empowered to make change. I like that I can be myself and work with amazing people!

Jennifer S.

EMPLOYEE SINCE MARCH 8 2007

Culture, to me, means smiling when I arrive because someone smiled at me on my way in. It means walking down the halls of the office and saying "Hi," to everyone along the way. It's seeing my team grow and become amazing buyers right before my eyes. But most of all, it's the laughter I enjoy all day long while at work or on the road. It makes me know we are not only having a blast, but we are making history. Cheers, Zappos!

Jessica L.

EMPLOYEE SINCE MARCH 13 2006

The Zappos Culture is unlike any other. There is a real sense of "team." Here, as we are all doing different duties to make the entire company come together and function. I think we have gotten to where we are now hugely in part to the Ten Core Values. These Core Values help us decide how to act and treat each other. No matter what we're going through, if we keep the Core Values in mind, we can make it happen. I am proud to be a Zapponian!

Jim C.

EMPLOYEE SINCE NOVEMBER 16 2004

2008 was an interesting year. The economy took a dive, business was okay and there were a lot of tough things we had to deal with both personally and professionally. Despite these rough times and the bad days, I still enjoyed coming in to work. Zappos has created a culture unlike any workplace in the world. It's hard to explain in a book, or trying to tell someone who has never been to our office, but it really is something special and unique. I have been fortunate enough to work with this company for the last five years and I've seen Zappos evolve from an empty office with scattered computers to a living, breathing, and well-oiled machine. This was all made possible by creating such an intense, friendly vibe that cannot be explained in words (and by selling a lot of shoes, of course :)) So, this year, I will keep my entry short and sweet – this company and its culture is the best in the biz! I have made a lot of friends through Zappos; I even met my wife here! So there is nothing more that I can add, except I can't wait to see what 2009 has in store for us!

Jonathan H.

EMPLOYEE SINCE JULY 9 2007

Zappos is a wonderful place to work. Why? First of all, I totally love the job that I do. I find it fascinating, interesting, and rewarding. Secondly, the people I work with here at Zappos are caring and interesting. We have many events throughout the year where we get to know one another and because of this there is a tight bond. One of the best things is that during the day, most of my co-workers have smiles on their faces and are truly interested in helping each other do their best. I have not experienced this at previous workplaces. There are many other reasons why Zappos is great. We can decorate our desks, wear whatever we want to work, have free lunches, and we always find time to celebrate!

Josh S.

EMPLOYEE SINCE SEPTEMBER 11 2006

So, 2008 was an interesting year, and not in the most positive of connotations. Times were tough in the retail world; sales were down, brands and retailers closed doors, there were layoffs, and the media insisted on telling us about it EVERY DAY. As a result, morale in the office was a bit lower than it had been in the past. But in times where we could have let this break our culture, we instead pulled together to combat the beast head-on. That is the best lesson that I have learned in this past year. It is easy to be happy-go-lucky when things are going well but when times are tough, that is when the real test of core culture rises to the surface. 2008 has proven that regardless of what is going on, we will stay as a close team, learn from each other, and persevere through whatever comes our way. I really believe that because of our culture, there will be no stopping us now.

Karl K.

EMPLOYEE SINCE JANUARY 14 2008

I have never experienced what I experience every day that I come to work here at Zappos. I never thought that a fun working environment existed, but here it is. I used to dread getting out of bed and going to my old job, now I want to come to work even when I have time off. I have been able to work with some remarkable people that I consider good friends now, and I feel that everyone tries their hardest to make each other's work environment as fun and comfortable as possible. I really feel privileged to be involved with a company that cares about their employees. I get to leave the office everyday looking forward to the next, that is what Zappos Culture is all about.

Karrie M.

EMPLOYEE SINCE OCTOBER 23 2006

Zappos Culture, to me, is about a feeling of family. The relationships I have with my co-workers and my vendors are unlike those at any job in the past. I feel blessed to have found such an amazing company and so proud to tell people this is where I work. I love to see the looks on people's faces when they are on a tour, smiling from ear to ear and amazed that everyone has taken the time to greet them – and of course, the occasional "How do you get any work done around here!?" I can't believe I've been working at Zappos for over two years now ... time flies when you're having fun!

Kathleen J.

EMPLOYEE SINCE JANUARY 28 2008

From the day I walked into the doors of Zappos as a prospective employee, I knew I had to work here. There was an energy that was hard to miss and it pulled me in and made me want to be a part of it. Within days of starting work here, I found out what that energy was: it's our Zappos Culture, the "WOW." I quickly found that we are an eclectic group of creative individuals who are working in an environment where individuality is cherished, nurtured and recognized. Our culture is a prime example of how well things can work when the employee feels like an integral part of the company's vision and mission. I wake up looking forward to coming to work, because I know that no matter what challenges I may face throughout the day, I am supported by an awesome team of talented co-workers who are really more like family members, who encourage me when I need it and are here working toward the same goal: to provide the best customer service imaginable and to "Live and Deliver WOW!"

Kathy K.

EMPLOYEE SINCE JULY 5 2006

Zappos Culture is a great, big WOW to me. I am fortunate to have built friendships and vendor partnerships that I cherish. I come to work every day confident that I can express myself without judgment while truly enjoying what I do. The people that I work with have helped shape me as a person and the core values have steered me in the right direction professionally. Zappos is an amazing place to work.

Kelly B.

EMPLOYEE SINCE FEBRUARY 6 2006

Three years ago today, I was sitting outside of Starbucks on a Sunday morning, after a long run. I was talking to friends about how excited I was to start a new job the next day at Zappos. I had heard from several of my sales reps that I "needed" to work there and that I would love it. I can't believe that tomorrow is my three-year anniversary! I am so grateful to be part of the Zappos family. When I hear my friends talk about their dread of returning to work every Monday morning, I realize how lucky I am to look forward to another day at Zappos. I think in order to work here and stay here, you must have an emotional connection to Zappos. You WANT to give 150%, not because you have to but because you begin to love this thing called Zappos! I love this place:)

Kenneth L.

EMPLOYEE SINCE SEPTEMBER 4 2007

The Zappos Culture is a lot of things. It can be as simple as holding the door open for someone or flashing a quick smile to someone you don't know. It can be this fancy metaphorical idea I've used to explain it to outsiders who haven't seen it in action: "You know ... the culture is like this idea that we can all be individuals, but still fill a specific role into something that's much bigger. Really, it's pretty cool." It can be the sense of pride we all seem to have when we see the Zappos brand steps into the spotlight, whether we're part of a Letterman joke or when we're prominently featured in Fortune magazine. It can even be as silly as Christopher Walken followed by a cacophony of cowbells. To me, the Zappos Culture is a lot of things but I know that it, above anything else – even the very items we sell – is what makes Zappos the successful company that it is today.

Kevin W.

EMPLOYEE SINCE OCTOBER 18 2004

After almost five years now with Zappos, I still consider myself very fortunate to be a part of this team. I get to work for and with people that I respect, admire and consider my friends. In good times and in bad, those things have remained constant. With that in mind, I'm extremely excited for the future and have tremendous confidence that we will continue to rise to the challenges we face. I look forward to seeing what we can accomplish over the next five years together!

Kim C.

EMPLOYEE SINCE SEPTEMBER 10 2007

Culture ... what does Zappos Culture mean to me? Zappos Culture is very unique, and unlike any other! Our culture and our Ten Core Values are really what make Zappos a very special place to work. I can honestly say that we do live, and breathe our core values on a day-to-day basis! It is something that is indescribable; something that you really need to experience to understand what I mean. Every day that I walk into the office, I can just feel the energy coming from everyone. Not every company has a culture, but after working at Zappos, it really shows me how important, and beneficial it is to have one! Ever since I have been working here, I cannot imagine working anywhere else!

Kimberly R.

EMPLOYEE SINCE APRIL 2 2007

Zappos Culture ... what can I say about our culture that has not already been said? I could say it's about my awesome co-workers and how work doesn't quite feel like work when we're all working together and having fun. I could say it's the environment and how every time I think I've seen it all, Zappos still manages to surprise me. It all just translates to my life outside of work. The smiles, the opening of doors, the general respect towards others is not just reserved for the office. Instead, I'd like to think of the culture as more of a way of life.

Latrira S.

EMPLOYEE SINCE AUGUST 15 2007

The Zappos Culture is the reason I come to work every day. It's the reason that no matter what, I continue to believe in Zappos and its future. I know that no job is perfect, but Zappos comes close to none. Just being here for close to two years I have learned so much about myself, gained the most amazing friends, and had the chance to experience life in such a different way. Zappos is more than a place to work, or a nine-to-five job. It's a 24-hour morale boost that keeps you opening doors and saying hello to everyone you meet at work or at home. Zappos is becoming a way of life and I'm just glad to be doing my part in such an amazing, talented company.

Lauren G.

EMPLOYEE SINCE SEPTEMBER 11 2006

Our culture here at Zappos is very special. We are constantly growing and changing. Each time I meet a new co-worker, it seems like we have known each other for years. The culture here is very contagious, but there is definitely something special in everyone who is hired. Work doesn't feel like work, it is a new adventure every day. "Work hard and play hard," is a great way to look at our company. We get things done, while having fun and being a little weird at the same time. Our culture is why I love being a part of Zappos, I feel very lucky to be here!

Leemarie S.

EMPLOYEE SINCE DECEMBER 18 2006

Zappos to me is a place where anything is possible. Ideas are heard and people have the opportunity to pioneer new ground. Change is a given at Zappos and it is what makes things exciting and new each day.

Lindsay R.

EMPLOYEE SINCE FEBRUARY 6 2007

Zappos Culture. What can I say? It's really a way of life. We come here each day and do the best we can to provide for the family we have here and at home. There are ups and downs with each week and it is NEVER the same. When I first started, I read the Culture Book and thought it was a hoax. Well, I am here to testify that this company is anything but. I am proud to be a part of such an innovative company; one that always tries to put its best foot forward even when times get rough. It's amazing to me to have a work environment where people really do care about other people, not just about a job. I am so very grateful to be a part of this family and hope to be here a long time.

Lynsey C.
EMPLOYEE SINCE MARCH 12 2007

"Be the change you wish to see in the world." – Gandhi. This is one of my favorite quotes. I read it every morning on my refrigerator while drinking my coffee to get my day started. To me, Zappos Culture is a collection of individuals being the change we all want to see. Our culture is a variety of people with many different personalities and qualities that have come together with one vision in mind. It is truly astonishing to see such vastly different people from so many backgrounds have one common goal that they sincerely live their life with, day-to-day. It's the little things where this commonality shines through. Like holding open a door, smiling in the hallway, saying, "Hi," to someone you may not know ... the list goes on and on. These little things are the building blocks of our culture.

Maggie H.
EMPLOYEE SINCE MARCH 6 2006

Many of the major corporations in America are proud of their "Mission Statements." These list the objectives of the company and how it is going to achieve them. At Zappos, we live our "Mission Statement" through our culture. Our sincere concern for our fellow workers, for our customers and for our vendors makes our company successful. Zappos is a "think tank" with an atmosphere that encourages us to constantly reinvent ourselves. We are always free to express ourselves and our ideas and energies are welcomed. There are no boundaries.

Maggie M.
EMPLOYEE SINCE JANUARY 2 2007

"Yesterday is history, tomorrow is a mystery, but today is a gift. That is why it is called the present." – Oogway, *Kung Fu Panda*

The Zappos Culture is the culmination of the best in every single employee. This became more apparent than ever as we navigated through a trying 2008. In the end, the employees of Zappos, valued partners across all areas of the business, and our rock star customers all came together and reached a $1-billion-dollar sales goal in the face of a tough economic downturn. That's pretty amazing! While we achieved remarkable financial milestones in 2008, we did not make it out unscathed. We experienced the loss of valued employees, friends, vendors, and brands. We definitely shed some blood, sweat and tears along the way while learning a hell of a lot. But no matter what, the driving force behind Zappos' successes and challenges was, and will always be, our Zappos Culture. It defines our actions and determines our outcomes. I believe the unwavering presence of our culture, paired with its inherent adaptability during tough times, has delivered us into 2009 with a pronounced focus and sense of opportunity. Our culture is our lifeblood and it runs within every single employee at Zappos.

Marisa R.

EMPLOYEE SINCE MAY 7 2007

When I go to work, I am surrounded by people who inspire me. The kindness, creativity, intelligence and passion of each individual employee at Zappos are tremendous. The realization that every employee does matter and is valued is evident. Our culture encourages you to take the lead when you feel passionate about an idea. You do not have to be a manager to head up a project or make a change; you just have to "own it." Zappos Culture truly creates an environment of freethinkers where everyone is encouraged to be a leader.

On that note, Zappos Culture, in turn, teaches you an even more invaluable lesson: when to follow. I am sure everyone, at some point in life, has been asked, "Are you a leader or are you a follower?" I believe it is important to be both. Once you have been a leader, you realize the significance of support and the necessity of a strong team. I am still astounded by the willingness of all of my co-workers to help in any way, and in the short time I have been at Zappos I have learned that nothing is more rewarding then helping someone else accomplish their goals. This is because in the end we are all working towards a common, more important goal. In the cutthroat world of corporate America, I think this aspect of humility is absent in many companies. People will do whatever is necessary to get to the top, to be the best, even if ultimately it is their customers who pay the price. This is not the atmosphere Zappos Culture creates and the success of this approach is apparent in the accomplishments of the company thus far. People have said as our company grows the culture will change. I hope they are right. I hope Zappos continues to grow and evolve. I hope we will persist in finding even more passionate, weird, driven individuals who will progress the culture in new and innovative ways.

Matt B.

EMPLOYEE SINCE NOVEMBER 8 1999

If I could rewrite one of our Ten Core Values, it would be # 5, "Pursue Growth and Learning." I think a more appropriate title would be "Anticipate and Adapt to New Responsibilities." My experience has been that the most valuable growth and learning at Zappos takes place when a new responsibility or role is thrust upon an employee. Implicit in our culture is the belief that if an employee truly buys into what we are trying to accomplish here, he or she will be resourceful enough to learn, and become a leader with just about any new responsibility or role. The real key to growing and learning at Zappos is making yourself open to these responsibilities and roles, and seizing them when they become available.

Matt T.

EMPLOYEE SINCE MARCH 12 2007

I first learned about Zappos through the Culture Book. I was at another job and my boss wanted us to read certain parts of the Culture Book so we could make our place of employment similar to Zappos. I asked, "What does Zappos do?" and she explained that it's a website that got started in shoes and handbags and now sells all kinds of stuff. Why would a company create a book dedicated solely to its culture? I was intrigued, so I started to read the book. From page 1, I was hooked. People actually liked working at Zappos! I had to be a part of this, so I decided to "Pursue Growth and Learning" (before I even knew it was a Core Value) and put in an application. Now it's two years later, I'm knee deep in "WOW" and couldn't be happier.

Megan R.

EMPLOYEE SINCE AUGUST 6 2007

Zappos Culture, to me, means constant learning and growing in an environment that makes it fun to do so on a daily basis. I'm excited to come to work each day, which is more than most people can say about their jobs! I work with some of the most talented buyers/teachers/mentors in the business, and yet, their humility and willingness to share their talents is what sets them apart and makes Zappos an amazing place to work and grow. I love working for people that encourage creativity and thinking outside the box. I believe that is why we have been blessed with so much success as a company. Everyone here has a voice and we are managed by people with the willingness to hear each and every voice. The Zappos Culture is what makes this place more than just another retailer! I thank God for blessing me with the opportunity to work for such a great company and I cherish the days I get to spend here!

Meghan B.

EMPLOYEE SINCE NOVEMBER 7 2005

The Zappos Culture is ...
Zaptastic!!
Awesome
Positive
Passionate
Outstanding
Service-Oriented

Melissa A.

EMPLOYEE SINCE JULY 14 2008

The culture at Zappos is unlike any corporate culture I have experienced in my career –
in a good way. Admittedly, it was a bit overwhelming at first. The idea of people being
genuinely happy and having fun at work made me a bit skeptical, perhaps because I have
spent the past 11 years working in a corporate retail environment where the vast majority
of people walked around looking slightly miserable. That's what I thought "work" was
all about. I am so grateful that I now work for a company where the people are truly
passionate, creative, bright and genuinely happy. Although today's economical challenges
will dictate an uncertain future for many companies, I believe that the unique culture and
the hard-working people at Zappos will keep us going strong.

Micaela M.

EMPLOYEE SINCE MAY 29 2007

Zappos Culture, to me, is a lifestyle. This "culture" will be studied over the years in
business schools and other companies will try to be the "Zappos Way" ... but really, it's all
common sense. It's about being good people and doing the right thing.

Michael F^ol.

EMPLOYEE SINCE JANUARY 7 2008

Today, I am sitting at my desk in a ridiculously ugly, yet remarkable, 80s sweatshirt with
an equally ugly 80s cap, acid wash jeans and some boots that just don't quite match.
On my way into work today, I thought to myself; I have really long hair, a beard, wear
awesomely ugly clothes and I ride a bicycle. I am pretty sure any other company would

call the cops if I even came close to the parking lot because they would think I was some homeless dude. At Zappos, I can be myself and I wouldn't want it any other way!

Michael F^{or}.

EMPLOYEE SINCE NOVEMBER 5 2007

Ten or five years ago, when someone asked me where I see myself in the future, I never once imagined I would be working at a place like Zappos. When I walk into work each and every day, I know that I work at a place that strives to make a difference in the lives of its employees, vendors and customers. What is so awesome to me is that I never know what will happen next; the opportunities for stimulating and meaningful life experiences are all around us. I write this knowing that I am a part of something very special ...

Michelle F.

EMPLOYEE SINCE DECEMBER 10 2007

Zappos is like no other, and I love that. It's so refreshing to wake up every morning wanting to come to work. Wanting to actually see and interact with all your co-workers. Because this isn't just a job, and they're not just co-workers, they're all great friends. And when you get to go to work every day and work with all your friends and do what you love, it isn't work at all. They say time flies when you're having fun and this last year has FLOWN by!

Mike N.

EMPLOYEE SINCE APRIL 14 2003

The Zappos Culture is very unique so it can mean different things to so many people. I have experienced the evolution since April 2003. That's when I took my leap of faith, which was three years in the making. I remember the office in 2003, with six-foot tables, wires on the floor, less than 200 brands and six buyers. We had around 75 people total back then. It amazed me back then that if someone had an idea it was put into place immediately. We have seen a lot of change and an evolution into one of the greatest customer service stories ever told. We have crafted a place that people want to be at. We have developed great relationships with so many people at so many different levels. It is mind-blowing sometimes to think about this culture, as it is ever-evolving and growing. It has become a way of life to treat people great and to always WOW people we come into contact with. So, in a nutshell, it is living the "golden rule," treat people like you want to be treated. I am proud to be part of this company, this growth and this culture.

Miranda W.

EMPLOYEE SINCE APRIL 23 2005

Never did I think I would consider my Zappos co-workers as friends, yet alone family. And after working here for a few years now, I still can't believe this reality. I still continue looking forward to each day. Each day is never the same as any other, which makes it all worthwhile. I like to think of Zappos as box of chocolates, you never know what you're going to get. The Zappos Culture is definitely unique; however, it's all about the Zapponians. We all treat each other with the utmost respect, share our experiences with each other, work hard and play together as well. All of this embodies our wonderful culture here at Zappos.

Monica V.

EMPLOYEE SINCE JUNE 18 2007

WOW – is what comes to mind when I think about the place I work. Zappos has been a great place for me to learn and grow, personally and professionally – the knowledge I have gained has been priceless. I honestly don't know how the company culture continues to grow stronger every year – but it does! I can only imagine where we will be in the next few years, and I'm excited to be a part of the journey.

Myra D.

EMPLOYEE SINCE OCTOBER 6 2008

Zappos is a company that is Powered by Service. Culture is a set of shared attitudes, values, and goals within a group. When you put the two together you have this amazing thing called Zappos Culture: a collection of values where we take care of each other by building a team and family spirit. It's hard to describe what it is, exactly. It's a feeling. It's a way of life. It's an energy that is contagious and spreads amongst everyone that it comes in contact with, whether it's a vendor, a friend, or a complete stranger. I have never worked for a company that believes in an enriched work experience the way Zappos does. I don't just utilize it in my everyday work occurrence but also I try to instill it in my personal life. Being away from my loved ones back in California didn't seem as bad when I started working here. Everyone is truly genuine and looks out for one another. The Zappos Culture has definitely changed my outlook in life.

Natasha P.

EMPLOYEE SINCE NOVEMBER 28 2005

Over the years, the Zappos Culture has come to mean to me:
Live Life.
Keep Learning.
Be ready for anything.
Don't get scared, step up to the challenge.
If it's never been done this way before, guess what? There's a first time for everything!
Endurance is survival.
And smile!

Nick P.

EMPLOYEE SINCE FEBRUARY 11 2006

The last year has been a whirlwind of emotions for me personally at Zappos. From receiving a totally unexpected bonus check in March that helped me purchase my first house to the unfortunate layoffs at the end of the year. Through all the highs and lows, everyone still seems like family, and just like family, you are going to have ups and downs. It's through these ups and downs that people really seem to pull together, really embrace our culture, and make this more than just another job. What does our culture really mean to me right now at this very minute? Knowing that I have a group of people I can count on no matter if things are good or bad. That's pretty rare this day in age.

Nicole B.

EMPLOYEE SINCE MAY 29 2007

Zappos makes me feel as if I am exactly who, what and where I am supposed to be right now.

Nicole S.

EMPLOYEE SINCE JULY 10 2006

Zappos Culture is about friendship and family that can stick through the hard times together.

Noel C.

EMPLOYEE SINCE MARCH 6 2006

How can I explain the culture here? I can't. If I was asked to fill a book I couldn't really explain or describe it well enough. However I can tell you ... that the culture does genuinely revolve around its core values ... that I've told multiple friends to work here after I started and now they do (seriously, heaven is working with your best friends!) ... I love going to work every day and after work, I love hanging out with co-workers ... I love our benefits and rave to strangers about Zappos every chance I get ... I feel the same way about this company that I did three years ago when I started. I'm still so excited to be a part of our strong culture. But ultimately you have to come in and see for yourself. So next time you're in Vegas, stop and see for yourself ...

Paul P.

EMPLOYEE SINCE AUGUST 13 2007

The Ten Core Values are a "How To" guide at Zappos. They help guide us in any situation that we may be unfamiliar with. I think that was most evident this year when times got tough; we were able to look to the core values and find guidance. The core values run from the practical ("Embrace and Drive Change") to the unorthodox ("Create Fun and A Little Weirdness). This is also very applicable to life outside Zappos; sometimes you must find a practical solution or sometimes the crazy may work. I think it's amazing how work can affect one's personal life in a positive way, and appreciate Zappos for it. Thanks.

Raina A.

EMPLOYEE SINCE JUNE 25 2007

The world of Zappos and its culture make my work so much more than just a job to me. I remember when I first walked through the front doors of the office I thought, "What did I get myself into?" A random parade had just walked by, and the really nice guy at the front desk offered me a breakfast sandwich that he had just brought back to the office. Little did I realize that I had just embarked on one of the best experiences of my life so far! Zappos has allowed me to grow not only professionally but also personally, which is something I never really felt at any of my previous jobs. Plus, I've had the opportunity to meet and work with a bunch of great people that I never would have otherwise met. Thank you, Zappos for all of the wonderful opportunities, and for allowing me to just be me!

Raven M.

EMPLOYEE SINCE JULY 28 2008

Dynamic and innovative. The Zappos Culture is always on the lookout for the next best thing. In this zany and wild environment, there is always a creative thought and new idea brewing in the midst. The Zappos culture is about not being stagnant – being able to move, adapt, and be the first to arrive. Zappos strives to be the leader in the industry rather than the follower. As always, Zappos seeks to be a step ahead of the rest. It's thrilling, fun and motivating to work for a company that allows you to push the limits and explore the possibilities.

Rebecca K.

EMPLOYEE SINCE AUGUST 12 2004

From my very first day at Zappos over four years ago, I was amazed and excited about the differences that set it apart from any other company I had worked for or come into contact with. There was no forced standard for employees to conform to. Every employee had his or her own personality and way of thinking –and it showed! I was greeted with enthusiasm and respect. It felt good to go into an office where I felt appreciated as a valuable employee and was given the freedom to share my ideas and act on them.

Zappos has maintained that culture since I started. I have been so fortunate to grow with the company. The longer I am here, the more I appreciate the incredible place it is. And that incredible atmosphere is directly related to the people surrounding me. The people drive the culture. The culture is unique, but so familiar – because it makes you feel at home. Everyone knows you spend a lot of your life with the people you work with ... I am very happy that the people I work with are easy to be around and encourage me to develop my talents.

Rico N.

EMPLOYEE SINCE APRIL 19 2004

Zappos Culture has always been something that has always been close to my heart. It means so many different things to me. When I think of the Zappos Culture, some of the words that come to mind are family, caring, fun, friendships, hard work and pride. I have never felt like that towards something other than my blood relatives. That is saying something special. After we had a tough year, I read a blog that said, for a company that promotes family, why did we do some of the things that we did? That really made me think. It really made me ask that question myself. We did what some families have to do and that is make sacrifices for the greater good. We do that every day in our real families. What made me even prouder is that the company felt stronger as a whole. I think that to really appreciate that, you have to be a part of it. Looking from the outside in does no justice to what it feels like to be a part of the Zappos family. I come to work for my co-workers. They are the reason I enjoy coming in to work each day. They are the reason I feel so part of something special. Each person I come in contact with just reassures me that Zappos is doing it right.

Zappos has been, is and always will be a very special place to be. I can still remember the very first day I walked into the SF office and every single employee greeted me. Now that we've grown to the size we are today, the feeling hasn't changed, it has just grown. It is such a pleasure to be a part of – and to watch the blossoming of – a company like Zappos. We are truly witnessing something great here. I am thankful every day that I can help make Zappos that much better and that much more fun.

To all the Zapponians out there, let's keep this thing going. This ride is far from over. We have some great people here that make every day worthwhile. Thank you for being you! For all those friends of Zappos or people just outside looking in, come on by and hang out a little. Maybe a little Zappos will brighten your day too. It still does for me.

Robert A.

EMPLOYEE SINCE JANUARY 18 2005

2008 was a turbulent year (to say the least) here at Zappos, but I think it's safe to say that without the culture, we would not have come through as well as we have. The willingness to do what's best for the company, coupled with the camaraderie that we feel for each other, has been an enormous help in making sure that for every step we take moving forward, we're still the same company that started way back when. I definitely feel that with our Ten Core Values firmly in place, we as a company were able to weather this storm and make ourselves ready for whatever 2009 will bring.

Robert P.

EMPLOYEE SINCE OCTOBER 29 2007

The Zappos Culture is not the norm. It is above and beyond anything you will find anywhere else. The culture is the employees of Zappos. Everyone brings their style and ideas together and creates one big strange but happy family. Look around the office and you will find a mixture of different lifestyles and backgrounds. Somehow, they all mingle together to form the culture we currently have. This makes coming to work more enjoyable because it's a fun environment and it's always changing. If you have ever felt left out, you won't feel that way here. You feel as if you belong and you're part of something special.

Robin C.

EMPLOYEE SINCE AUGUST 27 2007

The Zappos Culture is frequently compared to being a family. I agree that these are people that I not only work with but also get to have fun with. To me, though, that is only part of being a family. The other part of it is being there for each other in tough times. With the economic climate this past year being as difficult as it is, Zappos has had to make some tough decisions. This is the time that I am really reminded of being part of a family, because everyone has come together to help make sure that we are able to stay a successful company and stay true to the roots of our culture.

Rowena D.

EMPLOYEE SINCE NOVEMBER 20 2006

As I was thinking about what to write – because I felt like my entry would be similar to previous years – I realized that it is a great thing that not much has changed in the way I feel about Zappos Culture. I still feel like Zappos friends are like a second family. I like being at Zappos and enjoy the people I spend my day with.

Rudy R.

EMPLOYEE SINCE JULY 5 2005

Zappos is an adventure. It feels like a piece of my life that I was missing. It's like a roller coaster– you go up, down, on curves, around, and back again, riding with an awesome crew while we scream, have fun and let go.

Scott J.

EMPLOYEE SINCE SEPTEMBER 16 2002

This will be my 7th year at Zappos; what an amazing experience it has been and continues to be. I am thankful that I work for a company that provides so much opportunity for personal growth. The friendships I have formed through Zappos will last a lifetime. Looking forward to what 2009 has to bring! Edit and amplify!

Sean M.

EMPLOYEE SINCE APRIL 25 2005

I'm Sean, and this is my band EmoSean. Cryyyyy! I get sad when puppies cry ... Zappos Culture ROCKS! EmoSean 2009

Shanda F.

EMPLOYEE SINCE MAY 7 2007

For me, Zappos Culture means: I have zollars in my pocket, food in my tummy, friends at my house, and knowledge in my brain. What else could I ask for?

Sharon I.

EMPLOYEE SINCE MAY 7 2007

Everyone who works at Zappos knows it is a unique company that truly cares about its employees, as well as its customers. Everyone works hard, but there are plenty of times for fun and games among the co-workers. Management and employees strive to embrace the Core Values and by so doing, make working at Zappos more than just a job. There are very few companies that treat employees as well as Zappos does. Zappos never ceases to amaze me with everything it does to make Zappos the best place to work with the greatest of employees.

Shyloh C.

EMPLOYEE SINCE APRIL 16 2007

As I sit here on a Thursday evening at 9:00 p.m. in our Zappos office in Henderson, still working, I marvel at how much I actually don't mind it. Today, I rolled into work after spending a beautiful morning with my children, eating a large breakfast and getting them off to school. As I drove in, I decided to pick up a coffee. I didn't have to rush – we have flex hours at Zappos. I continue to sit at my desk this evening with my radio on, my shoes off, my feet curled underneath me while writing orders for what I expect to be one of the largest apparel brands to launch on the site (Levi's), and I am incredibly excited. Never mind that the orders are due in tomorrow and I have already put in a full week!! It never feels like overtime here at Zappos. I am empowered to handle my business the way I see fit and in the schedule I choose to fit it in. Deadlines need to be met, but in your own space and your own time. I love it. It is the human element missing in most workplaces ... the ability to trust your employees to make their personal and their professional lives mesh. I will most likely leave around 10:30 p.m. tonight and will decide whether or not I will come into the office tomorrow (Friday), or work from home (as we can do that). Maybe I will do both. After all, I love hanging with my team and find that it is often too lonely working from home. Right now I am going to finish my orders and not worry about tomorrow. I'll decide my schedule AFTER I have another beautiful morning with my children, eat a leisurely breakfast, and get them off to school. Oh and of course, AFTER I pick up my coffee!

Stephanie B.
EMPLOYEE SINCE JULY 10 2006

The past year has had its ups and downs, but for most friends and families, it's been a hard year. It's good to know that I still have a job, but even better, that I have a job here at Zappos. I've always looked at my job as more than a "9-5 job", and more than just a paycheck. It's always been a team and family feel here in the office, but now, more than ever, I feel so close to my co-workers. I feel like I can turn to them when I'm in need of something, whether it be big or small.

I used to brag about coming to a job that I can have fun, go to happy hours and just have a good time at. Now, I talk about how it's one of the best companies to work for, because of how I've bonded with my co-workers. They are true friends and in time of need, they know I would be there for them, as they have for me. That's what, to me, Zappos Culture is all about!

Stephen H.
EMPLOYEE SINCE SEPTEMBER 20 2008

Culture to me is the end result of the bond that a group of people has formed together over any length of time. We all maintain a personal and professional culture, and I am proud to work at a place where, more often than not, they are one and the same. Whether it's hanging out with friends, participating in outings, or communicating beyond the workplace via things like Twitter, MySpace and Facebook, our culture is shared and exposed to friends and co-workers all the same. This is a welcome change from having a rigidly defined "work mode" whenever dealing with work stuff!

Steve G.

EMPLOYEE SINCE MARCH 22 2008

Zappos Culture allows me the freedom to think independently and act collectively to get my job done well. Other companies assign responsibility without accountability ... not Zappos. Also, pretense is minimized ... breath of fresh air!

Steve H.

EMPLOYEE SINCE NOVEMBER 1 2004

It's impossible to put down in a few words what Zappos Culture means to me. We're a team, a family, a group of individuals and a collective soul aligned towards one goal. That goal is to make Zappos the greatest company anywhere. Everybody contributes in his or her own way, and every contribution is meaningful. We've been through some rough patches and emerged from every one stronger than before because of our culture. As our culture continues to grow and evolve, I feel privileged to be part of the Zappos tribe.

Steve P.

EMPLOYEE SINCE JANUARY 7 2008

The culture here at Zappos is simply amazing!!! It's what allows me to wake up every morning excited to go to work!! It's not a "9 to 5," it's not a job ...it's an incredible experience that you want to participate in, day in and day out!!!

Tara J.

EMPLOYEE SINCE JULY 31 2007

What I love most about working for Zappos is that I can be myself. Not only am I accepted, but I'm embraced. There's a feeling here that each and every employee really does make a difference and it's not just something that people say.

Terra E.

EMPLOYEE SINCE JANUARY 8 2007

So many amazing things have happened to Zappos in the last year. From hitting a billion dollars as a company, to being on "Oprah" and now, being featured in Fortune magazine for being one of the "Top 100 Companies to Work For." It's been such an exciting year that I was having a hard time deciding just what I was going to write for my culture entry this year when it just hit me tonight. I'm in NY for FFANY this week, and tonight I had drinks with some friends of some friends of some friends. As I was meeting all these new people for the first time, in each conversation that I had telling them that I worked at Zappos, I heard one of the following responses: "Oh, I've heard that's such a great place to work" or "Wow, Zappos is such an awesome company" and "You are so lucky!" All of which are true. I feel truly blessed that not only did I find my dream career but I also found a company that I am so proud to be a part of.

Terry I.

EMPLOYEE SINCE JULY 31 2007

Culture defines any population's beliefs, values and social practices. Zappos Culture is the treatment of putting co-workers, customers or anyone we meet ahead of ourselves. To go out of our way to help when or wherever possible, and to make people feel good about themselves – which, in turn, makes us better people ourselves.

Valencia F.

EMPLOYEE SINCE JANUARY 8 2007

I love the team and family spirit of Zappos. I think it's great how we all work hard but we are also encouraged to play hard. Having team outings and being able to get to know our co-workers outside of work is awesome and I think it builds a stronger relationship for us at work...like a family.

Valencia S.

EMPLOYEE SINCE OCTOBER 24 2005

Where has the time gone? It's been close to four years here at Zappos for me and what can I say? I have loved every minute of it. From the very beginning up until now, I have watched the company go through many growing pains. I seriously cannot imagine where else I could be but at Zappos. The "team and family spirit" here really shows everyday and just gets better with age here. I've made so many great friends here, some I can even call family members. Although I have lost some friends during my stay, it's great to see that Zappos can carry itself through these tough times. I truly believe in this company and I can honestly say that I make a difference here. I never hesitate to state where I work and I recommend everyone should know about this place. Where else can you bump shoulders and party with the CEO? Zappos is more than just a job to me. Zappos is almost like my second home. And if you're ever in my area, don't hesitate to stop by and say hello.

Whitney M.
EMPLOYEE SINCE MAY 27 2008

Zappos Culture is not like anything I have ever experienced before. When I decided to come on board, I knew that it would be different than what I was used to in my past professional world. I came from a very buttoned-up corporate job, the complete opposite of Zappos. I still find myself having to adjust to this new environment from time to time, but I am very grateful to have a job at Zappos. While some people see Zappos as a large company, I still see a huge opportunity for growth. I feel very lucky to be a part of this creative team; I can't wait to see, in time, the different ways Zappos will evolve.

Yevan C.
EMPLOYEE SINCE JANUARY 28 2008

What can I say – Zappos is the WOW! Working for Zappos is like a walk on the beach, on a warm summer day with your dog, watching all the happy people playing, swimming, running and just chilling. So much joy, so many smiles, people with happy hearts. It's like sunshine coming through a clear, clean window. Everyone has a vision and they work towards it. It is truly a breath of fresh air. The people are wonderful, kind, caring, giving and helpful. Everyone cares! WOW is the Zappos family and I am so very grateful to be a part of it. True happiness is found in giving and Zappos is about giving!

FIG V-4. This year, Zappos decided to give 6pm.com a redesign after we acquired them in 2007. Hope it really makes you shop, save and smile.

FIG V-5A. As we mentioned, people like to show affection to one another here.

FIG V-5B. But little does everyone know, it's not just people that like to do that. Ties do too.

Free Candy Inside!

(come alone, Crystal)

Some other things you'll never ... and a little (ok, sometimes a lot of) Weirdne...

Fun Facts for April 9th!

- Today is National Chinese Almond Cookie Day.

- On this date in 2005, Britain's Prince Charles married Camilla Parker Bowles.

ind a shortage of at Zappos: Fun

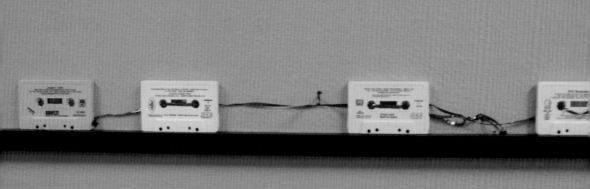

HAPPINESS IS WHEN WHAT YOU
THINK, WHAT YOU SAY AND WHAT
YOU DO ARE IN HARMONY.

THE MAN, MAHATMA GANDHI

VI.

TECHNOLOGY
PROJECT MANAGEMENT

FIG VI-1. The Technology department thought it was a good idea to build a bowling alley next to their desks. Everyone loves it, but we're not sure what the bowling ball thinks about it.

FIG VI-2. As some of you might know, Spiderpig (from *The Simpsons Movie*) likes to hang out with our Technology team when he's not hanging with Homer.

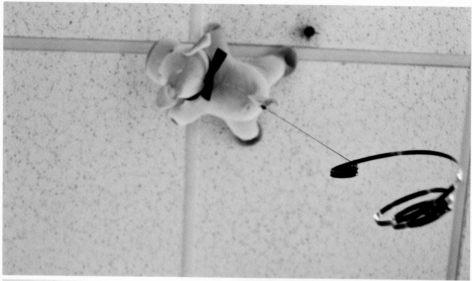

FIG VI-3. Desks to the left, bowling alley to the right. Makes complete sense, doesn't it?

FIG VI-4. A common sight when you happen to look up at Zappos. Nerf® wars, galore.

Adam G.

EMPLOYEE SINCE MARCH 12 2005

Over the last four years at Zappos, I've seen a lot. There have been great times, and there have been sad times. What makes the Zappos culture so amazing is that even during the hardest times, we've come through strong and retained a positive family spirit. People still smile in passing, people still drop everything they're doing just to open a door, people still care ... I still care.

Aki I.

EMPLOYEE SINCE JANUARY 2 2002

When I find myself in times of trouble, mother Mary comes to me,
Speaking words of wisdom, let it be.
And in my hour of darkness she is standing right in front of me,
Speaking words of wisdom, let it be.
Let it be, let it be, let it be, let it be.
Whispering words of wisdom, let it be.
And when the broken-hearted people living in the world agree,
There will be an answer, let it be.
For though they may be parted, there is still a chance that they will see,
There will be an answer, let it be.
Let it be, let it be ...
And when the night is cloudy, there is still a light that shines on me,
Shine until tomorrow, let it be.
I wake up to the sound of music, mother Mary comes to me,
Speaking words of wisdom, let it be.
Let it be, let it be ...

Alex K.

EMPLOYEE SINCE MARCH 26 2005

I'm writing this Culture Book entry right around my fourth-year anniversary at Zappos. As I look back on my time here, I think I've really seen both the company and Zappos Culture evolve and grow. When I first started, we didn't have parades or karaoke or some of the more superficial things that made it into the magazines and TV shows. Although they are part of the culture, there's much more at work here that makes the Zappos Culture special. To me, it's the mutual respect and camaraderie that has been a constant since I've been here and is at the heart of our culture. Even if Zappos were a farm out in the middle of nowhere and we plowed fields all day, it would still be a great place to work because of how we treat each other. Our work environment and our benefits will constantly be changing but the essence of what makes the Zappos culture great will probably stay the same: accepting, hard-working people who work towards the same goals with mutual respect and inspiration.

Austin K.

EMPLOYEE SINCE SEPTEMBER 15 2008

As a new employee at Zappos, I feel like I have stepped into a horror/ suspense film. I awaken every morning to walk into a strange place filled with ridiculously cheery people. I mean, seriously, people here are just TOO happy to be at work. I am still waiting to see what the plot twist is. I am told that some of the members of Development are vampires, but I don't know if that explains everything. My theory is that every employee is eventually replaced with a genetically-enhanced clone and that the original is either made to work in some underground mine or are converted into some kind of Soylent product. Only time will tell if I am correct, but I guess I will just enjoy the ride ... until I am replicated and eventually eaten.

Becky C.

EMPLOYEE SINCE SEPTEMBER 10 2007

Things I've learned during my last year at Zappos:
1. Nerf guns can cause eye abrasions.
2. Poison dart frogs aren't naturally poisonous.
3. You can be kicked out of a German beer hall for being too rowdy.
4. Russ lives next door to a pimp.
5. Fog machines do not set off smoke detectors
6. February 6th is Hug –a-Korean Day
7. Recalling a reply-all simply results in another email.
8. Hina can fit inside a Zappos box.
9. Always wear shoes while running through the office to avoid broken toes.
10. Eating too many doughnuts at one time can make you sick.
11. Three children will always beat ten engineers at paintball.
12. Chris is the creepiest person you will ever meet.
13. Turning off lights can cause an electrical hazard.
14. The smaller you are, the better you are at dodge-ball.
15. QA should be segregated at all times, due to its high infection rate.
16. It is possible to squirt Super-Glue into one's eyes by mistake.
17. Matt can rock thigh-high pleasers.

18. Hamsters eat popcorn on pianos.
19. Pascal is the name of a pricing cat.
20. When in doubt, blame John Peterson.
and lastly, working at Zappos rocks!

Bill W.

EMPLOYEE SINCE MAY 21 2007

Did you know that there are 92,349,933 mome raths that have the answer to the ultimate question of life, the universe and everything? Not really, but it's awesome that I work at a company that is willing to print its employees thoughts, no matter how silly. Here's to Zappos - showing that success doesn't have to mean being uniform! Thx!

Brhan B.

EMPLOYEE SINCE JULY 14 2008

Zappos Culture is a language unspoken but collectively understood by everyone who works at Zappos. This communication tool is recognized by all of the Zappos employees, vendors and partners. Thus, the company benefits from collecting unique talents and most importantly, is able to retain them. Understanding Zappos Culture has helped me grow both personally and professionally. I've grown to accept differences. I've made more friends and families within the seven months I have been with Zappos than I expected. I appreciate and feel lucky every day that I work at a company that I care about and vice versa.

Brian C.

EMPLOYEE SINCE MAY 1 2008

Our culture is just what the doctor ordered. We may work long hours and have stressful days, but so does everyone else in our field. What makes us different is the ability to have a full scale Nerf war with our neighboring departments and still get the job done. Company-sponsored outings have given way to employee-sponsored outings during tough times. (Paintball, anyone?) TLD is in full swing and our benefits keep getting better. We even seem to have made it through a layoff without the normal aftershocks I have seen at other companies. So, for my fellow geeks, I mangle the following quote: "Our Culture is what gives Zappos its power. It's an energy field created by all Zapponians. It surrounds us and penetrates us. It binds the company together."

Charles A.

EMPLOYEE SINCE JULY 16 2001

The Zappos Culture to me is a desire to be the best company to do business with and to work for. It's a culture of constant growth and of figuring things out.

Chris S.

EMPLOYEE SINCE JUNE 23 2008

Nerf / Japanese Hand Towels / being knighted with a toilet of chewing gum / Tra la la / people asking if everything is going okay because I haven't tweet'd in a while / Gunther / random applause / the warm fuzzy feeling from being applauded by a room full of people for just being you / thank yous / strange statues reading the newspaper / the sitz / D in a V / recover a duck fumble and you get a bonus / fog machines, strobe lights, and a well planned counter-attack / my faaaaaaaaaaace / Hamburglar Tuesday / Color Buddies / listening in addition to hearing / ninja co-workers (seriously) / "I am a Beautiful Animal..." / rabbits / Wu Chang Clan / absolutely and fantastic / Capt'n Crunch and frozen yogurt / DON'T REPLY ALL!! / Blue Steel / Thirsty Bat / haha / all the lights are too bright / Ein Prosit / penguins in July / postcards from Mexico /

.W rehpotsirhC

EMPLOYEE SINCE MAY 19 2008

.loohcS hgiH gnidnetta ot ralimis ,syaw ynam ni ,si soppaZ ta gnikroW
.elpmaxe na ylerus si siht hcihw fO .ssenmodnar htiw yllarebil desrepsretni ,erutcurtS
.adarP sraew liveD eht taht eveileb ew ,regrebsieW ekiL .efil rof tsul a evah ew ,hgoG naV
ekiL .ti gnignahc tuohtiw erutluc eht evresbo tonnac eno ,grebnesieH ekiL .detalpmetnoc
egami eht fo naht fles fo noitcelfer a erom si erutluc eht ni sees eno tahw ,hcahcsroR ekiL
.seye dnA .ssenippah ni sreveileb gib er'eW .sisab raluger a no gniyas siht tset ew ,veD nI
.tuo eye s'enoemos tup I litnu yppah eb t'ndluow I taht dias rehtom ym ,kcits prahs a htiw
gninnur elihw ,ecnO

.redro taht ni ylirassecen toN .hcaB dna ,rehcsE ,ledoG era eW

.noitcnuf nnamrekcA rieht naht ssel tahwemos hguohtla ,strap ruo fo mus eht naht erom
era eW .oicivres onis ,sotapaz se on somednev euq ol euq nua ,yenom ekam wohemos eW
sevlesruo dnif netfo os dna ,seirtne koob erutluc dne ot woh wonk t'nod eW

Crystal C.

EMPLOYEE SINCE JULY 8 2008

Interesting moments during my mornings at Zappos:

- I mentioned that it was "Hug a Korean Day 2009" on Twitter last night, and before I even reached my desk this morning I received six hugs. The first few scared me a bit because I was thrown off by it all, but the rest of the hugs weren't as "Awkward Turtle." I received seven more hugs throughout the rest of the day!
- The Finance department paraded into our Dev room yesterday morning and announced through a loudspeaker: "We are looking for ... CRYSTAL CHANG!!!!" I was the lucky victim (I mean recipient) of Finance's Random Acts of Kindness! They gave me a "Finance <3s Me" hat, a Starbucks gift card and I walked through their "Tunnel of Love." Pretty awesome.
- One weekend, there was lots of gossip on Twitter that I had suddenly become engaged (all false rumors spread by my lovely Zappos co-workers). By the time I went into work on Monday, I figured that a few people would ask me what that was all about, but I was not prepared to see a long banner hanging above my desk proclaiming "Congratulations, Crystal & _____!" (name excluded) adorned with hearts and an engagement ring. The infamous DEV-clap started up as I stared in horror. Twitter rumors + Dev = eeevil.
- I accidentally blasted music from "High School Musical" at 9 a.m. one morning when I opened up my laptop, because Brent Cromley had lent me the DVDs and I had watched it on the laptop the previous night. I couldn't manage to turn it off for a while because I was so flustered – I felt the eyes staring at me, and then everyone actually started clapping along to the beat of the music. Now I always make sure that my headphones are plugged into the laptop before opening it so that this would never ever happen again. But this doesn't mean that we never randomly hear clips from HSM songs in here though... we still get that via Brent's many HSM iPhone ringtones. :)

So what have I learned from these experiences?
1. Twitter can be very powerful. It must be used for good, not evil!
2. It's always an interesting day at Zappos, and I love it!!! *guido fist pump*

Daniel P.

EMPLOYEE SINCE JANUARY 7 2008

Now that I have worked at Zappos for a year, I can look back and barely remember what working in a company void of culture was like. I have had lots of fun times here, learned so much from my peers, and am very thankful to have such awesome people surrounding me, as they are the reason we are so "cultur-ific", or something to that tune ;)

David L.

EMPLOYEE SINCE OCTOBER 1 2007

Culture can be defined a million different ways by a billion different people. (I say a million because there could very well be conjoined twins who both share a single brain. A lot of them.) Like many others undoubtedly do, I view culture as something like a cousin of one of those talk show guests whose teen does what she wants because she has grown. Much like that teen, we are free to express the culture how we please. For example, I eat food while wearing pants. All in all, I feel the best example of what culture is to me is on page 194.

David R.

EMPLOYEE SINCE FEBRUARY 29 2008

The Zappos Culture means everyone has the ability to have personal and professional freedoms. You can be yourself at work and enjoy your career and at the same time contribute to a successful company.

Derek F.

EMPLOYEE SINCE JANUARY 8 2007

I'm not sure which day it was last week, but I remember waking up and thinking about everything that has happened in the last year. From economical and political tension, to personal events in my life that have had an impact at the way I look at the world as a whole. I can't express in mere words how grateful I am to work for a company that cares about its employees like family. Sometimes being a Systems Administrator can be a bit stressful, but I've found that working for Zappos, it never really is. Every day I wake up and look forward to taking on the challenges that lie ahead, and I am truly excited for the opportunity to learn and grow with a company that values my work. I'm not sure what else to say, except I <3 you Zappos!

Dylan B.

EMPLOYEE SINCE AUGUST 11 2008

Zappos Culture has instilled a standard in me that I feel all other businesses should work towards. A breakdown in the common suit-and-tie style of work is what I've always wanted. I feel like I can be myself and relax at work, and having that peace of mind does wonders for my productivity.

Ed L.

EMPLOYEE SINCE DECEMBER 5 2005

I started at Zappos December of 2005, just a couple of days after I moved to this city expecting a new life. At first, I didn't expect much. I said "Hi," and exchanged a few pleasantries with a few...and a few more, as each day passed. Fast-forward three years and my new life has become my Life: The person that sits in front of me is a close friend, the one behind a mentor. Zappos the company has become Zappos my family. I am very proud to be a part of something special as this.

Geoff B.

EMPLOYEE SINCE APRIL 7 2008

In so many words, Zappos employees share a common message of respect. Whether you are loud, shy, outgoing, quiet (insert your favorite adjective here), people amongst the company recognize and appreciate one another's differences. To me, that is the one thing we all have in common, respect and understanding for our fellow workers.

George T.

EMPLOYEE SINCE JANUARY 28 2008

Well, I just hit my one year anniversary at Zappos, so it got me thinking about how I got here ... In late 2007, I read my American Express credit card statement to find a mysterious charge on my account for a purchase at this place that I barely knew about called "Zappos." I thought to myself, "I think that's that shoe web site that I've been hearing about in the news lately. But I didn't buy anything there." I came home to see my wife wearing a shirt that said, "Will Work 4 Shoes." Mystery solved - or so I thought! She denied everything and opened up her vast shoe collection to prove it. I couldn't believe it. That meant my billing data was stolen! Not knowing that Zappos customer service was so excellent that I could have called them directly to settle things (and instantly have gotten a real, live human being on the line), I called American Express. Fortunately, AmEx customer service isn't that bad. They waived the charge and sent me a new card. Nonetheless, I ended up with a curiosity for the company and a not-so-positive first impression of this Zappos place.

A few weeks later, that curiosity would be piqued again. Destiny sent an e-mail! Her name was actually "Destiny!" Was it pornographic spam that slipped through GMail's spam filter? Probably - it was from "Destiny." So I skipped over it. But then the next day, Destiny e-mailed again. "Hmmm. Spammers don't usually follow up on their earlier spam," I thought.[1] I decided to open it. It wasn't spam - it was a recruiter contracted by Zappos to find software engineers looking to work in an exciting, dynamic, fast-paced environment, "where everyone can feel appreciated." I had to see the place where my credit card was fraudulently used. I wasn't expecting much. But after a phone interview, on-site interviews with the Dev team, and (especially) the tour, it became clear that this was not some shady, fly-by-night operation. This place was serious. Serious fun, too. And going places. It's a place where I can aim to do something and actually get it done without being impeded by bureaucracy. So, here I am now. And what do you know: One of the projects I'm working on is a re-write of the fraud screening software.[2]

[1] Okay, that part was embellished for dramatic effect. I actually don't recall the real name of the recruiter.
[2] Ooh! I should put this in my bio.

Hina J.

EMPLOYEE SINCE NOVEMBER 15 2008

You know what is the best part about working at Zappos, for me? The Ten Core Values we have don't just apply when we are at work. Even when I am not at work I apply them to my day-to-day life. A gesture as simple as holding a door for someone can put a smile on a stranger's face. Isn't that rewarding? Makes my day all the time. :-)

Ian M.

EMPLOYEE SINCE JULY 14 2008

I was taken in by our growing cobblery in the late 1920s, having just finished my apprenticeship in a small and remote end of this nation. I was impressed by the modern-day amenities we were afforded, things that I had only read about in the papers (the novelty of television still remains for me, these years later). However, the crash of 1929 and the subsequent Depression hit us hard. We stopped buying records for the phonograph, opting to listen to the radio instead. And, in early 1930, many of my colleagues and dear friends, excellent cobblers they all are, were forced to move on to the bread lines. In spite of the hard times, we managed to adhere rather strictly to our values. I believe that it is because of these values that scarcely an ill word was spoken of our cobblery. I, for one, am convinced that it is these values that make us the best darn cobblery in town. You bank on us being here through these trying times, repairing soles for many years to come.

Jamie W.

EMPLOYEE SINCE JULY 9 2007

The best part about working at Zappos is being surrounded by people who love to have fun and work hard! Whether we're working together on a project or shooting each other with nerf guns, we're a team. I always look forward to coming into work each day!

Jeff N.

EMPLOYEE SINCE SEPTEMBER 22 2008

I have been at Zappos for about 4 months now and it has been quite impressive. It is great to feel as if I work for a company that practices what it preaches. Zappos is one of the only companies I have seen that values its customers the way we all want to be valued. It is refreshing to be a part of something that challenges the norm of "customers as numbers", and sees them as humans instead.

Jen K.

EMPLOYEE SINCE NOVEMBER 20 2006

The Zappos Culture is about having fun, being comfortable in your work environment, and using your imagination. We have departmental outings to play paintball. Parades come through the office frequently, with people throwing candy and trinkets. Peoples' desks are decorated with zany toys, posters, and "swag." I've worked at Zappos for over two years. You'd think the shine would have worn off for me by now, but my thoughts and feelings about the company culture are about the same as they were in my first week of being a Zapponian.

Jennifer G.

EMPLOYEE SINCE JANUARY 29 2007

The culture at Zappos is inclusive of everything and anything. We are one big family that works hard & plays hard. It's a place where you can truly feel comfortable being yourself and you're excited to come to work every day because you feel like you're part of something much bigger. Thanks.

Jeremy A.

EMPLOYEE SINCE MAY 27 2008

Pancakes for breakfast in accounting, pirates in the R-Desk department, a nerf- gun territory war in DEV – a day at Zappos is always like a "choose-your-own- adventure" book, where you always have to decide the fate of your day. And you are the one that decides your fate, and enhances the culture at Zappos.

Jessica M.

EMPLOYEE SINCE JULY 10 2000

Whether you knowingly step inside Zappos Culture or have it painted on just by proximity, the unspoken rules of engagement manifest in all areas of one's life, as does a sense of hope and promise with what seems impossible. Zappos Culture arises from this optimistic attitude as a different type of education. It's not pronounced or implied, rather, it's infectious and irresistible, and Zappos has cultivated it to its fullness. Zappos Culture will infect you like a pop song ... you can't keep from humming and there's a little bounce in your step.

John F.

EMPLOYEE SINCE JULY 23 2007

Zappos Culture means being able to work for a great company while being able to be around close friends. How does this happen? Zappos enables and encourages its employees to use both company time and personal time to deepen their relationships with each other. What does Zappos, as a company, get in return? A very devoted, happy group of employees who can work across departments and through barriers to get the job done right – while keeping the friendly and fun culture alive. It is definitely a win/win for everyone.

John N.

EMPLOYEE SINCE JULY 30 2007

Well, Zappos as a company is an extension of your family – a real close family. Everyone here generally cares about you and your life outside of work. We are a close-knit company whose employees take care of each other. Our culture is out of this world and really should be looked at by other companies; we almost feel that we are all owners of this company.

We are allowed to express ourselves individually and really are allowed to just be ourselves. Zappos has a belief that if it takes care of the workers/employees, we will take care of the business. It's so true; each and every one of us does not view our job as just a "job," we view it as being part of something bigger then we can imagine. I love it here and hope I will be an old man when I leave.

John P.

EMPLOYEE SINCE JULY 29 2008

Culture ... everybody asks, "What does it mean?" Really, it is just a word. It doesn't mean anything without the actions behind it. Zappos Culture is about action, about success, and about people helping each other. It's intrinsic in all of us to be this way, given the correct environment. That is part of why our culture is such a success. So the things to remember are, "Say Hi," go hang out, and above all, always think, "How would I feel if I was in their shoes?"

Justin C.

EMPLOYEE SINCE SEPTEMBER 24 2007

It's okay to be you. It's okay to have a thought and express it. It's okay to be part of the team. It's okay to dress the way you like, and no one judges you for it. It's okay to have forward thinking. It's okay to be you.

Kevin C.

EMPLOYEE SINCE JANUARY 7 2008

I joined Zappos over a year ago and while being interviewed for the position, folks kept telling me how important Zappos Culture was to the company. I came on board thinking, "I have to check this culture thing out more closely." Being perfectly candid, I would not have been surprised if I had discovered over time that there was an element of spin with the whole company culture approach, as many companies talk it up, but do not consistently walk it – if you get what I mean.

Twelve months in, and I find myself pleasantly surprised – in fact, delighted – as Zappos Culture is very much alive, kicking and it's the real deal. Working for Zappos is like being part of a big extended family. It is a unique collective community that is oozing with creativity, innovation and it is a refreshingly different company to work for. I have worked for several good companies, and a couple that were well, shall we say, not so good. Zappos is out there on its own as the only fantastic one!

Kris O.

EMPLOYEE SINCE JANUARY 1 2005

I don't fit in, I never have. I don't dress the same as everyone else. I don't speak the same way as everyone else. Yet, somehow it works – because no one else around here fits in. People talk about culture fit all the time. It's not about being the same person as someone else to fit in. At Zappos, you need to stand out, not fit in.

Lee M.

EMPLOYEE SINCE MAY 7 2007

Zappos Culture is working hard and playing more. It's encouragement to run a marathon for the first time. It's making friends with someone you'd never thought would talk to you. It's about getting comfortable about being out of the comfort zone. Oh! And "Go Dodgers!" Congratulations on winning the 2009 World Series!

Lynn W.

EMPLOYEE SINCE JUNE 23 2008

What does the Zappos Culture mean to me? It means freedom. Freedom to be who I am. Freedom to try new things. Freedom to fail and learn from those failures. Freedom to succeed and learn from those successes. Freedom to care about this company and those who work there. Freedom to be the best I can be. I started with Zappos about seven months ago. I can't tell you how much of a gift it is to work for a company that gives its people the ability to be free. It's such a gift that I am still getting used to it and learning to trust it. Thank you, Zappos (and Tony), for being who and what you are and for giving us the freedom to be who and what we are.

Mallory J.

EMPLOYEE SINCE NOVEMBER 12 2007

Working at Zappos has been the best thing to happen to me in a long time. I thought I loved my job at the construction place where I worked before; Zappos tops it. I started in CLT and now I am an IT dispatcher and I love my job. I don't wake up every day dreading coming to work and to me that means the world. The environment and the people are amazing, and I wouldn't want to work for anybody else. Thank you, Zappos, for giving me a job I truly enjoy!

Mark M.

EMPLOYEE SINCE OCTOBER 6 2008

On my second interview, five different people told me that I SHOULDN'T have worn a tie.
I ate 11 Krispy Kremes in 20 minutes for a contest one day and immediately got diabetes. I
sang Madonna's "Borderline" at karaoke in the lunchroom. The Fortune magazine article
angered me … How are we not #1? :) It's a different, friendlier, happier world here at
Zappos and I'm proud to be a part of it.

Mary Ann C.

EMPLOYEE SINCE NOVEMBER 12 2007

Zappos Culture is a culture that should not be dictated by the department you work in.
With over 1,000 employees between Las Vegas and Sheperdsville, Zappos should have a
consistent "feel" to it, no matter whom you deal with internally or externally. At its core,
it is having respect and the courtesy to listen to whomever you are dealing with. It means
not taking for granted the ability to create fun and weirdness … but not at the expense
of others. The goal is inclusiveness versus exclusionism, an end to apathy, realizing your
potential, encouraging others' successes, using resources efficiently …"Put a little Zappos
in Your Day," extend it out to your daily routine and make the world a better place!:)

Matthew G.

EMPLOYEE SINCE OCTOBER 30 2007

Zappos Culture, to me, is what keeps my MTV-Generation brain happy, with just enough
change to keep me out of the unenviable "rut of habit." Thanks to the Zappos Culture, I
look forward to coming to work each day… and each day is different … and I get to share
my work day with like-minded folks!

Matthew R.

EMPLOYEE SINCE APRIL 10 2006

Zappos is the kind of place where a group of co-workers might take a few minutes out of
a day to watch the YouTube hit, "Hamster on a Piano." The kind of place where you're as
likely to hear "Boogie Woogie Hedgehog" as you would hear people talking to vendors on

the phone. The kind of place where co-workers hang out together after work, for bowling, drinks, or whatever. I never expected to have such a job merely months after graduating from college, and am very grateful to work with the people I work with. I really wish I had remembered to write this sooner – people always write the most wonderful entries, and mine, well, they're not as creative as I'd wish them to be. I've also vowed not to do the whole "I'm a programmer, so here's my essay in Perl or Java" that I'm sure someone will do. Maybe next year I'll remember in time to write a nice haiku or something. A great place to work ... yeah, I'd need to work on that. Next year! I'm setting a goal! Culture poem.

Miki C.

EMPLOYEE SINCE MARCH 6 2006

I've been part of the Zappos family for three years now, and it has been a fun and meaningful three years. I look forward to coming into work each day. As the company changes and grows, the team and family spirit grows with it. It takes the whole team working together to keep our culture alive, and I look forward to the coming years and hope we continue to grow as a family and create a positive experience for our employees and customers.

Nick V.

EMPLOYEE SINCE OCTOBER 6 2003

Driving forward ... without crashing

Pawel S.

EMPLOYEE SINCE JANUARY 2 2007

I'll be honest and say that I don't like writing these things. Squeezing down a year of Zappos life into a few lines is pretty hard. This past year wasn't all roses and hamsters on pianos (eating popcorn) but we held together and made it through some tough times. That being said, working here is awesome. I've been challenged more than at any other job I've held, and I've made some really good friends here over the years. I still look forward to heading in to work each and every day – and that's saying something.

P.S. As I write this, it's February 6th – Hug-a-Korean Day. Everyone put it in your calendars for next year and surprise Crystal.

Rachel M.

EMPLOYEE SINCE JANUARY 7 2008

I've been at Zappos for just over a year now, and I can honestly say I have never worked for a better company. It is always a pleasure to come to work, each and every day. It's been a rough year here at Zappos, and if it wasn't for the family atmosphere and strong culture base here, I'm not sure if we would have survived it. Previous to Zappos, I worked for a company that didn't care about their employees, and it was visible at every level of the company. To go from there to Zappos was quite a culture shock. To actually be at a company where the employees (at every level) mean something significant to the well-being of the company ... it's something I really didn't think existed. Working here has not only taught me things about how a company can be run and succeed, but what I want from a company I work for. Thank you everyone here for the opportunity to become something I didn't know I could become.

Ray M.

EMPLOYEE SINCE APRIL 16 2007

During good times and bad, the employees at Zappos remain dedicated to the idea of furthering the company and the family-like environment. I feel very privileged to work at a company that respects its own employees even in the times of layoffs. Thank you, everyone for adding so much good to the culture!

Robin C.

EMPLOYEE SINCE JULY 23 2007

Zappos is the first job I have ever had where on my days off, I actually miss coming to work and hanging out with my co-workers. Our culture is unique in that it encourages creativity and individuality. Because of that, I feel Zappos is awesomely fantastic! Best company EVER!

Russell S.

EMPLOYEE SINCE APRIL 24 2006

One of Zappos' core values is "Embrace and Drive Change" and 2008 was a year of change for the nation, Zappos, and myself as well. I'm originally from Boise, where I lived for

38 years before moving to Las Vegas to work for Zappos. Boise is a quiet place without much in the way of criminal activity. Recently, a pimp moved down the street from where I live in Vegas. Although not all change is good, such as having a pimp move two doors down from where one lives, embracing and driving change is necessary for growth. I look forward to being a part of Zappos' future – hopefully not of the pimp neighbor variety.

Ryan A.

EMPLOYEE SINCE OCTOBER 15 2007

Zappos is like a Fortune 500 company in kindergarten. People take a professional approach to their jobs, but with the attitude that their jobs are as great as recess and coloring. I really can't imagine working anywhere else. It'd feel too much like "work," and I don't think I'd get as much accomplished. And I like playing with all my classmates.

Ryan Q.

EMPLOYEE SINCE SEPTEMBER 2 2008

When I interviewed for my position here, I asked all of my interviewers the same two-part question: "Do you love your job? What was it about your last job (before Zappos) that really gives you perspective today?"

Here will be my answer to those questions: "Yes I do love my job. At my last job I was afraid to be anything; right, wrong, smarter, dumber, etc. At Zappos, being yourself is the best thing you can do"

Shannon E.

EMPLOYEE SINCE JUNE 25 2008

Culture is the underlying definition of any situation in any scenario. Culture defines the feel, the mood and the perception of the scene. The culture at Zappos, to me, means working with my best friends. The environment lets us share our lives and learn to understand each other's strengths and weaknesses and learn to love them. Culture at Zappos means fairness and openness, if someone has an opinion or a concern, they are allowed to express that thought to an open and understanding audience. Culture at Zappos means having fun and laughing, pulling the best from each other and becoming a family.

Sheldon S.

EMPLOYEE SINCE APRIL 30 2007

cul . ture [kuhl-cher] noun, verb, -tured, -turing. 4. Development or improvement of the mind by education or training. 5. The behaviors and beliefs characteristic of a particular social, ethnic, or age group: the youth culture; the drug culture. Things I like about Zappos Culture: a dedicated group working together towards common goals, people staying upbeat and positive even when things are not going well, feeling good about going to work in the morning, it's easier to overcome setbacks while learning from mistakes, having fun with co-workers, growing and improving our skills individually and as a team, being able to dress casually.

Sotheavy O.

EMPLOYEE SINCE OCTOBER 22 2007

We've had a tough year in some regards. The economy plummeted and people lost jobs and homes. Though there was some shifting within the company, the core culture held strong. While there may have been changes to company-wide infrastructure or just within some departments, it seems as if everyone has adjusted quickly and we all still manage to have fun. My job keeps me where I am – not because of the income, but because I truly enjoy being here every day.

Stacey A.

EMPLOYEE SINCE NOVEMBER 1 2004

"All cultures are inherently predisposed to change and, at the same time, to resist change. There are dynamic processes operating that encourage the acceptance of new ideas and things while there are others that encourage changeless stability."... I've been with Zappos for four years and seen many changes. Some good, some bad, but culture is what comes out of it – not what we force it to be.

Suchi Y.

EMPLOYEE SINCE FEBRUARY 18 2008

Zappos hasn't stopped surprising me. In my first year at Zappos, I thought this might be a honeymoon period, but I am on my second year and I must admit my enthusiasm hasn't faded a bit. For the first time, I have actually seen a company do what it says – such as the company's Ten Core Values being applied in principle on a day-to-day basis. I strongly believe that that Zappos values its employees as much as it values its customers, and provides not just service but only the BEST service. I have no doubt I work for one of the best companies, even if it wasn't ranked as one :)

Susan A.

EMPLOYEE SINCE JULY 9 2007

To me, Zappos Culture is being excited to come to work to see everyone's smiling face. Every day there is something new to be a part of. It is amazing to work with people who are enthusiastic about what they are doing and what they can contribute.

Photo
Challenge
2008-2009

SOME PURSUE HAPPINESS,
OTHERS CREATE IT.

ANOTHER ONE OF THE
MANY WISE ANONYMOUS
PEOPLE OUT THERE

VII.

KENTUCKY WAREHOUSE

FIG VII-1. On Gear Day, Zapponians get creative, loading as much paraphernalia as they can at one time. Looks like someone got a little happy with temp-tattoos this year.

Aaron O.

EMPLOYEE SINCE NOVEMBER 30 2007

To me, Zappos Culture means "A tradition that is carried on through the foundation of our economy and the expression of free will and the right to be ourselves and stay true to what we feel ... To do what we may feel is right and to only benefit the others that stay true to the culture that is created through a wonderful place." Some may read this and think that is copyrighted or plagiarized but this is truly how I feel and believe what culture is and what it stands for.

Abby B.

EMPLOYEE SINCE SEPTEMBER 24 2007

Zappos is, by far, one of the best places where I have ever had the privilege of working. It's the one place where you can go in on any given day and people are actually happy to be there. This really struck me when I first started working here over a year ago. I was amazed to see all the smiling faces as I walked through the warehouse. This made the job for me. Smiles are contagious and even if you are having what seems like the worst day ever, there will always be someone there for you with a smile. A smile is simple but it never fails. Still today, during the hardships of our current economy, you will find that when you take a walk anywhere at Zappos, you are bound to see more than a few smiling faces. Keep on smiling!!

Alex M.

EMPLOYEE SINCE JANUARY 7 2008

At Zappos, we are often reminded that our Zappos Culture is not just a sterile list of guidelines, but collectively something very tangible that can be applied to both our personal and professional endeavors. To me, our Zappos Culture is what sets Zappos apart from traditional Corporate America – a place that is often too stifling to allow people to behave like individuals. In fact, I will say that the amount of personal freedom that we are allowed at Zappos is pretty remarkable, and all too easy to take for granted. I do not know of many other jobs where I can write e-mails entirely in Snoop Doggy Dogg speak, pelt my co-workers with peanuts, have impromptu salsa dancing lessons, or just generally goof around and not earn myself a pink slip in the process ... or at least, a stern reprimand. To me, the freedom to just be ourselves is the first and most important perk of the job. And the free insurance is nice as well! But with the good comes the bad. We are encouraged to build and maintain a family spirit, which brings us all closer together but also makes the losses more painful. We are, in the end, a business, and difficult decisions have to be

FIG VII-2. Hat Day in Kentucky, January 21, 2009. It gets pretty cold over here, so next time it's cold where you live, wear a hat and call it Hat Day in your town too.

FIG VII-3. Easter egg hunts tend to bring out different sides of Zapponians...in this case, the sides are Hoarder, Hungry and Happy.

made, but there is a bit of comfort in knowing that a good effort was made by the company to take care of those who no longer work with us. In all, it has been an interesting time working for Zappos. I have learned the value of that old "rolling with the punches" adage. I have made some valuable new friendships, but most of all, I have found a place to work where I can feel comfortable in my own skin. A company can only be as strong as its people, and I do have to say, I love the people here.

Alma H.

EMPLOYEE SINCE DECEMBER 6 2005

I like the people I work with, and the benefits here are great. This is an awesome place for young people to work because of the opportunity for advancement. This is the only place that I have worked that makes you feel like part of a family. Zappos Rocks!

Amanda E.

EMPLOYEE SINCE DECEMBER 6 2005

I am unfortunate enough to live far away from my family and I miss them terribly. When I come to work, I am reminded that I have a second family here at Zappos. I love my family here in the photography department and while I will always miss my home, I know that they will all be here for me if I ever need anything.

Amber L.

EMPLOYEE SINCE DECEMBER 6 2005

Zappos has been a place that I have called home for five years now. I consider everyone I work with a family member. This company has given back just as much as I have put in for them and I could not say that for any other company I have worked for. Since I have started here, I have grown personally and professionally, and I continue to grow every day. The environment here is unbelievable and everyone here is fantastic!

Amy M.

EMPLOYEE SINCE JUNE 2 2008

So after being laid off from another retail company (I won't mention its name), I relocated here 3,000 miles away in Kentucky to continue my career as a photographer. The

FIG VII-4. Another example of Core Value #8, Do More with Less. On Gear Day, sometimes it's better to plop into an everyday mail box. Who knew butt-boxing would be so comfortable?

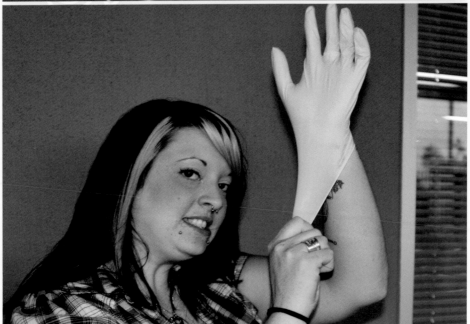

FIG VII-5. As questionable as this looks, don't fret. She was just putting on a glove to do some temp-tattooing on Bald Blue and Tattooed Day. At least that's what she *said*.

transition was very easy, thanks to my fellow workers who welcomed me in and went out of their way to assist me, helping me find an apartment, giving me directions to help me find my way around the area, even helping me unload the moving truck. I think it truly IS the people that make Zappos what it is.

Andi L.

EMPLOYEE SINCE MAY 8 2007

Time flies when you're having fun. I guess that's why I am quickly approaching my two-year anniversary at Zappos and it feels like I just started. I have never been able to fit in anywhere as quickly and as easily as I have here. The Zappos Culture really is a family. Everyone is there for you regardless of your situation. You could be celebrating the beginning of a new little one into your family, or morning the loss of a loved one. No matter what situation you are in, your friends and family at work support you in any and every way they can. This was proven to me this year when I almost lost my dog, who is very much my best friend. A few of my co-workers gave me money out of their own pockets. I couldn't believe it, and it truly touched my heart. They saved his life. :) We are blessed to be a part of a company with such strong values. Zappos provides our team with the real-life experiences that make us better people. I've grown, not only as an individual, but also as part of a team. The people I work with inspire me every day to be the best person I can be, at work and at home. Thank you to our CEO, CFO and all of the other uppers who started this team and continue to work so hard in preserving our Ten Core Values and team spirit, thus making Zappos one of the best places to work.

Andi P.

EMPLOYEE SINCE FEBRUARY 12 2007

The best way to sum up how I feel about Zappos is pride. I am so proud that our company is in the top 25 of the best places to work in Kentucky and the top 25 of the best places to work in the nation. I am so proud that the HR team works so hard to drive the culture at the FC in Kentucky and does such a great job. I am so proud that our employees get involved in the community, whether they are jumping in the Ohio River in February to support Special Olympics, or bowling to raise money for Big Brothers/Big Sisters or bed-racing during the Kentucky Derby Festival or walking to raise awareness for cancer or making sure local children have clothes and toys for the holidays. I am so proud that when I am out and meet new people and tell them that I work at Zappos, they rave about how much they love us. I am so proud of Zappos.

Angela T.

EMPLOYEE SINCE JUNE 4 2005

Working at Zappos has been an incredible learning experience. I love working for a company that lets all of us grow along with it. No one gets left behind when we try new things, get new technologies, make new procedures or even start new departments. We are always given the first shot at new opportunities and encouraged to expand our horizons so that we may reap the benefits of all that we see here every day. I look forward to continuing my education here, both for my career and my personal endeavors. Learning as much as possible and sharing that knowledge with the next person has been very fulfilling for me the past four years. Thank you, Zappos, for the amazing benefits, the fun, the friends and for keeping food on my plate in these hard times!

Angie H.

EMPLOYEE SINCE FEBRUARY 1 2005

I have been at Zappos for four years now and I have loved every minute of it. I look forward to coming to work every day. The people that I work with are great and the Zappos environment is like none I have ever worked in before. Absolutely, by far, the best place I have ever worked!

Anitra E.

EMPLOYEE SINCE MARCH 2 2004

Way back when I was on the search for a job, a friend told me about Zappos. I don't like to commute far from home, but after I started, I was hooked. We have the best discount known to women. What other job has a cheer contest, Ken-duck-y derby and the best holiday parties ever! Oh did I mention my KIVA bot "Ms. B-Haven?" She works just as hard as her owner. I think it's great when you can pick up the phone and start talking with the LV office. I have not found this kind of a bond anywhere. THANKS ZAPPOS!

Annette S.

EMPLOYEE SINCE MAY 15 2006

Diversity and a team-oriented company, WOW! What a great place to work, Happiness and joy and desire to be here. Friendships and the opportunity to expand your horizons.

Annie R.

EMPLOYEE SINCE JUNE 26 2007

Zappos is great! Thanks for making my grocery bill smaller!!

Anonymous.

Zappos is a wonderful place to work. Everyone here is joyful, lovable, caring. Zappos Culture means a lot because it's great to see how other team members feel about their culture.

Anonymous.

It is a very unique and unusual way of handling the day-to-day business. Takes you back to the time when the customer is always right. Not like the attitude that "when in doubt, say we're out," like most businesses today.

Anonymous.

I haven't blocked out the past. I wouldn't trade the person I am, or what I've done – or the people I've known – for anything. So I do think about it. And at times it's a rather mellow trip to lay back and remember.

Anonymous.

The culture of Zappos is an excellent way to get the job done and have fun while doing it. Just a little bit of fun during the workday does not take much time, but makes the job a lot more enjoyable. Taking some time to do creative activities with your co-workers is good for the employees and the company. In no way is it wasting time, because it puts employees in a better mood and helps them work better together. So taking time to have fun actually is more efficient for the company. This is what makes our culture so awesome.

Anonymous.

Zappos Culture is a place where I can be myself in a supporting environment that promotes personal and professional growth.

Anonymous.

They make it a nice place to work. They have good benefits.

Anonymous.

Zappos is a great place to work...

Anonymous.

Zappos Culture is everything that goes on at Zappos ... the events, jobs, people, etc.

Anonymous.

Zappos Culture means keeping work interesting. You come to work never knowing what is in store for you that particular day. Zappos rocks, baby.

Anonymous.

Zappos is a great place to work ... everybody gets along and really cares about what they do. Being here at Zappos you can have a lot of fun and be yourself ... it's a great place to grow and make friends. ZAPPOS IS AWESOME!!!

Anonymous.

Zappos will teach you that there is more to life than money. Zappos sets goals for you. You will hit them. All of them. Then you should feel good about hitting them. Because that is more important than anything, right?

April S.

EMPLOYEE SINCE NOVEMBER 26 2007

Zappos Culture to me is all about family. I come to work every day knowing that I will have a blast. My co-workers are hilarious ... even when they don't mean to be! I love my job!!!

Ashley P.

EMPLOYEE SINCE MARCH 24 2008

To me, Zappos Culture is about living the Ten Core Values in everything you do ... not only in your work, but also in your personal life and in the way that you interact with everyone you meet.

Ben V.

EMPLOYEE SINCE JUNE 21 2006

Zappos Culture is the mojo of the company. How many people can honestly say that they have fun at work? Not many that I know. What is the culture made of? The people. Those I have met since I started fully embrace the ideas and essence of Zappos. These people make it a point to make sure their coworkers are having fun and actually like coming to work. This gesture spreads from the veterans to the newbies and evolves to make sure that the culture is just as strong through our growth over the years.

Benjamin K.

EMPLOYEE SINCE MARCH 16 2007

It means a fun place to work where the company actually cares about its employees and treats them like family. You have to love the benefits: free food and drinks and a fun atmosphere that makes you enjoy the job here.

Betsy D.

EMPLOYEE SINCE AUGUST 4 2008

When I came home from working at my last job, complaining and upset because I didn't think I could go on there one more day, my husband surprised me with a job posting he found. It was for this company I had never heard of before. It was some online shoe store called Zappos. My first reaction was "I don't know. An online shoe company?" But as I started looking at the job description, I thought, "I could do that." So I looked up the company online. I began reading about the history and the Ten Core Values, but it wasn't until I began reading the blogs that I thought to myself that I had to get a job at this company. From that point on, getting a job at Zappos became my only priority. Finally, after several phone calls and meetings, I became a Zapponian. I have looked forward to work every single day that I have been here. Even the crazy stressful days are better then any day I have ever had at any of my other jobs. The constant changes keep every day interesting. I have finally found a job where I feel like I can be myself.

Brian P.

EMPLOYEE SINCE JULY 15 2008

What does Zappos Culture mean to me? Well where to start. I guess the only way to explain it is by telling you about my last job. Every day I would arrive to work an hour early and sit in the car staring at that grey steel door, stomach churning, in a cold sweat and white knuckles gripped and twisting on the steering wheel, knowing I had to go in there again. I never told a soul how I felt. People would ask me where I worked and what I did, and then say "Oh, wow, that sounds nice." I would just smile, lie and say "Yeah." Not even my family knew how I honestly felt and I hope no one ever has to know how it feels to be trapped. You can't leave or quit; you have bills to pay. You put applications in everywhere; call and e-mail job listings, but never hear a word. For five years I worked there, and for the first three, I just kept thinking, "You'll find something else, someone will call, you'll be okay!" Then for the last two years, I would think "Hey how long can you live, you don't take care of yourself you smoke like a freight train, an end won't be long." I'd hope anyways. Then my family would come home and tell me how they loved their jobs, how great it was to work at Zappos. And I would think to myself "SHUT UP!" So I thought "Maybe, just maybe." So one day I filled out an application, got my manager's phone number and e-mail and proceeded to pester the HELL out of her. The day came ... the phone rang and the person on the other end asked, "When can you start?" I replied "NOW." So for me there was a happy ending or beginning. Now when someone asks me where I work, I immediately say, "Zappos, and I LOVE my job!" I've heard and seen people around here point at me and say "You know, the one with that silly grin on his face all the time," and I think "If you only knew, you'd have a silly grin on your face too." I still get to work an hour early and sit and stare at that door but now I'm happy and very proud to say "I WORK AT ZAPPOS". I want to say to everyone I work with and especially Laura, Thank you! I love you all and yes, even you, Harley Brian P.

Brigid B.

EMPLOYEE SINCE JULY 17 2007

The culture at Zappos is, bar none, the best I have ever experienced. There is a certain feeling I get when I am here that cannot be summed up in a few sentences. I enjoy what

I do, and I enjoy all of the people I have the pleasure of doing it with. I would tell all my friends and family to work here, and I feel so very fortunate to have the opportunity to work for – and with – the team I am on.

Bryan P.

EMPLOYEE SINCE AUGUST 12 2007

I worked a lot of jobs in my day, around 20, give or take. I have to say this is by far the best job I have ever had. They treat you like family here, the benefits are great and the parties are awesome. You can be yourself around here and nobody judges. Sure, jobs have their rough edges but what job doesn't? At this job, the good outweighs the bad.

Burba.

EMPLOYEE SINCE JUNE 26 2007

Zappos rocks my socks off while my shoes are still on. You may ask how this is possible but some questions are best left unanswered =D

Byron S.

EMPLOYEE SINCE JUNE 20 2005

After being with Zappos for the past three plus years, I have had the pleasure of experiencing the existing culture and watching the creation and growth of our core values as the company has grown. As many companies grow, they quickly forget the building blocks that made them successful to begin with. I take great pride in the fact that, despite our rapid growth, we have stayed true to our culture and values. We not only have maintained our culture, we are continually looking for opportunities to grow and promote it internally and externally. Our culture is unique in the fact that it is not set in stone and is constantly changing and adapting. We have core values that are the building blocks of our culture but are encouraged to continually build the culture. When looking at new ideas, ventures, or areas of opportunity within our culture, Zappos is very different in the fact that instead of questioning "Why?" we ask "Why not?". Zappos is the last job that I want to have. This is not due to pay or benefits, but due to the company culture and the way the company conducts itself from top to bottom. Zappos is the only company that I have worked for which treats its employees with respect and actually listens to their ideas. I have worked for several organizations in which at the end of the day I felt as if I was a number no matter what the contributions I made. At Zappos I can honestly say that I feel as if I am an individual.

Cameron T.

EMPLOYEE SINCE OCTOBER 24 2006

As I head from Indiana to Kentucky, across the bridge, down I65 South to exit 116, I have the time to reflect about my day. What will I be photographing? Will I have a shirt buddy? What will be the question of the day? Soup or salad? What will Tony twitter today? I realize that everyday is a new adventure and as I pull into the parking lot of Zappos, I say a little prayer of thanks to Zappos and to Tony. I am so blessed to have this job and to be working for such an awesome company.

Carla B.

EMPLOYEE SINCE MARCH 2 2006

Zappos means family and friends. I love working here.

Cheryl S.

EMPLOYEE SINCE MAY 1 2008

Zappos Culture to me is a way to make Zappos unlike any other warehouse. It also helps create a good environment for the employees.

Christina Y.

EMPLOYEE SINCE JUNE 17 2006

Zappos Culture is Culture to the EXTREME. So take the act of developing the intellectual and moral faculties, especially by education, expert care and training; enlightenment and excellence of taste acquired by intellectual and aesthetic training, and times that by 1000. Thanks, Zappos. You still rule when it comes to working!

Craig A.

EMPLOYEE SINCE SEPTEMBER 12 2005

The Zappos Culture is unique and special. I had a hard time coming up with something new to say that I hadn't said in previous editions of this unusual compilation of comments by the people in our Zappos family. The new thought I'd like to add by way of comment this year is sort of an echo of what Tony says. The culture is not determined by him or by other leaders in the company. Everyone in the company determines the Zappos Culture. This means we all take a part in it and we all own it. That's not only pretty cool, but it's incredibly powerful. Kind of like a Wiki-culture. This has created and nurtured an environment that is welcoming to everyone. If you look at me, I wouldn't be what you would think of someone that would be part of a hip, cool, Internet Company. I'm not cool or hip, never have been. However, I'm accepted, loved and welcomed just like those who are. :) Being in a great place where I love to spend my time is the by-product of our culture. I think our people our more motivated to do well and contribute in a positive way because of our culture. This makes us better for ourselves, better for the company and better for our customers.

Dan C.

EMPLOYEE SINCE JULY 21 2005

Zappos Culture took on a whole new meaning for me in 2008. With all of the events that took place during the year, the sense of family took on a deeper meaning. I realized that I am a part of something bigger than myself, and yet melded so seamlessly into it that my minor actions affect the entire makeup.   It started when one of our own decided to move on. Having been here for almost four years, it didn't surprise me that someone's life had taken a different direction. What made it difficult was that it was my supervisor and my realization that it was someone that had been here before me. After that happened, I felt that the number of people I could rely on to set an example became that much smaller. At most companies, the business model has been established for years, there is a structure to everything and all you have to do is follow the leader. Here at Zappos, the book was written as it happened and it took the absence of one of the authors for me to realize that I had been writing along with them the entire time. The second event took place when I was promoted to supervisor. It was a role that I had wanted since the first day I walked through the doors and my hard work had finally come to fruition. Suddenly the responsibility of leading a group rested on my shoulders and it was one that I didn't take lightly. Zappos gives its leaders unlimited opportunities to help spread the Ten Core Values and I was determined to do my part so that the photo department could live up to its full potential. Fully aware that I now had influence over the direction the department was headed, I set to the task of helping others feel that they were a part of something bigger. The final events that brought the year full circle were the layoffs that occurred and the death of Max M. While the first two events could have been anticipated, the two that followed were strictly reactionary. For me, the most difficult part in each situation was putting myself in everyone else's position. Layoffs are always going to occur in business and death is a part of life, but to have both occur in such a tight family and in such close proximity to one another was something I really struggled with, particularly as a supervisor, because others looked to me for leadership, explanation, an ear to listen and a shoulder to cry on. Over the course of a year, I have discovered that somehow I have become the sharp end of the stick. What once was me looking to others for guidance has become others looking to me in similar fashion. I am fully aware of this and I look to my future here at Zappos with a lot of nervous anticipation. Nervous because what once was the responsibility of others now rests on my shoulders, nervous because there are 70+ sets of eyes watching me embody the Zappos Culture, and nervous because I want to set the best example I can for those that follow.

Darrell B.

EMPLOYEE SINCE OCTOBER 31 2007

It is a great place to work, especially with the recession. This job has a great pay wage and spectacular benefits.

David G.

EMPLOYEE SINCE SEPTEMBER 10 2007

Culture is something that I was never concerned about before I was allowed to join the crew here at Zappos. All other places that I have had the chance to work for never even mentioned culture. That alone makes Zappos' culture unique. What this company does for the people who work here is almost unthinkable. I tell people all the time that I couldn't imagine working for a better company. Nothing compares to the environment of this place and how we go about doing out business. Change is always inevitable, but as long as Zappos stays true to its core values, it will stay a special company.

Debbie A.

EMPLOYEE SINCE APRIL 22 2008

Zappos Culture, to me, means you can be yourself. The culture also allows you to meet many different people, like the wonderful crew in photo. You all rock!

Debbie N.

EMPLOYEE SINCE SEPTEMBER 22 2008

The culture of Zappos treats employees in a very positive way and that makes happy employees.

Dennis.

EMPLOYEE SINCE APRIL 5 2004

The culture at Zappos gives me the confidence to do what needs to be done. In most instances, I don't have to ask permission to do the right thing. I can act in the essence of "WOW!" At the same time, we have not "settled" for things. As we continue to grow, we are empowered to challenge things that don't make sense and improve them. The culture also creates a fun working environment. Zappos is not like any other company. We promise the customers the best service available and we follow through on it. Zappos promises us the best place to work and does a great job on delivering on that. Go, Cards!!

Derek H.

EMPLOYEE SINCE AUGUST 11 2008

Zappos is an energetic, fun and diverse workplace.

Derek L.

EMPLOYEE SINCE MARCH 12 2008

Being able to have a little bit of fun while I work is what Zappos Culture means to me. I've never had a job that not only focuses on the actual work but also the aspect of having a good time while I'm doing so. It definitely makes the work day not as monotonous.

Diana R.

EMPLOYEE SINCE OCTOBER 6 2004

Zappos thrives to maintain its core values. While many companies are struggling due to the economy, Zappos has taken precautions so it will not be one of those struggling companies. It has done this while maintaining all the special benefits (free health insurance, lunch, vending and that awesome Christmas party). I feel very fortunate to be a part of the Zappos family.

Donna W.

EMPLOYEE SINCE AUGUST 25 2008

This is the best job I have ever had. Everyone here is like family. If there is a way to WOW the work force as we do our customers, I would tell them to just come to work here and you can't help but to be WOWed. LOVE IT!!!

EB.

EMPLOYEE SINCE JUNE 6 2007

To me Zappos is one in a million!!!!!! The people, the culture, the excitement... Every day is something new. I love my job and I love my team members. I have been at Zappos for about a year and a half, and they have yet to let me down. This place has become a big part of my life; working here has really taught me a lot about myself and who I want to be in the near future. I HEART ZAPPOS LIKE RICK DYE LOVES THEM CARDS!!!!! GO UL!!!!!

Elmer K.

EMPLOYEE SINCE AUGUST 20 2007

It's like a family atmosphere. Good place to work.

Erick H.

EMPLOYEE SINCE SEPTEMBER 20 2007

The culture is great, whichever department you go you can feel the camaraderie. It's always good to come to work when you know that you can have fun everyday while doing your job.

Erin R.

EMPLOYEE SINCE DECEMBER 16 2004

Zappos Culture means having fun at work. It's wheeling over to the next cluster in my comfy chair to share in a laugh. It's watching faces light up with an entrance of arms carrying Krispy Kreme donuts. It's watching team members try to eat 6 saltine crackers in 1 minute. It's watching chair ballerina-type poses glide through the studio. It's making post-it faces and including them in your conversations. It's performing the chicken dance with fellow supervisors after a meeting. It's wide eye staring at someone's sexy dance ... you know who you are. It's simultaneously lips pursed, head bopping with your cluster mate. It's trivia Fridays. Zappos Culture really means having fun at work and I can't think of spending my work days any other way.

Erin T.

EMPLOYEE SINCE SEPTEMBER 14 2006

ZAPPOS ROCKS!!!!!!!!!!!!!!!!!! THE BEST place I have ever worked!!!!!!!!!!!!!!!!!!!!!!!!! I LOVE ZAPPOS!

Fred D.

EMPLOYEE SINCE NOVEMBER 13 2008

Life and fun.

Grace H.

EMPLOYEE SINCE AUGUST 16 2007

The people make the difference here at Zappos. I love my job and I look forward to coming to work every day!

Greg P.

EMPLOYEE SINCE NOVEMBER 25 2007

I have made it through a year plus, and am really happy with my job in maintenance. As with any job, I have my good days and bad. I'm still learning about why we spend money on some things that I feel could be better spent elsewhere (my opinion).

Gregg B.

EMPLOYEE SINCE MARCH 23 2008

Having spent a good portion my life in the fields of higher education and the private and public high school, I was quite surprised at the core values, which the Zappos corporation had designed and adopted; unlike most institutions and corporations, Zappos is an employee-based company. My Zappos orientation sessions left no doubt as to the value of the individual and team spirit. My first day on the sales floor of the outlet store was an enjoyable experience, due to the conversations with the store's assistant manager, John. I was not given the traditional "this is what this company will do for you" speech; instead, I was questioned and requested to give ideas that might advance the outlet store. My previous experiences were both welcomed and sought, making me feel valued. To say that my first impression of Zappos was WOW is the hyperbole of understatement!

Harley C.
EMPLOYEE SINCE SEPTEMBER 24 2007

Zappos has been a great experience and I hope will be one for many more years to come. This place feels like a second home. Everyone here is like family, and why wouldn't you want to work for a place like this? If I had inspirational quotes for my job these are what they would be!

1. "Your work is to discover your world and then with all your heart, give yourself to it."
2. "Thank God – every morning when you get up – that you have something to do which must be done, whether you like it or not. Being forced to work, and forced to do your best, will breed in you a hundred virtues which the idle never know."
3. "Be thankful that you don't already have everything you desire. If you did, what would there be to look forward to?"

Heather L.
EMPLOYEE SINCE AUGUST 25 2008

Even though this is my job, at the same time I feel like part of a family here at Zappos. Everyone in split shift is so different personality-wise, yet we get along so well and work together as a team and also help each other with anything. I look forward to coming to work every day.

Heather P.
EMPLOYEE SINCE AUGUST 18 2008

Coming from a retail management background, I know what it is like to work for a company that would rather make its employees conform versus letting them be themselves. Being new to the area when I started at Zappos was a bit overwhelming, but I quickly learned that I could be myself and have made some wonderful friendships within the walls of our building. I take pride in my job and what we stand for as a company. I hope that the current economic situation looks up because I know that this company can achieve so many great things in the future with the people we have today.

Helen W.

EMPLOYEE SINCE OCTOBER 13 2008

Zappos Culture is unique and inviting! WOW, it is great to work for such a wonderfully diverse company! I look forward to coming to work everyday to work and mingle with all of my teammates. Everywhere you look, and in everyone you meet at Zappos, you see creativity, kindness and a true teambuilding environment!! Everyone from the upper ranks to the team members is unique, friendly and inviting. I Love My Job!! PHS ROCKS!!!

Isaac S. Sr.

EMPLOYEE SINCE SEPTEMBER 12 2005

"The time has come for YACE (Yet Another Culture Essay). So what does culture mean to me now, after all of these years with Zappos? Well, I think all things should be condensed into what you love. I love Pie. So:

Pride: I'm proud of working for Zappos. I wear the employee T-shirts practically everywhere. It is always nice to hear people tell me that they love Zappos.

Impressive: What we've accomplished is very impressive. The dream to sell shoes online at first seems just weird, but everyone has pulled together behind that goal and transformed it into a service company that has everyone talking about us.

Edible: Okay, not all acronyms work out well. However, there is still free catering, so let's go with that!

So hopefully, ten years down the road, I will be writing another one of these culture essays and I'll come up with a word more creative than pie! (Which is tasty.)

Jamie S.

EMPLOYEE SINCE FEBRUARY 1 2005

Culture to me is about coming home but yet working. Culture is talking to the VP or anybody else about how the other family is doing. Culture is knowing everyone as more than just a team member. Culture to some may be the hot meals, the free vending, the sodas or the parties but culture to me is the things that are free to Zappos. The people, the work, the attitude and knowing you're free to be yourself. Zappos accepts team members for who they are, not for what they wear or how they talk. Culture is being able to take your problems to your manager, or HR, no matter what the cause. Culture to me, well, culture to me is Zappos.

Jason R.
EMPLOYEE SINCE JUNE 26 2007

Zappos is a great place to work! I recommend it to all of my friends and a few even switched jobs to work here. We get tons of benefits; fun people and we have superheroes on the wall! It's always fun to be here.

Jennifer H.
EMPLOYEE SINCE FEBRUARY 25 2004

I've been at Zappos going on six years now and I continue to say this is the best job I'd ever had. Year after year, Zappos goes the extra mile to WOW their employees. Zappos provides great health benefits and free lunches. Zappos is the best.

Jenny H.
EMPLOYEE SINCE MARCH 26 2007

Zappos Culture to me means a new way of living at work. Zappos creates a place to work that is fun and creative. Who knew you could come to work and play in a rock band? No other company in the world offers better benefits than Zappos, not only health benefits, but the benefits of the variety of people to work with and the different activities that include your friends and family. I don't believe there is a better place to work than Zappos!!!

Jerry K.
EMPLOYEE SINCE SEPTEMBER 27 2007

It's pretty cool working here. Zappos is a fairly progressive company that puts a lot of emphasis on the employees, as much as it does on the customer. Being powered by service is never a one-way street. Fortunately, Zappos understands this. "It's going to be a shared set of values, a shared ethical framework that's going to be the glue that will hold together societies struggling with enormously difficult choices." – Peter Singer. Here at Zappos, our "shared set of values" that are supposed to hold us together are part of our culture. However, sometimes it seems these core values are used when we want them to be used, instead of across the board. It's not really a value if we are willing to trade it in for a little security. "Any society that would give up a little liberty to gain a little security deserves neither and will lose both." – Benjamin Franklin   I'll translate this into what I'm talking about, so we can see how it applies here: "If we are willing to trade in our values for a little security, then we deserve neither and will lose both." I sure would hate to see the company culture here begin to crumble because we are willing to "punish" the majority for the idiocy of the few.

Jessica A.
EMPLOYEE SINCE NOVEMBER 20 2006

Zappos Culture to me is a way to be yourself at work. The culture is an important way for employees to be treated like people and not just numbers. It's a creative way of making work a positive and not a negative. We are all here in the same place so why not make the best of it and have a little fun along the way. Work hard=Play hard!

Jessie B.
EMPLOYEE SINCE MARCH 1 2005

The following words were first sent to me by email, by a fellow employee of Zappos. "Our company is one that strives to employ genuine thinkers." These words describe what Zappos Culture means to me.

The McSkillet Review

So McDonalds has a new breakfast burrito, the "McSkillet." The size and cost of the McSkillet puts it in a new competitive bracket than its predecessor, the breakfast burrito.. It directly competes with some of the higher-end breakfast burritos on the market. An example would be the Sonic Steak, Bacon and egg breakfast burrito released earlier this month. But the big question is does the McSkillet deliver? So I took a drive to my local McDonalds and plopped down my $2.69 and here are my thoughts ... Size-wise it's on par with Sonic's hefty breakfast burrito. The flavor of the burrito is very good, the sauce inside is a new twist on an old theme. The cheese and egg are very good. Here is my first problem; with the burrito at $2.69, I expected the meat to be steak. The picture in the drivethru doesn't depict the meat well. The sausage though, is savory, serves its purpose and is not the biggest flaw of the burrito. The biggest flaw and by far my biggest disappointment in the burrito is the potatoes. They are huge, soggy, and uninspired. I longed for crispy hash browns inside the burrito as an alternative to the soggy, lifeless, potato chunks. The Bottom Line: The McSkillet is a solid entry into the breakfast burrito market and satisfies despite its shortcomings. The price is a little hefty for the thrifty consumer, who may chose to get two breakfast burritos for 2 dollars. If you're expecting perfection, you may want to drive on past McDonalds and hit Sonic, but if there is no Sonic available, the McSkillet does great in a pinch.

Jim R.

EMPLOYEE SINCE APRIL 7 2008

Zappos has been an amazing change for me. I have never worked for a company that cared as much or treated me as well as Zappos. Things that are commonplace here for everyone are reserved for executives in other places. Some people are concerned about a yearly bonus – I feel like I get one every day. What a great place to work.

Jimmy M.

EMPLOYEE SINCE JANUARY 7 2008

Today, my job consisted of scaling a 40-foot-high ladder onto the roof of the old Zappos warehouse to shoot a group photo. Yesterday, I was photographing protein candy bars and then got to eat them. Tomorrow ... well, tomorrow I'll probably get back to shooting adult apparel, children's apparel, footwear, electronics or housewares. My point is you that never know what each day is going to bring at Zappos. To be successful, you really have to embrace and drive change, and we do! I have been working here just over one year and while my first year has zipped right by, I feel like I've known everybody in our department for years. Through so much change, we have been able to stick together as a team, all the while maintaining a positive atmosphere.

Joe M.

EMPLOYEE SINCE AUGUST 19 2008

Good relations and communications.

Joe S.

EMPLOYEE SINCE APRIL 17 2006

I have been with Zappos for almost three years now and this has to be one of the best companies I have ever worked for. All the small things it does for the employees really add up and make it a pleasure to come to work. Management really seems to care and listens to everyone no matter how minor the issue. I am excited to see where Zappos is heading in the future and I will be there to help through good times and bad.

John J.

EMPLOYEE SINCE DECEMBER 2 2006

I have never worked for a company with a culture similar to the one at Zappos. I look forward to coming to work and I'm proud to wear my Zappos t-shirts when I'm out and advertise where I work. I'm always telling people about the great place I work and that this is the job I plan to retire from. I feel that I can be myself at Zappos. I can do my job and have a little fun too, and there are opportunities to advance within the company should I choose to do so. The way Zappos takes care of its people is unique as well. Catering lunches every day, parties twice a year and my insurance is paid 100%. What more could you ask for?

Johnny R.

EMPLOYEE SINCE DECEMBER 6 2007

I feel like this has been the best employer that I have ever worked at in my entire life. Everything that goes on at Zappos is great and the environment is the best. Thanks for everything.

Jon B.

EMPLOYEE SINCE JULY 18 2006

From the very first day here at Zappos, I knew I had fallen into a great opportunity. It makes me feel good when I tell people outside of Zappos about my job and all the great benefits/perks we get here. Coming up on my third year here, I couldn't be happier that I am still around and working to help this company be the best it can be!

Joon K.

EMPLOYEE SINCE OCTOBER 20 2006

Now that I have been here for two and a half years, I am truly qualified to answer this question. What does the culture mean to me? First the facts ... 1. I love the people I work closely with. Great people, all different but all equally great. 2. At least we try! Nobody is perfect. We all know this. This company has its good and bad days, but at least we try. As a company, we ask questions and we try to make everyone happy. 3. Vegas = #3. Create fun and a little weirdness and Kentucky = #8 Do more with less FUN! I know, I know, we are based on numbers and production here in Kentucky. If we don't photograph it or ship it out fast enough, the customer won't become a raving fan, but can we at least try to have

NERF gun fights in Kentucky as well as in Vegas? It looks like a lot of fun. The culture of Zappos reflects the attitudes of the people within. It means something to those who embrace it. I embrace it. I see the culture being embraced by many. But maybe some people forget to embrace the culture or are not allowed to embrace it. So to me, the culture is about being honest to myself and to the people around me.

Jordan S.
EMPLOYEE SINCE JUNE 26 2007

My coworkers rock my zocks!

Jordan S.
EMPLOYEE SINCE JUNE 30 2008

To me, the culture here at Zappos is all about creating an environment where people enjoy coming into work. We have all worked jobs where you wake up in the morning and absolutely dread going into work every day. I worked in the service industry for three years before I began working here, and it is definitely a dog-eat-dog environment, where nothing REALLY matters except for the bottom line. You see, the biggest expense in most service companies is labor, and managers are constantly getting pressure from those higher up in the chain to get it for as cheap as possible. It is inevitable in such a situation for an employee to not get over-worked and burnt-out, and burnt-out employees don't provide good service to their customers. That's where Zappos differs from the majority. In my department, we do a lot of things to try and keep ourselves from getting burnt-out. We have paper-rock-scissors tournaments, random dance parties, we listen to lots of old school hip-hop, we play Rock Band on our breaks, we have a "Question of the Day" at all of our start-up meetings so that we can all learn a little bit more about who we work next to, and the list goes on... There are still days when I dread coming into work, but usually within the first ten minutes of being here, someone does something that makes me laugh, and the rest of the day just doesn't seem so bad anymore. I guess that is what Zappos' culture is all about.

Julie R.
EMPLOYEE SINCE DECEMBER 5 2005

I think that Zappos is a great place to work. Zappos tries to make sure it lets us put our family first. We have great benefits that I have never been able to find anywhere else. We try to have fun even while working to make it more enjoyable and help the time go by. For this reason I enjoy getting up every day and coming into work.

Julie V.

EMPLOYEE SINCE JUNE 5 2007

Zappos Culture is so much more than a list of core values. Working for a company that does so many amazing things for its customers and employees is something I am very proud of. Reading all the emails that we get from customers, explaining what amazing experiences they have with us, always reassures me that my job is one of substance and importance. It can be stressful and tiresome at times, but I love what I do. I know it all sounds so cheesy, but I love the people I work with and I love what we stand for as a company. It's something that I strive to stand for personally. Going ABOVE AND BEYOND what is expected of us in order to make someone else's day better ... that's a good thing.

Justin M.

EMPLOYEE SINCE APRIL 3 2007

Zappos Culture is like a family environment to me. I enjoy coming to my job and treat it like it's my second home. There is always someone in the house. It's now come to a point to where the people I work with and see every day are like siblings. So, the culture to me is a "home away from home" feeling.

Justin W.

EMPLOYEE SINCE FEBRUARY 26 2007

Zappos culture means to not only be open to diversity, but to embrace diversity. All people have special skills and talent and Zappos tries to find that in each employee. It means to be free to be yourself as long as you are a positive contributor to the company and your team. It means that leaders are willing to sacrifice for the group and to give a little extra when the company most needs it. It means to find something bigger than yourself that you can contribute to and be proud of. Go Zappos!

Karen R.

EMPLOYEE SINCE AUGUST 18 2008

Zappos Culture brings people of various backgrounds together as a team with a common goal. It is this variety that makes working at Zappos fun. Everyone here helps one another. It is about the team and not just individuals. Zappos is a great place to work. Everyone here is like family. I really enjoy coming to work every day.

Katie B.

EMPLOYEE SINCE NOVEMBER 20 2006

Zappos Culture means everything to me. The fact that I still love coming to work every day is just amazing to me! I love what I do here and I love the people I work with. I also love how I can be myself here, no matter how goofy or crazy or "weird" I am (and I get pretty goofy). I have been able to grow personally and professionally so much since I've been here. Zappos has given me the support of a wonderful new, extra family and the experiences that I have needed to grow as a person. My extra family is awesome! We've laughed and cried together. We grow as a team together, from learning cheers to working hard together to keep up with new products to singing Christmas carols to breaking out the "stanky leg". We are building experiences that we will never forget. Zappos is awesome because it has created such a great culture where everyone can come together as a family, despite their differences. Zappos provides so much for its employees, free food, fun, awesome health insurance, but most important of all a wonderful atmosphere and family! P.S. Handbags still rock!

Katie F.
EMPLOYEE SINCE AUGUST 9 2008

They have a diverse group of individuals. You have gothic, rednecks, preps, jocks, etc. Everyone seems to get along.

Kaya F.
EMPLOYEE SINCE FEBRUARY 25 2008

Zappos Culture means coming to work every day with my friends and family, and thoroughly enjoying my experience at my favorite job ever each day that I am here. Zappos Culture makes me want to get up in the morning and come to work every day.

Kaycee C.
EMPLOYEE SINCE JULY 1 2005

After working here for almost four years, I cannot find enough words to express how much Zappos culture means to me. Working in the photo dept. I believe that we envelop every core value there is and live each day with at least one in mind, if not more. We strongly uphold all of them so much that I cannot pick just one to talk about. Whether it is a work function, or just a bunch of us hanging out listening to a co-worker's band, or Happy Hour on Friday or some crazy dance club, we maintain family and team spirit, no matter what we approach. I find that everyone is astounded to hear that my company pays 100% of my insurance, buys me lunch and snacks and goes out of its way to make sure we have fun at work, with a karaoke machine, rock band or some crazy event "just because." Oh yeah, let's not forget the soft-serve ice cream machines or the ice cream cooler with the variety of scrumptious items in that. Meeting new friends and learning interesting facts about your co-workers sure makes for an interesting work environment here and I would NOT trade this for the last piece of chocolate on earth ... well, maybe not the last ... LOL.

Kelly G.

EMPLOYEE SINCE AUGUST 9 2006

Our culture to me is best described in 3 words: Pride – I am proud to tell anyone that I work at Zappos and how much I love it here. Resourceful – I have never worked for a company that has "rolled with the punches" as awesomely as ours. We have reacted to every situation put in front of us with not only caring, but with forward thinking. "What will help us now and in the future?" seems to be the question when we are faced with tough situations. Desire – We are also stretching for that next step whether it's a "Big Hairy Audacious Goal" or a plan of action to make us the best service company out there. We desire to be the absolute best and want to do what it takes to get there, even if the steps to get there seem scary and out of reach. Zappos Rocks!

Kelsey W.

EMPLOYEE SINCE NOVEMBER 29 2007

When I think Zappos Culture, I think of Family. I have been here at Zappos for a little over a year now and I absolutely love my job. The team that I work with is awesome! We are like one big "happy family". I have never had a job where I could be myself and where I had so many great friends. So, Zappos keep up the great work and let's WOW everyone this new year!

Ki M.

EMPLOYEE SINCE NOVEMBER 3 2006

What does Zappos Culture mean to me? Tasty Cake. And that means a lot.

Kyle S.

EMPLOYEE SINCE NOVEMBER 29 2007

Zappos has the ability to capitalize on capitalism. I'm nothing less than ecstatic to see this movement take place right before my eyes. If we keep working together as one unified team, even though it's West and Midwest, and even though we have different departments and personalities, we can accomplish anything. We could make the prequel to the Transformers. Maybe even cryogenically freeze Sly for our ever-longing need for action movies. Ponder that.

Laura S.

EMPLOYEE SINCE NOVEMBER 19 2004

So what can I say about our culture this year that's different than my past year's entries? Hmmmm ... not as much humorous dreams or soapbox behavior, dear friends. I feel the need to leave a more personal entry and express what I am thankful for after finishing this long, winding and bumpy path called 2008.

Our culture stands for more than just the Ten Core Values we have in place. To me it gives a standard of what I should work towards, what I can improve on and what I can do on a personal level to make our company better. I feel this year has tested my resolve more often than it has provided me rest sometimes. I have grown as a person and feel the need to thank those who have helped me throughout this trying year.

To the rock in my life: My wonderful husband, Chris, I am so very proud of you for putting in these four long years to complete your nursing degree. You are an incredible man, son and grandson. I love you more than you know and cherish each day I get to wake up next to you. I hope our future children get your brains (... and my hair :).

We had a lot of ups this year: Zappos made it to a billion in sales (a milestone many said we would not achieve so early), we were named #23 in the Fortune 100 Best Companies to Work For (and became the highest-ranking newcomer EVER!), we got SHARP certified here in KY (HOOPLA! to Miss Leah, you were #1 in making this happen), the KY Content department welcomed several great newcomers to our team (you guys rock!) and we've kicked off our greatest mission of becoming a profit center.

We saw several people transition into promotions, different positions and facing new experiences in their lives. To Stephanie T., I miss you often and still get teary-eyed looking at your jersey. To the supervisor and management team (Betsy, Erin, Dan, Jenn, Linda, Mike, Mark & Michele), thank you for your courage and willingness to face any changes that were ahead and will continue to be in 2009. I am proud to be a part of this great department! But where there were ups, there were many downs. I feel I have confronted my most challenging year yet here at Zappos. Facing this troubled economy has not only rattled my personal life but also shaken my professional one to its core. Our department has gone through restructuring and changing divisions, shift changes and new startup schedules, even new management and new studios.

I delivered the news of an employee layoff to seven of our photo and imaging team members who were directly affected. My hopes go out to them often and I miss you all.

We also lost a dear friend and team member, Max M., who passed away late last year. My prayers remain with his family and friends.

In the good times and bad, I have considered myself fortunate and blessed to have a job I love to go to every day. Aside from the projects and responsibilities I have enjoyed managing, the one I am most thankful for is the team of people I get to spend every day with, working alongside them.

To Matt and Brian, thank you for your guidance, direction and motivation. Your willingness to put your trust in me has helped me grow more than I imagined. Thank you for this tremendous opportunity. To Anji and Rico, your support has been unwavering and I appreciate your help tremendously. For our vendors, investors and many partners, thank you for being a part of Zappos and contributing to this great company. And to Tony and Alfred, I do not say "Thank you" as often as I should, so please know that every day I walk through the door, I do so because you have built a company I want to be a part of. You have shown me through your actions what it means to be respectable, upstanding and humble leaders as well as business owners. Thank you for everything that you do and for keeping our culture at the core. See you all in 2009!

Laurie W.

EMPLOYEE SINCE FEBRUARY 14 2006

This past year was difficult for everyone. What was amazing was how much everyone pulled together to make sure we moved in an awesome direction as a company. It feels like second nature to always think of what's best for the company. I often ask myself, "Would I feel this way if I worked anywhere else?" The answer to that is no. No one really cares about a job, or how his or her company does. But they do care about a family, and how their family does.

Leah M.

EMPLOYEE SINCE AUGUST 24 2005

It has been a year since my last Culture submission and WOW ... things have changed! Zappos thrives on continual growth and achievement. The statement by Buzz Sullivan, "A champion is someone who goes so far they can't go another inch – and then they go that inch," reflects the motivation and inspiration that Zappos encourages! HOOPLA!

LeAnn W.

EMPLOYEE SINCE MARCH 10 2005

I enjoy working here at Zappos. I really enjoy everyone I work with. We are like family. It is hard to find a place like this. Thank you for all our benefits.

Linda H.

EMPLOYEE SINCE SEPTEMBER 13 2005

What I love most about Zappos is the atmosphere, which makes you want to come to work everyday. I can finally say that I have a job that I enjoying coming to and that's because of the culture. You can come to work, be yourself, and have fun at the same time. Zappos cares about its employees.

Lindsay E.

EMPLOYEE SINCE JULY 6 2006

Culture is a big thing for me. You have to enjoy the people you work with in order to have fun and want to come to work everyday! Zappos Culture means many things: a fun family to be around everyday, great benefits (free lunch!) and a place to call home. Zappos has been the best place I've EVER worked because they truly care about their employees and their customers. Everyone here really goes above and beyond to do what he or she can for co-workers and customers alike. Even in unpredictable times, you can still count on the culture at Zappos to remain the same. I also like how you can grow, grow, grow into a better worker and person while you're here. The Ten Core Values are something we truly live by, not just a plaque on the wall, like in most companies. The best part of my job is that Zappos makes it easy for me to WOW my team on a day-to-day basis! I hope to stay with Zappos for a long time and make us even more successful!

Lisa M.

EMPLOYEE SINCE FEBRUARY 28 2007

The People. A job is just a job, but it's the employees here that make Zappos worth coming in everyday for. They really put the Zappos Culture into action. Co-workers here have become great friends. These are people that have fun no matter what is going on and yet, can still hold an insightful conversation. We are all random and even the lamest and quirkiest among us feel apart of the group.

Lloyd P.

EMPLOYEE SINCE SEPTEMBER 4 2007

Zappos Culture is fulfilling in the business sense with its family surroundings.

Logan R.

EMPLOYEE SINCE JANUARY 3 2007

The Zappos environment is unlike any job I have ever worked. It was here that I found an "at home" work environment. Every day is a new adventure. Thanks to Zappos, I also found the love of my life. The knowledge I have gained and friendships I have made will follow me for the rest of my life. Thank you again, Zappos, for all you have done for me.

Lynn E.

EMPLOYEE SINCE APRIL 5 2004

I have been at the warehouse for a few years, and as time goes by, I continue to be WOWed by the culture that is Zappos. To me, it is based on the Ten Core Values. The work ethic, the friendships that are made, the fun activities, the continuous support from HR (thanks, Sarah) and the encouragement from the management staff ... I could go on and on. I have made friendships and memories that will stay with me for the rest of my life. It's a great place to work and I am thankful every day for my job.

Lynn G.

EMPLOYEE SINCE MAY 8 2007

Our culture is imperative to our future. With our Ten Core Values, we move forward, always looking for ways to do things better. Something we must all remember is we are a team within a team. We each have our own departments, but we are all dependent upon each other in some way. Nothing would happen without the receiving department; what would we sell? The photo department gets to present the product to the customer; hopefully in such a way they just have to buy it! From there, the pickers efficiently select orders from the shelf and send it to shipping, which expediently packs it up and sends it on its way to the customer. From there, customer service may have to help our customers who may have gotten the wrong color, it doesn't fit or they just aren't happy. Because of them and their dedication, those customers will come back and buy from us again! Without our returns department, where would all of the unwanted product go? Someone has to put it back into the system. For the product that can't go back into the system, we have to thank our outlet stores. They tend to the product that was rejected and try to find it a new owner. We must not forget our support departments, like development, who keeps improving our site to please our customers. IT, systems & maintenance who keep it all going so our customers can purchase from us, not to mention keeping our internal systems moving so we can do our jobs. Finance, because what good is everything unless we take care of our money! Human resources, because someone has to take care of us! Administration and management, because someone needs a vision of our direction. In the end, we are all important and our roles are vital to the health of this company. Let's all embody the core values each day and make Zappos bigger, better and stronger than ever!

Mandy R.

EMPLOYEE SINCE APRIL 18 2006

Zappos culture means to live, have fun and love. We work very hard at Zappos, but we are shown that our hard work and dedication are appreciated. This appreciation enables me to give 100 percent. I enjoy coming to work with my family at Zappos!

Mark M.

EMPLOYEE SINCE JANUARY 3 2004

Every year we reflect back on the goals met and the achievements thought unreachable obtained. It gives you a sense of pride and belonging to know that you are a part of this amazing adventure. We redefined the business matrix, put the customer experience first and put the employee experience first as well. It works. Keep watching.

Mark S.

EMPLOYEE SINCE SEPTEMBER 25 2005

It is great working for a company that not only thinks of its customers, but its employees as well. We definitely are a model company to all the rest of them, and should be looked upon as what the work force should be.

Matt W.

EMPLOYEE SINCE MAY 8 2006

Counting my temp time, I've been with Zappos for just over three years. So many changes have come about since I've been here; moving into a new, much larger warehouse and technologically superior picking, sorting and distribution processes as compared to hand labeling and whatnot, as was done in the past. One thing that has not changed, I've found, is how Zappos reveres its employees. Free lunch and vending are always worth mentioning. Oh, and the benefits are very generous. Whenever possible, it seems Zappos gives back to the employees for their hard work and perseverance. Little pick-me-ups throughout the year in the form of t-shirts, special meals and theme days or Rock Band events add some fun into the workplace that goes a long way. We have a very nice party every year to cap off the holiday season, where everyone can cut loose and enjoy each other's company away from the office. I feel it's important to mention that a lot of times, team members will go out after work or get together on free time during weekends, which proves that there is a deep core of friendship and spirit with the folks that work here. Zappos Culture to me means all of the above – a laid-back, fun workplace that still prioritizes production goals and customer service, caring, helpful individuals from management down to box making and all the areas in between. Zappos encourages you to be your unique self, which is rare in most companies these days. This is definitely a culture like no other, and I'm so very happy to be a part of it. The people make the difference, and as long as that is a strong conviction of this company, well, I think we'll do all right. Keep on rockin' in the free world!

Matthew S.

EMPLOYEE SINCE MAY 27 2008

Well, Zappos means a lot to me ... my co-workers are more than a family to me. I care more about hanging out with them than I do with my own family. It turns a long day of work into a great day. Most jobs you would walk into work and not want to be there, but when I walk into Zappos I just get a feeling that it's going to be a good day! There are times when you don't want to leave 'cause you just have so much fun with your friends. I could go on and on but I'm not, 'cause I don't have much time! Words can't really explain what Zappos means to me. Thanks for a great year and I'm looking forward to another one!

Maureen D.

EMPLOYEE SINCE SEPTEMBER 14 2006

Zappos is a place where you can be as comfortable as you are at home with your family. My supervisor and co-workers are there in good times and bad. Everyone here treats you as they would like to be treated and cares about you when things are not going so smoothly. It helps to like your job and the people you work with and here at Zappos that is very easy to do.

Melanie W.

EMPLOYEE SINCE JUNE 9 2008

Zappos Culture means, in my definition, freedom of expression and individualism. It means that I can come to work and be myself, dress as I like and have fun. It has taught me to accept people as they are, because they accept me as I am.

Melissa L.

EMPLOYEE SINCE AUGUST 7 2006

When I think of the Zappos Culture, I think of fun, friends and family. Each employee is appreciated and viewed as an integral part of the company. One of the most unique things about Zappos is that our personal ideas and suggestions are actually encouraged and often turned into company-wide activities! For example, a team member in the fulfillment center suggested a unique way of packaging shoes so that the customer wouldn't just receive a plain box when the original box was damaged. Not only was his idea implemented, but he was also rewarded with his very own VIP parking spot, presented to him by the CEO himself!

Other unique activities that were generated from employee ideas: the karaoke and rock band stage in the Zappos Café, Spirit Week where we have dress-up days and cheering contests, our annual Fall Festival designed for fun for the whole family and an art show where employees can showcase their creative sides! At Zappos, it is realized that people don't necessarily work because they want to, so why not create a work environment where people actually look forward to coming to work every day! When it comes to employee morale, Zappos does many things to show employee appreciation, from our free health benefits and free catered lunches, to Customer Service Week where the managers serve lunch to the employees and shuttle employees to and from their vehicles in a golf cart, company t-shirts, holiday and birthday gifts, our amazing holiday parties and of course our very generous 40% discount! Overall, Zappos is by far the best company I have ever worked for and I hope it is the last! Rock on, Zappos, and keep on WOWing!

Melissa W.

EMPLOYEE SINCE MARCH 4 2008

It means A LOT!!! My favorite is the Build a Positive Team and Family Spirit! My family has been through a HUGE experience this last year with the premature birth of my grandson! Everyone in my department, along with HR – Kudos to Sarah O.– has been very understanding of my family situation, and has gone out of the way to accommodate me. I could not ask for a better company to work for. The whole B Shift receiving team is AWESOME!!! Thanks to my team leader, Suzanne and a HUGE Thank you goes out to GARY B!!!! You guys ROCK!!!! ZAPPOS ROCKS!!!!! What a GREAT company to work for! THANKS SOOOOO MUCH!!!

Michael J.

EMPLOYEE SINCE MARCH 22 2007

WOW, a lot has changed in ONE YEAR!!! Zappos is still number one. I am proud to be a Zapponian. It is exciting when you say where you work and people get excited, "Oh, I love Zappos!!!" I am looking forward to a long career at Zappos.

Michele K.

EMPLOYEE SINCE AUGUST 5 2008

Zappos Culture is a way of life. The Culture here at Zappos is accepting, real, happy, ever-changing and has a family atmosphere. This is one of the first jobs that I've worked that has such a positive atmosphere, every day. If you walk around and smile at 100 employees at least 99 will smile back – that is special. The people that are employed here at Zappos are very special and unique. There is no discrimination of any kind here, people can be themselves and not have to worry about someone looking down on them or looking at them differently just because of our differences. Everyone is accepted. If I'm ever in a bad mood and I come into work, my mood usually changes from negative to positive instantly. I love that this job helps change my mood and my outlook on life.

The Ten Core Values here at Zappos are very important in helping my outlook on life and my everyday encounters with people. My favorite Core Values are: #4 Be Adventurous, Creative and Open-Minded, #6 Build Open and Honest Relationships With Communication, #8 Do More With Less, #9 Be Passionate and Determined and #10 Be Humble.

Zappos is a one-of-a-kind company and I'm proud to be a part of it!! Not many companies thrive on making the employees happy; it's usually just the customer. Here at Zappos, that is not the case. We are treated with such awesomeness it's amazing. Everyone employed here at Zappos gets free catered lunch every day, vending machines, free insurance with no co-payments (medical, dental and vision) and free goodies all the time. There are many more great things that Zappos does for us on a constant basis; it's unbelievable. It can't get any better!!

Micki G.

EMPLOYEE SINCE MARCH 27 2007

When I came to Zappos it was just another warehouse job. I would keep it just long enough to get a better one. I very quickly found that this was the best place for me. We are a strange family that works. We look out for each other and for the most part work very hard to make Zappos a productive and happy place to work. I plan to make this my last stop on the job hunt. Zappos cares for its employees like no other company that I have come across. That shows a lot in all the things they do for us and for the community.

Mike B.

EMPLOYEE SINCE SEPTEMBER 26 2006

How cool is it to work for a company that is #23 of the top 100 companies to work for. Zappos has to be the best company I have ever had the opportunity to work at. I am having a blast.

Mike D.

EMPLOYEE SINCE APRIL 5 2006

To whoever may read this, I hope I have helped you. Our #1 is deliver WOW and we get a 10 for that. You can embrace and drive change in a New York minute. I started working here on Oct. 13, 2005, but had to wait until April 4, 2006, to officially be a Zapponian. I started in the warehouse for two years. There, I met a lot of people and made friends. If you believe in yourself, you can do anything you want. I love coming to work every day; I never have a bad day. Here you can pursue growth and learning. Just be humble and you will go far. I am almost 60 years old and I would love to retire from Zappos. So Zappos, "Thank you for believing in me. I believe I give 110% every day!" Thank you Zappos, I love you!

Mike M.

EMPLOYEE SINCE JULY 12 2006

As I look back over the past two and a half years that I have been employed by Zappos, I am reminded of all the great friendships that I have made along the way. The people that work at Zappos genuinely care for one another and that makes for the best possible working environment. When you have the opportunity to work with people that actually care whether you succeed or not, your outlook on the job changes tremendously. I no longer dread going to work; I eagerly anticipate reporting to work every day. How many people can actually say they enjoy going to work? If you can find someone that does, I bet they work at Zappos!

Mindy B.

EMPLOYEE SINCE OCTOBER 12 2006

I believe in order to love where you work, you must love the people you work with. I have been here over two years now. It truly has been the people, co-workers, supervisors, leads, HR, maintenance, IT, (all departments) etc; that make Zappos a wonderful place to work. Without them there would be no WOW in Zappos. Because of their hard work, Zappos is still here when so many other companies have had to shut down during these hard times. Thank you to all Zappos employees for doing more with less and working so hard every day. You never get to where you want to be in life if you give up when it gets tough!

Morbid T.

EMPLOYEE SINCE SEPTEMBER 10 2005

The Zappos Culture to me is the people. We have a unique group of amazing people in KY and Vegas that keep us moving forward daily. We treat people like they are the most important assets that we have, and that is because they are! That is what makes Zappos so unique. We don't just say the company is great and leave it at that. We make sure that it is known the company is great because each person on our team makes it that way. By the way, we also know how to party like no other company!

N.M.

EMPLOYEE SINCE JANUARY 19 2004

The culture here at Zappos is awesome. What I like most is the family spirit. Anyone that knows me has figured out that I am quite shy, which usually makes it hard for me to walk up and talk to just anyone. But it's different here. I have to say this is the first job I have ever had that I am not at all afraid to walk up to my manager or supervisor to talk about anything. Another great thing is that Zappos, as a company, takes care of us. They keep us well fed, give us clothes to wear and make work fun with indoor inflatables, book sales, health fairs, etc. ...

Naomi S.

EMPLOYEE SINCE MARCH 7 2008

I've been working for Zappos for almost a year now. I can remember when I first started that I couldn't believe what an amazing place it was to work for. I had just left my job of seven years that was stressing me out to the max and then I walk into a work place filled with fun things to do. I actually like working! Here at Zappos, there are so many different types of cultures. It is really amazing. We are able to be ourselves and it's wonderful getting to know different types of people. For me, that's culture. Just being together, working together and having fun together. We are all different, but we make it work. Being able to accomplish that is amazing. Way to go, Zappos!

Natashna S.

EMPLOYEE SINCE APRIL 17 2007

It means wonderful, wonderful times with joyful memories of all my co-workers who are now like family. Boooyyah! HOOPLA!!!!! LETS DO THE WAVE PEOPLE!

Nathen S.

EMPLOYEE SINCE JUNE 30 2008

Personally, I believe Zappos Culture is best defined as living to the fullest of your potential. While many people may disregard the amazing amounts of benefits and accommodations brought forth to the Zappos employee community, I guarantee that most who separate from the company never find the same kinds of luxuries offered to Zappos employees. Therefore, living and working to your fullest potential should be a small token of appreciation in return for Zappos' gratitude.

Nour E.

EMPLOYEE SINCE FEBRUARY 1 2005

This is my fourth year at Zappos and I'm still amazed. This is more than a workplace. There is more respect towards employees and what Zappos does for them ... So I say that I'm fortunate to be part of this company and its culture.

O Keane.

EMPLOYEE SINCE AUGUST 1 2007

Zappos culture, to me, means building and growing through communication and team spirit. In all previous places I have worked, there has never been as much emphasis on the family value in the workplace. It is truly a joy to come to work every day and a better team I have never worked with. Go Raibh Mile Maith Againn (A hundred thousand thank yous to all).

Pam H.

EMPLOYEE SINCE NOVEMBER 6 2006

When I think of Zappos Culture, I think of a company that does all it can to stay on top of its game. WOW the customer! WOW the employee! This is a company that knows happy employees are more productive employees. There are several things that Zappos does to keep us happy. Topping the list has to be free health insurance for all employees and very affordable insurance for our families. This is virtually unheard of anymore. Then there are free, catered meals and free vending in the break room. This helps add more value to our benefits. Zappos also gives us lots of free t-shirts and other goodies. By the way, we don't want to forget it puts on AWESOME company parties and family picnics. Very few companies show their appreciation to their employees like Zappos.

At Zappos, everyone is free to be themselves. In fact, individuality is encouraged. Hey, a little weirdness is one of our Ten Core Values. There are no strict, archaic dress codes. We are encouraged to dress safely but comfortably. Our core values are what define who we are. We are frequently asked for our ideas about what would make our jobs more fun or better. Not only does Zappos ask, but it also listens! To sum it all up, I need to use only one word – WOW!!!

Pam W.

EMPLOYEE SINCE FEBRUARY 1 2005

WOW, is it culture book time already? I started Zappos as a temp in October, 2004. It didn't take me long to realize this was the job for me. My co-workers were great. Sarah B. and Bubba taught me a lot about receiving and I thank them. They are very dedicated employees and I wanted to show them I was too. A lot has changed through the years, but the culture is still the same. We are a group of people working together that has made this company what we are today. I am in the photo department now and love my job and my peeps, even though we are a little weird. Let's keep up the good work and embrace and drive change.

Pamela I.

EMPLOYEE SINCE JUNE 30 2008

WOW!!! I think Zappos is a great place to work. Zappos treats us like customers not just employees. We have great benefits like free daily lunches, cool, fun giveaways and awesome insurance. I like the fact that I can get up in the morning and know I am going to a place where I can work and have fun at the same time. I LOVE ZAPPOS!!!!

Patricia C.

EMPLOYEE SINCE APRIL 29 2006

I enjoy coming to work at Zappos. The people are friendly and fun to be around. We are given opportunity to shine with programs like Creators of Culture. Zappos takes good care of their employees, they provide our snacks and drinks, t-shirts, functions for our families and let's not forget the great parties. I believe that Zappos as a company values me as an employee.

Paula P.

EMPLOYEE SINCE DECEMBER 6 2006

I love working at Zappos. My favorite Core Value has to be #7 ... Build a positive team and family spirit. There is such a strong sense of family here. When something bad happens, we all seem to band together to help each other through the worst of situations.

Pauline S.

EMPLOYEE SINCE NOVEMBER 21 2005

The people! Liking the work you do. The great benefits. And where else can you work that will send you to Vegas for a "GREAT PARTY!"

Rachel G.

EMPLOYEE SINCE OCTOBER 24 2007

It means for the first time in my life, I look forward to coming to work. No more thinking of what I can call in for, no more dreading coming into work. I love where I work and anyone who knows me, knows that. I have never worked for a place that fed me everyday, gives me t-shirts (being a t-shirt and jeans girl, yeh!), gave me a bonus, gives awesome holiday parties and best of all – insurance with no co-payments! Go Difference Card! And no manager has ever cursed at me! Wow, not like in corporate America! If people don't like working here, there's something wrong with them! You WILL NOT find another company out there that does what Zappos does.

Reatha M.

EMPLOYEE SINCE OCTOBER 24 2007

The Zappos Culture is astounding. I work in PHS and love it. I have a lead that promotes the Ten Core Values. When a change comes to the department we may not be too happy about, he says "Embrace and Drive Change." So whatever the situation, he's known to quote the Core Values to help keep us in focus. Zappos is just a great place to work. The managers and leads trust their employees to do their jobs. Employees have the freedom to perform their job without someone watching their every step.

I've been at Zappos for about a year and a half. It amazes me as I walk around to have people call out "Hello," to me by name. It feels so warm and personal, like they really care. And they do. Everyone is so friendly. It makes me feel that I really belong. There aren't many places today where that type of environment exists. There is such a diverse age group of people who gather into groups at breaks. It's not just a group of young people or a group of more mature people. The groups are mixed and there is such an exchange of conversation on all kinds of topics.

Creativity is encouraged. Ideas are encouraged. The Culture Book is a good example of where we can express ourselves. It's almost like being a published author. We are all encouraged to be ourselves. After all, this is our home away from home. If we can't feel comfortable at work, then where can we?

Rick D.

EMPLOYEE SINCE OCTOBER 31 2006

The culture at Zappos is so unique. When I first started working here in 2006, I never dreamt that a company that prides itself on creating such a great culture would actually have a great one. Each day, I look forward to coming to work, being a part of the team and working with such great people. To know a company cares so much about their team members and managers in this day and age is a comforting feeling. I am truly blessed.

Rick R.

EMPLOYEE SINCE MARCH 17 2008

When I walked in the door at Zappos, I could tell it was going to be a whole new experience. It is the first place I've worked where the employees are valued for who they are, not just as numbers doing a job.

Roger L.

EMPLOYEE SINCE JUNE 13 2008

To me, Zappos Culture means working as a team in celebration while accomplishing the same goal, which is ensuring our customer's satisfaction.

S Dawson.

EMPLOYEE SINCE SEPTEMBER 7 2006

I have worked for Zappos for two and a half years and I love it here. This is the best place to be. I feel like all those years I spent working in other places was such a waste. I also feel like this is a true family. I work in pack/ship and I have the best boss – I can really talk to her.

Sam R.

EMPLOYEE SINCE NOVEMBER 7 2007

Zappos Culture to me is all about being yourself at work and following the Ten Core Values. They make work fun and unique so everyday doesn't just become a regular routine. Zappos is by far the best job I have had. GOOD TIMES!!!!!!!!!!!!!!

Sandy H.

EMPLOYEE SINCE JANUARY 12 2005

What can't I say that's good about Zappos Culture? I have never known any company where people put so much into what they believe in. It is really awesome the way we are treated as one big family. (I LOVE IT.)

Zappos has been a blessing to me in every way. After I spent 28 years in my previous job (the plant closed), Zappos hired me and I consider Zappos my HERO. I love everything about you. I hope to grow old and retire with you guys. Keep up the good work.

Sandy S.

EMPLOYEE SINCE JULY 1 2005

Zappos has been a great place to work for the last four years. It is a company that strives to be the best at everything it does. Whether it's service for customers or benefits and parties for the employees, it is the BEST. Thanks Zappos.

Sarah J.

EMPLOYEE SINCE MAY 25 2005

Zappos Culture is unlike anything that I have ever seen. At one time there was only one place that I could truly be myself and that was at home. Then I started at Zappos ... No matter what you do here, no one looks at you and thinks "What a weirdo!" Nine times out of ten, they are doing the same thing that you are! At any given moment, you can walk through the warehouse and see someone singing karaoke, playing Rock Band®, relaxing at the internet cafe, or enjoying a free (yes, free) snack or drink! I think that holidays are my favorite time. Where else are you encouraged to dress up in all green on St. Patrick's Day, or in costume on Halloween? Sometimes I stop and think WOW, am I really at work?! That is the best feeling in the world! I love Zappos!!

Sarah O.

EMPLOYEE SINCE MAY 23 2005

The culture here is what helps me get up each morning ... I know that when I get into work, there are hundreds of smiling faces waiting to greet me and share their day with me. Everyone is here because they want to be here, that makes all the difference in the environment! I love knowing that each of us is willing to give 110% of ourselves because we know that the company will also turn around and give us 110%. It's a wonderful relationship we all share with this magical thing called ... our culture :). I'm very thankful to everyone I have ever had the pleasure of working with here at Zappos, for helping me understand what makes us so unique and so wonderful. Here's to many more fabulous years!

Scott Z.

EMPLOYEE SINCE APRIL 1 2005

Our culture and core values are all about creating story worthy experiences, in my opinion. It just isn't about our end customers being WOWed by their experience. It is just as much about our employees and vendors having the same experiences that make them want to talk to their friends and family about Zappos and what we stand for.

Shaina M.

EMPLOYEE SINCE AUGUST 25 2008

Zappos is so many things; we're a family, we're friends and we create a workspace that is never boring. Our determination to improve every day makes us better individuals personally and more efficient Zapponians. Zappos is a great place to work. YEE-HAW!

Stefanie W.

EMPLOYEE SINCE FEBRUARY 4 2008

Someone pinch me! I must be dreaming! That pretty much sums up my job here at Zappos. I remember driving by the Fulfillment Center as it was being built, thinking to myself how nice it would be to work so close to home. I was content in my previous employment, but kept hearing about what it was like to work at Zappos. I would just roll my eyes and think, "Yeah, suuure." Here I am, years later, working for this unique company and loving every minute. I look forward to coming to work, no matter what the workload may be for the day. It can be challenging at times, but it is always rewarding. It's so nice just to be appreciated and encouraged to grow in my position. I feel like I'm finally where I need to be and have no desire to ever leave. As a result of feeling that way, I consider my co-workers as extended family. And just like I am with my family, I'm loyal to Zappos and thank my lucky stars daily that I have the pleasure of being a Zapponian!

Stephanie S.

EMPLOYEE SINCE NOVEMBER 22 2004

Zappos means growth and opportunity to me. Every day, I think I grow more and I think we grow more as a company. We have opportunities and drive that are endless. Zappos is the best!

Steven B.

EMPLOYEE SINCE SEPTEMBER 9 2008

Since I've been here, I have been very impressed! Zappos is the best facility I have worked at and the many small benefits are great. I have been in other settings where people were not team players and things were very inefficient. Most everyone I work around will help you without thinking twice! I also loved the amount of time and money spent on the holiday party to show how much Zappos appreciates its own!

Steven P.

EMPLOYEE SINCE MARCH 1 2005

Zappos Culture is about being different, having fun and change. I have worked here for four years so it is like working with family each day. Zappos is about taking care of the employees to the fullest, such as free lunch every day. Zappos Culture is about helping the ones that want to help themselves and no dream is too big.

Steven T.

EMPLOYEE SINCE JUNE 27 2006

When I think of Zappos Culture and what it means to me, several images and words pass through my mind. Fun, creative, family, parties, alcohol, Vegas, discounts, free food, great benefits, happy, #1, karaoke, charity, best place to work ... ever. I love Zappos and every day that I get to come to work, I think how awesome it is that I get to come and be myself. I can be as crazy and weird as I want to, and no one says a thing. I live the Ten Core Values in and outside of work and try my hardest to tell everyone about the GREAT company that I work for. I am very lucky to work here and will continue to do my part to make Zappos what it is today.

Susan D.

EMPLOYEE SINCE JANUARY 6 2005

I have been with Zappos for four years now and this is my fourth entry in these books. The culture in this company is like nowhere else I have worked. It is, for the most part, the best place to work. As with any growing company, I have seen hiccups along the way and they always work it out to keep growing and keeping the culture alive. All of the extras Zappos gives us still amaze me, from the free lunches to the free insurance. I still get up pretty much every morning looking forward to coming in to work. My family in photo is just that;

they have seen me through so much in this past year. Without that support I'm sure things would have been a lot worse emotionally. In our department, my managers, supervisor and senior assistant always have time to talk to me and are always making sure we progress into any job position we want. So, Zappos is still the last job I ever want to have and hopefully I will be here for a long, long time.

"Zappy Wishes and Shoestring Dreams."

Susan W.
EMPLOYEE SINCE NOVEMBER 27 2006

Working at Zappos is awesome! Being part of such a great team that really cares about you is something that I have not found anywhere else. I truly enjoy coming to work every day! Everyone loves to hear what I did at work because you get the best stories from working at Zappos. I don't know of any other place where you are playing dodge ball, painting your face or shaving your head between meetings and don't even get me started about the parties. ZAPPOS ROCKS!!!!

Suzanne H.
EMPLOYEE SINCE JULY 10 2007

Working for Zappos is awesome. Not only do you receive the free health insurance, free catered lunches everyday, and free soft drinks and snacks, you receive a family atmosphere. That makes coming to work joyful. I love working in the Outlet division. Everyone in the processing department and in the outlet store makes me proud to call him or her my co-workers and my friends. I love each and every one of them. Zappos brings the family spirit to realization and there is nothing better than to come to work every day and know that you have a family to support you. The culture that Zappos has is amazing in its own right. It provides nurturing, growth, happiness, diversity, laughter, amazement (WOW factor) and honesty. What else could you ask for?

Tammy B.
EMPLOYEE SINCE APRIL 17 2007

Freedom to be myself, I can act a little weird and nobody notices!

Tammy E.

EMPLOYEE SINCE AUGUST 18 2008

I truly believe Zappos is a great place to work. The way the economy has been, and we're still standing. I work another job besides Zappos, Zappos being my priority job. I deal with customer service at my other job! In today's society, people are much more moody, but if you've ever had to deal with Zappos customer service, you can't tell that the economy is in bad shape. The person on the other end of the phone is cheerful and eager to serve you. You can sell me the crappiest pair of shoes, but as long as the service is a great experience, I'll always come back. So keep up the WOW, Zappos Customer service!!!!!!!!! To me, being a part of a company like Zappos makes it easy getting up on those days you just want to sleep in.

Thanks, Zappos for this opportunity.

Tasha F.

EMPLOYEE SINCE OCTOBER 1 2004

When I started at Zappos in May 2004, I thought this would just be just another job that I could work until something better came along. It is now 2009 and I can't imagine working anywhere else! The benefits and extras that Zappos is always giving us isn't anything they are required to do. They WANT to go the extra mile to make Zappos stand out and above everyone else, from the never ending t-shirts to the free snacks and lunches to the climate control! Most importantly, we have Ten Core Values that stand behind everything we do as a company. Other companies say they have "values", but do they really live up to their word as a company? I say not. The company has grown so much in the 5 years I have been here, yet everyone still knows everyone else. When you walk into our building, you will see and feel a family spirit that will not be found anywhere else. I dare you to try.

Taurie M.

EMPLOYEE SINCE FEBRUARY 11 2008

Who else at any other company can say that they have ROCK BAND? There have been many nights where I've stayed after hours jammin' it out. Do you know of any other company that has a Collector's Edition Monopoly game modeled after their culture? I don't. That's my favorite gift ever! What about the lunch and brand-name snacks provided every day for free? Or how about free co-payments to see the doctor, along with an attractive benefits package? Not many. I REALLY appreciate everything Zappos has done and continues to do for me, for our customers, and for the community. Zappos has proven to the cutthroat business world that the impossible is possible. Moral of the story: Zappos is my role model and this company makes me feel like a rock star!!

Teralane S.

EMPLOYEE SINCE SEPTEMBER 10 2007

Culture to me means family. I love a lot of people here more than some of my own family. I enjoy working with them. Zappos has helped me out with insurance and free lunch. I have a husband and three kids and I need the great benefits provided here. The money I'm saving on free lunch goes to my kids' school lunch. All around, it is a great place to be and I'm proud to be here.

Theo G.

EMPLOYEE SINCE NOVEMBER 26 2007

Working for Zappos has truly been a life-learning experience. I have never seen a company that does so much for their employees. Everything from free vending, lunches and even free benefits! I can honestly say I've never worked for a company that treats their employees with such a sense of sincerity. Furthermore, the Ten Core Values that we practice daily have been instilled in my life outside work. With the remarkable success of Zappos, I am looking forward to growing and moving up within the company. Giving WOW + 1!

Thomas C.

EMPLOYEE SINCE MAY 7 2007

Until I came to Zappos, I never knew how to have open and honest relationships. I never knew how to be humble. And I definitely never knew how to WOW someone. My world has changed. I am very humble now. I also have hundreds of open and honest relationships. And I WOW more people than sham wow. WOW, what a life. WOW, what a culture.

Tonya H.

EMPLOYEE SINCE NOVEMBER 11 2003

Zappos has changed so much since 2003. The change is great. I started out in Receiving, unloading the trucks. It is about the same today. The process has changed a lot; we didn't use computers, we had scan guns, and they weren't the RF guns either. After we got finished scanning the new product, we had to download our guns and then put away. I was also in Putaway; before we could leave we had to find all the lost shoes that didn't show up in a location. After we put our pallets away, we would download our guns again. We used to come in an hour early and make boxes or stay an hour over and make boxes. We had worked on Saturdays just to make boxes for 8 hours. That wasn't all we did, we had certain aisles that we had to straighten and rescan before we could leave. During the busy season, we couldn't leave unless all the departments got to leave. I do remember our manager telling us "If you see me running, you better take off running also." I was also in returns, back then we only had four stations. We had to complete all the returns before we could leave. Zappos is awesome!!!!!!!

Tracy B.

EMPLOYEE SINCE OCTOBER 1 2004

Where to start? This will be my fifth year here at Zappos. WOW ... to be honest, when I first started working here as a temp in the receiving department, I never thought that I would still be here five years later. However, after I started, I saw that Zappos was different then most other companies I had worked for. It really cares about its employees. This is shown by the awesome benefits Zappos provides, such as free lunch, free health insurance and an outstanding culture. Our culture is what separates us from the rest of the companies out there. We are always doing something fun and exciting. We are always looking for new ways to WOW our customers, internally and externally. I look forward to being here for many years to come!

Tracy P.

EMPLOYEE SINCE JUNE 26 2007

Zappos Culture means family to me. This is a loving and friendly environment. Everyone cares about everyone else. When we lose a family member, we cry together. When someone has a baby, we cheer and party together. We go out together on weekends and have fun. Most of us see our work family more then we see our home family and it just makes that bond stronger. I'm thankful for the friends and family I've made working here.

Travis R.

EMPLOYEE SINCE MARCH 20 2008

It means coming into a job that is more than just that. It means that I can look forward to coming in day after day and truly enjoy what I do each and every day. Ever since I have started, I have never dreaded coming to work like I have in past jobs. I can honestly say that I am doing what I really want to do. Not many people can say they love their job and love what they do; I can.

Tyler H.

EMPLOYEE SINCE AUGUST 24 2008

Deliver WOW through service. Be passionate and determined. Embrace and drive change. BE HUMBLE. Build a positive and family spirit. Do more with less. Pursue growth and learning. Create fun and a little weirdness. Build open and honest relationships with communication. Be adventurous, creative and open-minded – all of these things because shoes are freakin' awesome.

Valerie M.

EMPLOYEE SINCE SEPTEMBER 7 2006

With working in the pack/ship area, I have found out that we really do WOW our customers every day. I enjoy being part of the process in making a difference so customers get their packages on time.

Vicky H.

EMPLOYEE SINCE AUGUST 13 2008

Zappos is a great and fun place to work.

Zella K.

EMPLOYEE SINCE JULY 9 2007

What Zappos means to me, is a place that I can look forward to coming every day, because it's a positive environment. I can come to work and the people I work with have a great attitude. Most important I have the greatest boss, Tony. He cares about the people who work for him, and that is rare, unfortunately. He has made Zappos a great place to work.

Fɪɢ ᴠɪɪ-6. Life's not all fun and games at Zappos. Sometimes you get tasked with hair clean-up or, as his shirt says, you have to survive KY Boot Camp before becoming an employee. No, Zappos is not for the faint of heart.

SxSW

I-1. When we attended South by SouthWest in 2008, we passed out ponchos. Lucky for us, it rained. This year, we wanted others to get lucky and gave away a trip to Vegas. Now that luck's on both sides, wonder what's going to happen next year...

I-2. Sunni Brown created this illustration *AS* Tony was giving his 'Delivering Happiness' presentation at SxSW. Another reminder of how inspiration oftentime goes both ways.

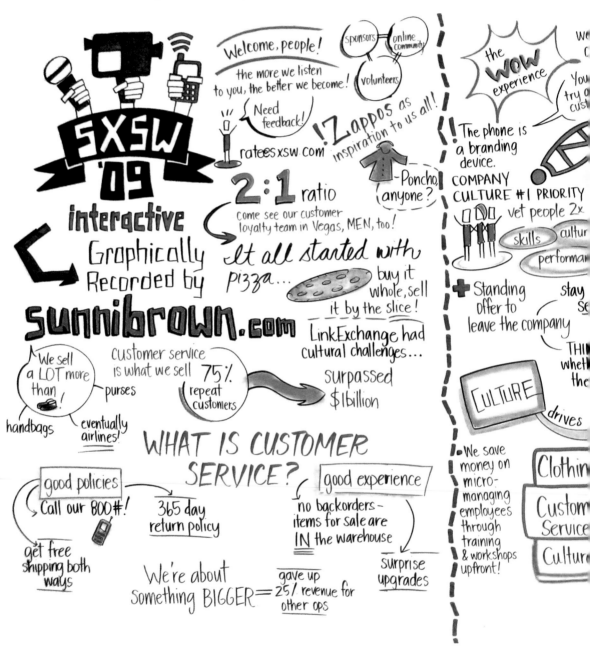

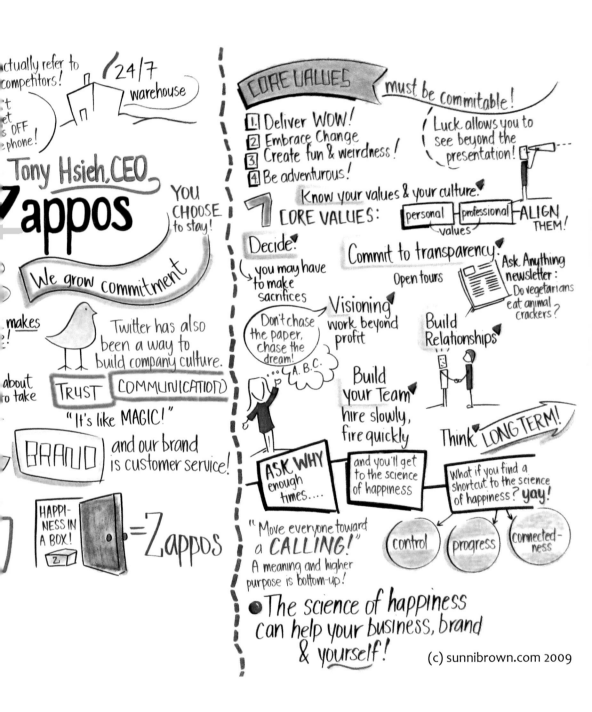

actually refer to competitors!
...t
...et
...OFF
...phone!

24/7 warehouse

Tony Hsieh, CEO
Zappos
YOU CHOOSE to stay!

We grow commitment

...makes ...!

Twitter has also been a way to build company culture.

...about ...o take

TRUST COMMUNICATION

"It's like MAGIC!"

BRAND and our brand is customer service!

HAPPINESS IN A BOX! = Zappos

CORE VALUES must be commitable!
1. Deliver WOW!
2. Embrace Change
3. Create fun & weirdness!
4. Be adventurous!

Luck allows you to see beyond the presentation!

Know your values & your culture.

7 CORE VALUES: personal — professional — ALIGN THEM!
values

Decide!
you may have to make sacrifices

Commit to transparency!
Open tours

Ask Anything newsletter: Do vegetarians eat animal crackers?

Don't chase the paper, chase the dream! A.B.C.

Visioning work beyond profit

Build Relationships

Build your Team hire slowly, fire quickly

Think LONG TERM!

ASK WHY enough times....

and you'll get to the science of happiness

What if you find a shortcut to the science of happiness? yay!

"Move everyone toward a CALLING!"
A meaning and higher purpose is bottom-up!

control progress connectedness

● The science of happiness can help your business, brand & yourself!

LET US BE GRATEFUL TO PEOPLE WHO
MAKE US HAPPY; THEY ARE THE CHARMING
GARDENERS WHO MAKE OUR SOULS
BLOSSOM.

MARCEL PROUST

v.

PARTNERS

Bill A.

EARTH

When you are in the office one gets the overwhelming sense of a large group of people all on the same page and pulling in the same direction. You can almost imagine Zappos switching their business to a whole different industry and seeing them adapt, re-focus and succeed in a short period of time ... of course, a few theme parties would be thrown in along the way for inspiration.

Cliff J.

SUPERGA

Culture... hard to define, difficult to invent, and nearly impossible to achieve. The business world is full of also-rans, companies that feel they know the importance of culture but never grasp the fundamentals of actually how to achieve this most elusive value. In terms of culture, Zappos has not only "talked the talk" – it has "walked the walk" each and every day since the company's inception. And herein lies the secret... at Zappos, people think about culture, they talk about it, they plan it, and they reinvent it every day. I have watched Zappos grow from day one, losing my good friend Fred Mossler from my team to this most curious group ... a group out of nowhere that felt they could sell shoes on the internet! How absurd. Now, some 10 years later, Zappos is a force to be reckoned with in the footwear business, the new leader in customer care. There are no limits to what the Zappos team can accomplish, as they have achieved the most difficult step of building their business model ... the establishment of COMPANY CULTURE. They have wonderful people working within who believe in the Ten Core Values. They trust that these core values will take them to the next level, and they undoubtedly will find those next levels. I would be remiss here if I didn't thank everyone from Zappos for doing something for me that is most unusual in the business dynamic of "accounts and sales reps"... treating me with utmost respect and kindness each and every time I work with them. I am proud to service Zappos and honored to be considered a friend.

Dan S.

BROOKS

Zappos is a breath of fresh air. It is great to work with energetic, motivated people that love their jobs.

Danny M.

DEERSTAGS

Around the time that Zappos began, a Wall Street Journal article ran, listing the businesses that could and/or could not make it on the Internet. Shoes were a prime example of the "won't make it" list.

I recall this often when thinking about Zappos. It's not the fact that Zappos did indeed become such a successful business that amazes me. It's that in these ten short years, Zappos' culture has evolved so quickly and definitively, that it has become a model which any other company or person who interacts with surely strives to, in some way, make their own.

My own company has felt a kinship with Zappos from the beginning. We're a family business, loaded with loyal and smart people, who happen to be a little quirky, diverse and generally shy away from the norm. Work is a way we can be together, support each other, see the world and hopefully have a lot of fun. Sound familiar?

In the past couple of years, we have made a concerted effort to embrace these qualities and use them as points of strength. We don't aim to emulate Zappos. Zappos is and always will be a truly unique company and culture. But the Zappos culture has inspired us and helped us realize how powerful being a little different can be.

Greg B.

HOUSEPARTY

Zappos is a billion-dollar company that still feels like a family business. I live 2,500 miles away, but the Zappos team still makes me feel like I'm just around the corner. I'm excited to be part of the Zappos family!

Jan B.

RIEKER

Zappos.com, how do you do it? You are getting bigger and better. Unbelievable service, huge selection, speedy delivery and the customer is ALWAYS first! Zappos.com, the new (ten year old) synonym for SERVICE! Your biggest fan!

Jim H.

BROOKS

A relaxed environment where you can flourish as an individual. Great people who truly love their job.

Ken P.

TWIG FOOTWEAR

What do I enjoy most about working with Zappos? The answer is not as obvious as one may think! The salesman in me loves the depth and scale at which they buy my product. The credit manager in me loves that they pay their bills when the invoice is due. The marketing manager in me loves that they give me incredible exposure on their site. The traffic manger in me loves the fact that their routing guide, while at first may seem a bit daunting, is actually straight forward. The inventory planner and analyst in me loves the fact that you have unfettered access to your results. As a person who wears multiple hats in my company, I can tell you that I adore working with Zappos. However, none of the above-mentioned reasons is what I love most.

Have you ever been on a flight going to a destination like Cancun? Cancun is the kind of place that 98% of the people on the plane are there because they are going on vacation. The mood on the airplane is festive and generally devoid of the angst, rancor and contempt that greet travelers on a flight between say ... Chicago and Newark. People going to Cancun are excited and optimistic about their journey. People going to Newark hope that they arrive without too many delays.

Talking to the employees of Zappos is like being in seat 12B of the flight going to Cancun. They love where they are and are generally excited about their future, and the future of the company. The spirit is remarkable! They simply adore their jobs. How often does someone walk into a department store (or a big box store) and deal with people who look like they just came away from an Amway meeting?

I happened to be at Zappos HQ last week. As I got ready to head back to the airport Jo, the shuttle driver grabbed my case and luggage and started to take it to the door. I protested, insisting that I tote my own baggage but Jo kept on going. As we drove to the airport, I asked Jo how long she had been with Zappos. "One year, and I can tell you that I am the luckiest girl in the world to have this job ... I am a rocker chic who loves being able to be myself here at Zappos." One could look upon Jo's job as mundane, but that is not the way Jo sees her responsibilities. She loves what she does and her enthusiasm is contagious!

About a week later, I emailed Tony, the CEO of Zappos, and recounted my experience with Jo. I commended Tony on creating an atmosphere of extreme contentment among the employees. Fifteen minutes later, I received an email back thanking ME for my support and for taking the time to email him about Jo. He told me that he shared my sentiment. Obviously, Tony loves his job too. What a pleasure it is to be a part of this environment!

Lionel O.

THE FRYE COMPANY

In the 30 years that I have been in the shoe business, I have never experienced a company who treats their vendors with as much respect and professionalism as Zappos.

They treat each an every employee in the company, regardless of their responsibilities, as if they were the most valuable employee.

When I visit Zappos, which is often, the exuberance and enthusiasm of each and every employee is contagious!

Miles O.

UGG AUSTRALIA

2009! Zappos is now a decade young and I say young because nothing they do gets old. Every time I walk in the door, the office has evolved into a new theme or has freshly redecorated rooms. Everyone is smiling and having so much fun, yet the work always gets done. It is simply brilliant that, ten years later, there is still so much motivation by all the employees to work hard to provide the greatest experience for their vendors, co-workers and ultimately their customers. This takes so much energy and genuine caring.

Sure, most everyone is motivated by money, success and goals to achieve success, but that is not what is most important in life. Happiness should be the ultimate measure of success. If you are always having fun, that can surely lead to some level of happiness. And everyone seems to be having fun at Zappos. If you are having fun, it makes working hard a lot more enjoyable.

Ok, lets define culture: cul·ture d. The predominating attitudes and behavior that characterize the functioning of a group or organization.

Something that has really amazed me over the years, is hearing the stories of all the events that many of the employees get involved with outside of the daily work routine. I mean how many companies organize three-day hiking trips, sporting activities, crazy parties and the list goes on.

I feel very fortunate as a sales rep, but more importantly as a person to still be involved ten years later in the incredible relationship that we all call work, when it is really just so much fun. So many of the people that work for Zappos have become good friends with each other and some have become my good friends. I always look forward to every day I walk in the door just to see everyone and catch up.

Zappos continues to provide an untouchable record of service, fun and human touch, which no other retailer or company can match. This is Zappos, this is their culture.

I look forward to the next ten years!!!

Paul H.

OAKLEY

Well, congratulations on another ground-breaking year. It is great to see success come for such a well-deserving team. Zappos has come so far, yet I know Zappos is still in its infancy. The way that Zappos treats its customers, employees, venders and other partners, is a business model that has a tremendous potential.

The word "business" for some businesses tends to mean decisions without emotion or, in some cases, a heart. I can even think of a TV show where the individual takes pride in it. It is great to see a very successful company like Zappos embrace emotion and even run with it. The Zappos "heart" is why customers trust Zappos with their purchases and why I treasure being a Zappos vendor and partner.

Zappos has won me over as a customer in addition to a vendor. The more I can shop at Zappos, the better for me. Thank goodness Zappos has tackled new product categories. I love that I can now buy apparel, accessories, houseware, electronics and more from Zappos. Buying my new camera and the season's latest denim in one stop was very rewarding.

Living in Las Vegas and sharing a hometown with Zappos is what I appreciate about Zappos the most. Zappos' involvement in community is second to none. For a city where luck can be king. Las Vegas was truly lucky the day Zappos arrived in Las Vegas. As much as Zappos raises the bar in business, they also raise the bar for community involvement. Zappos you have "WOWed" me. I look forward to many more happy and prosperous years.

Piyush S.

DELOITTE CONSULTING LLP

Singing Karaoke during a merchandising happy hour...$0

Dressing up for Western Day, Pajama Day, the Purple Cow video...$0

Consuming 18 Krispy Kremes to win the annual donut-eating contest...$5 (for the Pepto Bismol)

Working with Zappos... priceless.

The culture at Zappos is not only unique, but also a coveted asset. Zappos is able to develop deep, family-like connections with employees, customers, and vendors, which has farther-reaching effects than traditional advertising methods. More than ever, the success of a company is contingent upon its ability to foster positive relationships inside and outside of the organization, and Zappos is certainly leading in this front. Speaking as a third-party provider, we were immediately welcomed into the Zappos family and we will be forever thankful.

PricewaterhouseCoopers Team

PWC

Impression of Life at Zappos – from the perspective of an "auditor"...

Energetic, happy, hard-working, relaxed, teaming, open, caring, creative and of course, a little weird!

As accountants, we get labeled as "auditors" and sometimes encounter customers who are less than enthusiastic to see us. Being the accountants for Zappos offers a completely different environment. The positive energy in the buildings can be felt upon entry. Seemingly simple things like a genuinely happy greeting in the lobby sets the pace for the day. Everyone around is hard at work, but not stressed about work (as is usually the case in Corporate America). There's something about the openness and encouragement of creativity that puts the mind at ease, which permits heightened collaboration and teaming. Political barriers seem diminished and creativity welcomed. A little weirdness abounds and serves as a welcome break from day-to-day tasks. Looking out the window at guys in sundresses, tiaras and roller skates, or at a bubble parade (complete with the queen of bubble in bubble wrap and a bubble-making machine) incite random giggles for months to come. Zappos always offers a great "reset" of perspective –the balance between the responsibilities of life and fun!

Sam G.
SAUCONY

Zappos means "YES, IT IS POSSIBLE!!!" Whether it is a deadline, fixing a problem or taking care of a customer ... every single time. In this day and age that is a very, very special thing!"

Tom A.
CLARKS

After writing what almost reached novella status last year, I have promised to keep it short this time around.

The year just past has been interesting in many respects, not the least of which were the challenges of the radically changing business environment in the second half.

These truly are times that test one's integrity, commitment to a stated mission and business core values. Many business leaders, some iconic on a national scale, have been found wanting. Some of the shenanigans that have been perpetrated on the American public have made headlines. Some of the smaller, less public nonsense that is going on is shameful and to my mind has left many of your competitors wanting on the honorability scale.

Thankfully, and not surprisingly, Zappos has not only risen to the challenge, but has continued to treat everyone who touches their organization with integrity, honesty and respect. The communication remains open and honest.

As a vendor I particularly appreciate the humility and openness with which Zappos employees conduct themselves. Zappos has grown to the point that their weight could be thrown around with their vendors, but rather than take that disagreeable course (which is so often the route taken by big players), you have continued to honor the partnerships that you have so carefully nurtured over the years.

This doesn't happen by accident and it reflects with infinite clarity the direction and attitude of the leaders of your company. It is something that is not just unusual, it is truly unique. I think it is just in your DNA.

Every day I feel honored to have the privilege of working with such an amazing company.

FIG VIII-1. Vendor Appreciation Party at the Palms.

FIG VIII-2. With the pyrotechnics, aerial acrobatics and dancing, it got pretty hot inside.

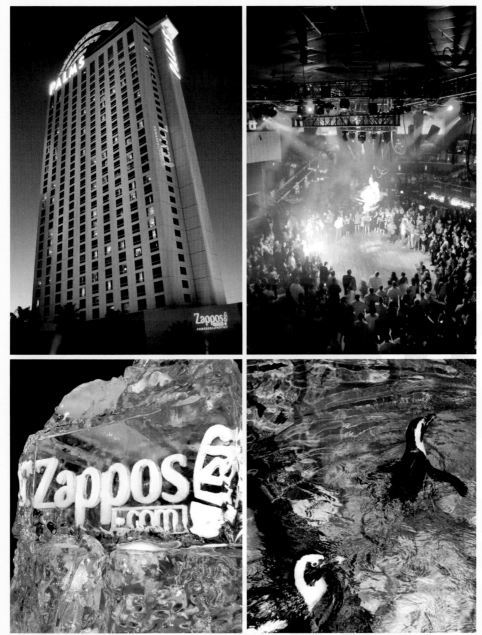

FIG VII-3A-B. But even in the desert, we were still able to enjoy the cool ice and penguins cavorting in the pool.

Joanne Cooper likes to be fun, creative and open-minded (especially when nose-picking).

Bill Cody, William Schwalbe and Christopher Rauschnot at the Twestival Charity event. They're still searching for the culprit that photobombed their pic. Any leads, please advise.

Zappos wants to create happiness
customers we want to WOW ever
appropriate to include them in our C

NAS team, Boston. They set the bar as high as their heels.

Skytypers type a little sky for Zappos.

Jon Levine contributes to the Ball of Guest Passes after his
tour of the Nevada offices.

Amanda Woolley's favorite Zappos accessory needs to be
safe when she rides with her.

very chance we get. Since it's our
day, we thought it couldn't be more
lture Book this year.

Elinor Shapira-Portnoy captures the irony of a hectic ballet.

Diana Kreider explores intimacy in San Diego, CA.

Derek Raguindin's reminded of his grandpa when he wears his New Balance. It's what he always wore too.

Kei and Koa forgetting and remembering in Hawaii.

Core Value #7: Build a Posit

Noelani Wong thinks Zappos helps take care of her family...

... so she sent in pics of her most valuable assets.

Debra Bouchegnies' daughter runs in the snow. Seattle, WA.

Wyatt and Marlon believe "Crazy Dead Eye Man" lives on Bonita Beach Road. Bonita Springs, FL.

ve Team and Family Spirit

"No matter what our last name, no matter what our political beliefs, at the end of the day, we're all Americans."
—Michelle Buros in Keens from Zappos.

"Long-live Jah (and Zappos)!" —Derek Raguindin

Converse worn with dust, spackle and paint from home
renovations. Bought at Zappos by Michele Catalano.

"My trip with Nona" Positano, Italia.
Taken by Alan Sutovsky.

Core Value #9: Be Passion
And in the case of these customers,

"Run with the little guy...create some change." —Mike Spear.

"Balance is Everything." Chennai, India.
Taken by Laura A.B. Brownlee.

Columbia Karasi shoes in Manizales, Columbia.
Bought at Zappos by Sergio DeLaRiva.

Kyna Rosen loves the saying on her shirt, "Lead or be led".
Taken by Darren Stevenson Photography.

ate and Determined.
'd say they're pretty Inspired too.

Inspired at the Cathedrale d'Images paying homage to
Picasso. Les Baux-de-Provence, France. Taken by
Apryl Zarfos Anderson.

"Time for Zappos." —Ed Kinnally.

'Anna' competing in the drag queen contest.
St. Mark's Square, Venice. Taken by Cyn Burton.

"Free-spirited, simple pleasures, nature, in the moment."
—Laura Dickinson

Core Value #3: Create Fun
We believe, if it brings you joy and

Dave Brown comes to terms with his love for shoes.

Debra Bouchegnies' daughter (future Zappos fan) running
her toes through the sand in France.

Kimberly Jones says her son, Miles, loves searching by color on Zappos and will only wear the ones he picked himself.

Annie Weierman looks forward to fall and winter because of one thing—the Frye Campus boots she bought from Zappos.

and a Little Weirdness.
appiness, why not?

Kathryn Jackson says two things bring pure joy in her life: her grandson Deuce and Zappos.

Shira Lazar loving life (and the internet) in Pantagonia, Chile.

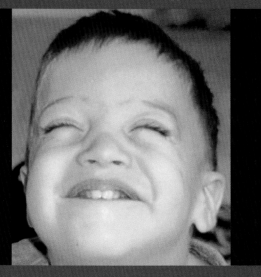

"So culture on my friends...y

In March 2009, Zappos customer Joseph F. watche
took a tour of the Nevada offices. Afterwards, he v
Tony enjoyed it so much, he wanted to share it with

Thistlewaite Falls, near the birthplace of recorded jazz in
Richmond, IN., inspires Zappos customer Joseph Gunn.

Aarti Sharma, his shoes and and wine glass take a break from
rock climbing in Quebec, Canada.

If someone had told me the l
shoe company, I would have
hundreds of companies, indus
have – Culture. I always knew
all the difference. You must h
in your office on a Friday a clo
workplace of Nirvana.

From the moment I stepped
popcorn machine sitting o
and business savvy new media
new for the world to see. Ever
me from time and memoriam,
didn't want to leave! I wanted
what culture I could contribut

Although the IT departmen
couch were our first intro
personalizing what they do, ho
relations, had a Peruvian Jung
the best assortment of wine I l
they do. I also loved the sophi
With that much ambiance why
hard times western hunting lo
Wahoo! Yet, the guy who still
demonstration of destroying a

Listen, I have worked for si
can compare with what yo
know how good your office en
worst agency to work for, prin
Affairs in the Air Force helpin,
DoD with great Feng Shui, and

u have made 'culture' a verb."

Tony speak at the Social Media Conference and subsequently
ntarily wrote this email to Tony.
of you.

part of my week in Las Vegas would be an end of the day tour at an online
aced a healthy wager against it – and lost. In my lifetime, I have visited
s, government agencies, non-profits, and none of them had the one thing you
e some kind of secret dream in the recesses of your mind, that culture makes
found Robert Frost's road after all. What a mind-blowing experience to come
g time, and find thoughtful, kind, receptive and cool people situated in the

to the lobby, I knew I was not in Kansas anymore, Shangri La maybe. With a
e front desk of the Lobby, to the laid back lounge with self-improvement books
p sellers on bookshelves everywhere, I knew that you had created something
e in your entire company impressed me that day. They all acted like they knew
y shared their lives, work and hobbies with all of us and you know what? I
be fully integrated with the company too!! I already started having ideas about

as gone for the day their Bedouin tent over their cube-farm and the powernap
how things are done there. The distinction – people taking ownership and
could that not succeed!! Another group that I thought was international
handing over their swank space complete with vines screaming monkeys and
e seen since Napa Valley. Kudos to that department, I'd join, no matter what
ates, i.e. the graphic artist group, with their smooth Jazz and dim lighting.
ould you ever want to go home! Your meeting rooms utterly rocked – from the
e motif, to the smooth 1940's Hollywood-esque room, to the massage parlor,
kes the cake, for the best part of the tour was de' boot man, who gave us a
d laptop!! You go bootman!! (It was already broken so don't worry.)

fferent federal agencies, several non-profits, and corporate America. Nothing
ave. Relish it, enjoy it, live the dream while the rest of us suffer. You will never
onment is till you work for the Department of Homeland Security, ranked #2
ly because they run it like a medieval fiefdom! Presently, I work for Public
orge a new world of web policy and new media. The Air Force is the "Zappos" of
s good chi as you will find anywhere in the Feds.

"So culture on my friends...y

continued...

I have to say, I found your lecture on happiness in a box, Tony, one of the best I ha social media (blitz) conference. That is not because I am sniffing the glue off you you fully integrated life with work. You did not compartmentalize people's lives, yo encouraged self-expression and now the lines between life and work are fully erase tour and yes, yes...yes it even topped my tour of the Jack Daniel's distillery in Lynch that is saying something. You can always give your best to anyone, when you know part to play.

L astly, I want to confess (reverend mother) that I hauled off a ton of booty from y (who shall remain nameless) let me. I have a ton of great reference books, cultu and a monopoly game which you should have seen me hauling my goodies through Airport in Chicago. Everywhere I went, people said, "Oh, you work for Zappos, I lov had to relate my revelation of taking your tour. Even at my most recent trip to Kans bottom of every TSA tray going through security. So culture on my frien something, and you have made "Culture" a verb.

A ll the best Zappos people. Kudos to making this world a better place to walk, ru

Sincerely,
Joseph F.

u have made 'culture' a verb."

yet experienced at the
ew shoes, it is because
nriched them, you
hanks for the amazing
rg, Tennessee, and
u belong and have a

r tour, because they
ooks, two backpacks
e terminals at O'Hare
heir shoes!" and I
City, you were at the
s, you are onto

stroll or just look good.

Customer Jon Levine takes a breather on the throne in Dr. Vik's office.
At Zappos, employees, customers and partners alike, are all VIP.

Tomme Fent loves Zappos and her pair of RSVP boots.
Sioux City, IO.

And there you have it! W

sense of what Zappos

We hope you have a better

Culture means to us.

People may not remember exactly what you did or what you said, but they will always remember how you made them feel.

—Tony paraphrasing various authors

Thanks for being a part
of the Zappos family.

We hope we continue
making you feel the

WOW

we feel from you.

FORTU
100 B
COMPA
TO WORF